The Natural History of the
British ISLES

The Natural History of the
British Isles

Fascinating Flora and Fauna and Beautiful Landscapes

Bath · New York · Singapore · Hong Kong · Cologne · Delhi
Melbourne · Amsterdam · Johannesburg · Auckland · Shenzhen

This book is dedicated to Ian and Anita MacFarlane.

This edition published by Parragon in 2011
Parragon
Queen Street House
4 Queen Street
Bath, BA1 IHE, UK
www.parragon.com

Pictures courtesy of Oxford Scientific Films. For details of copyright see page 380
Text © Parragon Books Ltd 2003
Designed by Julie Crane, Sue Neate and John Dunne

Produced by Atlantic Publishing
Origination by Cambridge Publishing Management Ltd
Designed by Julie Crane, Sue Neate and John Dunne

A catalogue record for this book is available from the British Library.

ISBN 978-1-4454-4441-3

Printed in China

CONTENTS

INTRODUCTION

The natural history of Great Britain is rich and diverse: from the moth in a fusty pile of old clothes to the majestic stag on a windblown mountain crag; from the frantic whirligig bugs in the village pond to the serene minke whale in the open sea; from humble mosses to mighty oaks. Wherever we are – at home, in the garden, out for a walk or drive in the countryside or down by the shore – there is wildlife all around us, sometimes just hidden from view and waiting to be discovered.

This book is designed to help you to recognise what you are looking at and inspire you to find out more. It is not intended as a field guide but as an introduction to some common species and some species which, though rarer, are beautiful or interesting. There are plenty of other publications which go into far greater detail about all the flora and fauna in this book and we would recommend using them for detailed study.

To help you make sense of your immediate surroundings this book is divided into different habitats, starting around the home and moving outwards to the wide open spaces. The species are not arranged to conform with modern field guides but are roughly in the order in which you would notice them: from the largest or most colourful to the smallest, dullest and most obscure, or from those nearby to those that keep their distance. It is not always possible to absolutely define habitats as many species occur in several different settings – fox, grass and gulls being perfect examples – but we have chosen the habitats where the reader is most likely to come across each species.

Many recipes and traditional potions are referred to but readers try these at their own risk. And although some of the recipes include wild flowers, please don't pick them if they are protected species such as cowslips.

House,
Garden and
Park

But this one, cramped by houses
  and fences, walls,

Must have slept here all winter
  in that heap

Of compost, or have inched by
  intervals

Through tidy gardens to this
  ivy bed.

HEDGEHOG
ANTHONY THWAITE

LEYLAND CYPRESS *(Cupressocyparis leylandii)*

SIZE: Up to 30 m tall

HABITAT: Very common in gardens

IDENTIFICATION: Single trees are conical. Dense green leaves, inconspicuous green (female) and yellow (male) flowers, round brown cones. Bark reddish-brown, fissured

SIMILAR SPECIES: Lawson cypress

The cause of many inter-neighbour disputes, this fast-growing tree is a popular hedging plant and grows to a prodigious height at up to 1.25 m per year. The resultant legal cases over loss of light and encroachment have given this conifer a reputation as something of a nuisance plant in the suburbs, but if clipped to a reasonable height and width it makes a perfect boundary line. 'Leylandii' is a hybrid between cypresses of different genera – Nootka and Monterey – and comes in two forms: Leighton Green (Nootka pollinated by Monterey) and Haggerston Grey (Monterey pollinated by Nootka). These crosses occurred on the Leighton Estate in Welshpool in 1888 and 1892, respectively. Haggerston Grey is more commonly grown in gardens and the small, densely packed, scale-like leaves vary from grey to bright green.

COMMON LIME *(Tilia x vulgaris)*

SIZE: Up to 40 m tall

HABITAT: Parks and avenues

IDENTIFICATION: Smooth grey bark, fissured when old; large (6–10 cm) heart-shaped leaves. Hard-cased, ovoid seed. Flowers in clusters of 5–10

SIMILAR SPECIES: Large-leaved lime, Small-leaved lime, Silver lime

This ornamental tree, a favourite in parks and alongside avenues, is the tallest broadleaved tree in Britain and is a hybrid between large-leaved and small-leaved limes. Many car owners curse it as, when it is planted alongside roads, the aphids which commonly infest it drop sticky, part-digested leaf sap onto the vehicles parked beneath; if left unwashed this sap is turned black by a mould fungus and can permanently deface the paint finish. For this reason, many municipalities now plant the aphid-immune, weeping silver-leaved lime (*Tilia petiolaris*) instead. The lime can live for 500 years and many examples in country estates date back to the early 1700s. The inner bark, called *bass* or *bast*, is stringy and was once used to make ropes. The fine-grained wood is used for carvings and musical instruments.

JUNIPER *(Juniperis communis)*

SIZE: Up to 6 m tall

HABITAT: Gardens, uplands, forests

IDENTIFICATION: Conical tree or low shrub, spiky blue–green needles (1–3 cm) in whorls of 3. Berries dark purple when ripe. Inconspicuous yellow (male) and green (female) flowers on separate bushes. Rich red–brown bark shreds off in strips

SIMILAR SPECIES: Pencil cedar, Chinese juniper

Although juniper is commonly found on mountain slopes and chalk downs, it is also a plant of the garden and park, where it has been cultivated in a variety of forms, from the slender, pointed columns of 'Hibernica' to the creeping, dwarf varieties in rock gardens, such as 'Depressa Aurea'. Juniper has been put to many uses over the years. Egyptians used the oil extracted from its leaves as part of a recipe for mummifying potions. Whereas medieval Europeans took to burning the branches and leaves to ward off evil spirits. The berries were found to yield brown dye and were said to cure the plague, heal animal bites and counteract poisoning. The berries are still used to flavour gin, and the wood is used to smoke meats.

COMMON YEW *(Taxus baccata)*

SIZE: Up to 15 m tall. Widespreading

HABITAT: Churchyards, garden hedges and parks

IDENTIFICATION: Flat, dark green needle leaves. Dense foliage. Male flowers yellow, female flowers (on separate plant) green becoming bright red fruit. Smooth, light brown bark, flaking reddish

SIMILAR SPECIES: Irish yew, Plum-fruited yew

It is an irony that this immensely long-lived tree (1000 years or more) is usually found where we are reminded of our mortality: in churchyards. The explanations for this common setting include myths referring to the yew's sacred qualities and the theory that its dense, spreading foliage gave shelter to itinerant missionaries, who founded churches nearby. The elastic yew wood has another association with death: it was used to make the weapon that changed medieval history, the English longbow. So many yews were felled to make bows that the remaining trees are the descendants of inferior plants. The attractively grained, orange–brown wood is a favourite with wood-turners and takes a high polish. The bark, foliage and seeds are poisonous, although the fleshy red seed cap is not and is eagerly eaten by birds. However, one of yew's toxins, taxol, is an effective treatment for some cancers.

WALNUT *(Juglans regia)*

SIZE:	Up to 30 m tall
HABITAT:	Parklands, country houses, large gardens
IDENTIFICATION:	Yellow–green leaves, alternate on twig, comprise 7–9 leaflets, larger towards tip. Young leaves bronze. Inconspicuous female flowers, male catkins. Smooth, grey bark with deep fissures. Green fruit with walnut inside
SIMILAR SPECIES:	Black walnut

A handsome, spreading tree with a majesty that both the Greeks and the Romans recognised: they both called it the 'royal nut'. The familiar nut, found within a green fleshy covering, has a distinctive crinkly shell protecting the kernel. The great challenge of nut lovers is to extract the kernel in one piece, preserving the appearance of two tiny human brains linked base to base. This brain-like appearance gave the nut a reputation in medieval times as a healer of mental illnesses. The tree came from Persia to Greece then to Rome about 2000 years ago; before being brought to Britain by the Romans, who used the nut for food and for cooking oil, just as we do today. Cabinetmakers prize the timber, which has a whorled grain and rich, velvety feel, and the oil has been used to make soap.

GOLDEN WEEPING WILLOW

(Salix x chrysocoma)

SIZE:	Up to 20 m tall. Widespreading
HABITAT:	Parks, gardens, riversides
IDENTIFICATION:	Long, trailing branches and twigs with long, pointed, green leaves. Grey–brown bark laced with ridges. Male catkins yellow on separate trees from female
SIMILAR SPECIES:	White willow, Crack willow

From the banks of parkland lakes and rivers to suburban front lawns, this distinctive hybrid is one of the classic motifs of the romantic English garden. Its drooping golden branches speak of long, indolent afternoons in a deckchair, slow strolls in the park, boating on the pond and of a peculiarly English disciplined relaxation. Willows hybridise easily and this common ornamental is thought to be a cross between *Salix babylonica*, which originated in China, and *Salix alba*. Like all willows, it grows very quickly and can be propagated by simply pushing a twig into the ground. This ease of propagation, and the fact that willows were among the first trees to grow in Britain after the Ice Age, mean there are hundreds of different species.

LONDON PLANE *(Platanus x hispanica)*

SIZE:	Up to 30 m tall
HABITAT:	City centres, avenues and parks
IDENTIFICATION:	Alternate, clear green leaves, 5-lobed with toothed margins. Rough green fruits like small footballs ripen from reddish-brown female flowers. Yellow, globular male flowers. Flaky bark
SIMILAR SPECIES:	American plane, Oriental plane

Take the plane trees out of London and the city would probably suffocate in a miasma of exhaust fumes. These pollution-tolerant trees are the mainstay of the many squares which are the city's lungs and cast their shade along the paths and avenues that criss-cross the major parks. The London plane, a hybrid of American and Oriental planes, literally shrugged off the choking soot of pre-Clean Air Act London through its characteristic shedding of strips of bark. The tree constantly renews its outer surface, revealing dashing streaks of creamy fresh growth. Rain also sluices dust easily off the shiny leaves. In this way some specimens have survived in the capital for more than 200 years, firmly establishing themselves as an essential part of the city's character. The hard, fine-grained wood is also known as 'lacewood'.

WHITE POPLAR *(Populus alba)*

SIZE:	Up to 20 m tall
HABITAT:	Widely grown as an ornamental tree
IDENTIFICATION:	Alternate, dark green leathery leaves, pale and hairy underneath. Greyish-white upper bark with black pores. Male catkins crimson, female green on separate trees
SIMILAR SPECIES:	Grey poplar, Italian poplar, Aspen

A highly prized addition to any park or large garden, the white poplar pleases both the eyes and ears with its spectacular foliage. The wide leaves on their flattened, whippy stalks flutter and dance in the slightest breeze, revealing their silvery undersides and whispering with the sound of gentle rain. To add to its grace, the trunk, which shades to a pale grey as it rises, often leans to give an oriental bonsai note. Greek legend has it that the tree used to be completely black. Hercules wore a garland of it while he fought the three-headed dog of hell, Cerberus, and his sweat bleached the bark white. It is particularly suited to urban and seaside environments as the white leaf hairs protect the breathing pores from air pollution and salt.

Norway Maple
(Acer platanoides)

Size:	Up to 27 m tall
Habitat:	Parks and city streets. All soils
Identification:	Light green, opposite, 5-lobed, toothed leaves. Yellow flowers ripening to winged fruits. Smoothish grey bark with many fissures
Similar species:	Sycamore, Cappadocian maple, Field maple

Like all *Acers*, the Norway Maple makes the little 'helicopter' winged seeds which give hours of aerobatic delight to easily amused youngsters. The tree also satisfies the more aesthetically sophisticated with its autumnal display of yellow and scarlet–brown leaves. Although a native to the bitterly cold mountains of the European north, this frost-resistant tree also tolerates the grime of cities and has become a favourite in parks and open spaces. Its only enemy is the grey squirrel, which eats the bark and then sups on the sweet sap beneath. Bees also feed on its pollen in the early spring when other food sources are scarce. It is shorter than its cousin, the sycamore, and the angle between the wings of its 'helicopter' is wider.

BOX *(Buxus sempervirens)*

SIZE:	Up to 11 m tall but usually a small bush or hedge
HABITAT:	Ornamental gardens and hedges
IDENTIFICATION:	Opposite, shiny, oval, evergreen leaves, dark green on top, paler beneath; notch at tip, inrolled margins. Tiny, green–yellow flowers. Rarely fruits in Britain. Bark light brown, greying with age
SIMILAR SPECIES:	None. Many varieties of different colours and sizes

Box is a rounded tree. It can also be described as peacock shaped or pyramidal, turned like a table leg or looking like a chessman, a cottage loaf or even a motor car. All these shapes and even more fanciful ones are crafted from the dense foliage by the nimble clippers of topiarists, whose creations adorn many ornamental gardens and hedges. Rare now in the wild, where it grows on chalky soils (as at Box Hill, Surrey), box is also in demand by carvers and instrument makers, who value the hard, heavy, stable wood. It was once used for engravings and is so dense that it will not float in water when green. The blue–green, tricorned fruit capsules, which turn brown and release black seeds, are seldom seen in Britain.

HOLLY *(Ilex aquifolium)*

SIZE:	Up to 20 m but usually much shorter
HABITAT:	Garden hedges, parks, hedgerows, fields and woods
IDENTIFICATION:	Stiff, leathery or waxy leaves with spiny margins, dark green above, paler below. White, 4-petalled flowers ripening to bright red berries. Green bark ageing to smooth grey
SIMILAR SPECIES:	None. Many cultivated varieties with smooth or bi-coloured leaves and variously coloured berries

Where would Christmas be without holly? The rich green leaves and vibrant red berries are the quintessential colours of yuletide when most other trees have paled into leafless austerity. Holly is surrounded by myth, principally in the role of warding off evil. So powerful a charm was it deemed to be that it was thought unlucky to cut down a holly. German legend says the person first bringing holly into the home each year rules that household for the coming year. And an old Scottish tale tells how holly saved the world from perpetual winter when the magic staff used by Cailleach Bhuer, the giant hag symbolizing the season, was captured by Spring and flung into a holly bush, robbing the hag of her power. The hard, heavy wood is used for carving, inlays and woodcuts, and caterpillars of the holly blue butterfly feed on the leaves.

SYCAMORE *(Acer pseudoplatanus)*

SIZE: Up to 36 m tall

HABITAT: Parks, gardens, avenues, farmsteads. Introduced to Britain

IDENTIFICATION: Leaves opposite and five-lobed, upper sides dark green. Tiny yellow–green flowers in hanging clusters. Winged fruits. Huge domed outline, dense foliage. Grey or pinkish–brown bark and creamy white wood

SIMILAR SPECIES: Norway maple *(A. platanoides)*

The chorus in one of the versions of the song 'Big Rock Candy Mountain' starts 'Oh, the buzzin' of the bees and the sycamore trees', which is apt as these trees, Europe's largest maples, are an excellent source of nectar. In the 15th century people wanted to banish the tree from towns because its honeydew-coated leaves putrefied after falling. However, the many mature sycamores around farms indicate that 19th century farmers favoured them for their shelter (Montgomeryshire folklore held that sycamore kept fairies away and stopped them spoiling the milk). Today, we hate the tree for covering our cars with honeydew but it will probably become important in lowland Britain as agricultural land is converted to timber. It was a preferred tree for hanging in Scotland because its large lower branches wouldn't break accidentally. Its timber is used in furniture, musical instruments, veneers and household utensils, and the sap was once used to make ale and wine.

CREEPING BUTTERCUP
(Ranunculus repens)

SIZE:	5–50 cm tall
HABITAT:	Very common in gardens, meadows and arable land
IDENTIFICATION:	Single or clusters of bright yellow flowers from May to September
SIMILAR SPECIES:	Meadow buttercup, Bulbous buttercup, Celery-leaved buttercup

Creeping buttercup is a real villain in the garden, as it seriously depletes the ground of potassium and other elements. Because it creeps, it is difficult to eradicate and can completely swamp garden plants. Damp meadows can become a yellow carpet of creeping or meadow buttercups which, being poisonous, are avoided by cattle and left to flourish. The celery-leaved buttercup is even more poisonous, affecting the milk supply if dairy cattle do eat them. Gardeners are advised to wear gloves when handling them, as they can produce sores on the skin. The buttercup flowers are popular with children, who like to hold them under their chins to see whether the reflection shows that they like butter.

DAISY *(Bellis perennis)*

SIZE:	20–60 cm tall
HABITAT:	Lawns and other short grassland throughout the UK
IDENTIFICATION:	Rosette of oval or spoon-shaped leaves with solitary white flowers from March to October. A yellow centre, surrounded by petal tubes, sometimes tipped with pink
SIMILAR SPECIES:	Ox-eye daisy

Wimbledon must have the only lawns that are not subtly improved by a few daisies. The generic name is derived from the Latin for 'beautiful' and writers and poets have sung their praises: Chaucer said he rose early to see them open with the sun, and Shelley compared them to earthbound stars. The name 'daisy' is a corruption of the old name 'Day's eye', so called as the flowers opened at daybreak and closed at dusk or in dull weather. Herbalists used the plant to treat scurvy and varicose veins and now daisy flowers can be made into a country wine known as 'Daisy Whisky'. Children sometimes sit on lawns in summer, picking daisies to make daisy chains by splitting the stalks with a thumb nail and threading the next flower through. The chains are then made into fragile crowns, garlands or necklaces.

GRASSES

There are many different grasses that grow in gardens, farmland, verges, downs, heath, moors and marshes. They might seem similar until closely examined. They all have narrow, green leaves and, usually, insignificant flowers. Sedges could be mistaken for grass, but if in doubt roll the stem between thumb and finger and remember that 'sedges have edges'. The common reed grows up to 3 m tall and is Britain's tallest grass. It grows on marshland and around brackish water. The tallest grass grows to 150 cm.

Red fescue (*Festuca rubra*) is often used for lawn grass and is usually seen mown and groomed. The creeping rhizomes spread to form a thick sward. However, a number of variants grow wild, particularly on sand dunes, salt marshes and heaths, where the red or purple panicles appear in early summer.

Sheep's fescue (*Festuca ovina*) is similar to red fescue but produces less foliage. It provides valuable grazing for sheep particularly on hill farms, as this hardy grass grows from sea-level up to 1220 m.

Other commercially grown grasses include **Annual meadow-grass** (*Poa annua*), **Perennial rye grass** (*Lolium perenne* ssp *perenne*) and **Timothy** (*Phleum pratense* ssp *pratense*). Timothy was named after Timothy Hanson, an American agriculturist who proved its value for making hay. It is also known as Meadow cat's tail.

Many grasses have delightful common names: 'Sweet vernal grass' has the smell of new-mown hay, 'Yorkshire fog' might have been named after the Old Norse *fogg* meaning limp, damp grass.

COMMON DANDELION
(Taraxacum officinale)

SIZE: 5–30 cm tall

HABITAT: Gardens, verges and wasteground

IDENTIFICATION: Single yellow flowers on hollow, leafless stems, from a rosette of long, deeply divided leaves. Flowers from March to October

SIMILAR SPECIES: Hawkweed, Nipplewort, Smooth hawk's beard, Cat's-ear, Great lettuce, Bristly ox-tongue

Children's games have helped to make this one of the most common weeds in Britain. Blowing the seed heads and counting the breaths was said to 'tell the time' and dispersed the seeds in the process. Gardeners despise the plant, which absorbs about three times as much iron from the soil as other plants. However, the lush flowers encourage bees for pollinating garden crops. All parts of the plants are used by herbalists: tea infused from the leaves or roots is said to stimulate the bloodstream, digestive organs, liver, kidneys and bladder. Over-indulgence can over-stimulate the latter, hence the French name of *pissenlit* or 'wet-a-bed'. Our name dandelion comes from the French *dent de lion* or lion's tooth, which some say refers to the shape of the leaves. In the past, dandelions were grown in old kitchen gardens and blanched like chicory. The slightly bitter leaves can be used in salads.

COMMON NETTLE OR STINGING NETTLE *(Urtica dioica)*

SIZE:	Up to 150 cm tall
HABITAT:	Gardens, verges, woods, hedgerows and wasteland all over Britain
IDENTIFICATION:	Upright stems with leaves toothed and lobed, the whole plant covered with stinging hairs
SIMILAR SPECIES:	Small nettle, Red deadnettle

'Nettles may be found by feeling for them in the darkest night,' wrote Nicholas Culpeper in the 17th century. Although hated for their sting and invasiveness in the garden, nettles are edible, and cooking dispels the venom. They are a rich source of vitamin C and contain more iron than spinach. Cooked like spinach, finished with cream and nutmeg, they make a tasty vegetable and the leaves can be used to make soup, pudding, wine or beer. Nettle tea is used in herbal medicine to relieve bronchitis, rheumatism, asthma and gout. A valuable liquid plant food can be made by steeping nettles in rainwater for 2 or 3 weeks, and this leaf feed is also effective as a pesticide in the greenhouse. The red dead-nettle *(Lamium purpureum)* and white dead-nettle *(Lamium album)* are in the mint family and not related to the stinging nettle.

BROADLEAF DOCK

(Rumex crispus)

SIZE:	50–100 cm tall
HABITAT:	Gardens, wasteland, grassland
IDENTIFICATION:	Upright plant with broad leaves with wavy edges. Green flower spikes from June to October
SIMILAR SPECIES:	Curled dock, Sheep's sorrel, Common sorrel, Common bisort, Knotgrass, Redshank

The dock is a tough perennial weed with long persistent roots, almost impossible to pull up without breaking. Its saving grace is its use to neutralise the sting of nettles, and fortunately it grows in similar habitats: 'When your fingers nettles find, be sure a dock is close behind,' says a traditional rhyme. The leaves were also used on burns, scalds and blisters. The low-key flower spikes are followed by more distinctive reddish-brown fruits. The leaves are edible, although those of the common dock are even more bitter than those of the curled dock. The leaves of common sorrel have a clear, sharp taste and can be used in salads or cooked in the same way as spinach.

GROUND ELDER *(Aegopodium podagraria)*

SIZE:	30–60 cm tall
HABITAT:	Gardens, particularly kitchen gardens and monasteries, wasteground throughout the Bitish Isles
IDENTIFICATION:	Aromatic leaves, each having up to nine leaflets. Umbrella-shaped flower heads have 10–20 branches carrying white flowers with prominent yellow stamens during May to July
SIMILAR SPECIES:	Fool's parsley, Burnet saxifrage, Pignut, and others of the large *Umbelliferae* family

Commonly found in shady places and under hedgerows, ground elder is one of the most difficult garden weeds to eradicate as the creeping roots run in among garden plants. In the 16th century, John Gerard wrote 'Herbe Gerard groweth of it selfe in gardens, without setting or sowing and it is so fruitfull in his increase that where it hath once taken roote, it will hardly be gotten out again'. It has many other common names in various parts of the country including 'goutweed', as in the Middle Ages it was served in roadside inns as a quick palliative for traveller's gout. Still used by herbalists today as a kidney-flushing herb and as a sedative, and by country housewives as an unusually aromatic vegetable.

SUN SPURGE *(Euphorbia helioscopia)*

SIZE:	20–50 cm
HABITAT:	Gardens, verges and waste ground
IDENTIFICATION:	A single thick stem carrying umbels of greenish yellow flowers surrounded by whorls of bracts
SIMILAR SPECIES:	Dwarf spurge, broad-leaved spurge

The gardener regards sun spurge as a weed that must be handled with care as it is poisonous, but it is sweetly scented and an attractive foil to other flowers so is sometimes used in wedding bouquets. The stems produce a white latex when cut and this was once used to burn off warts. Medieval herbalists used the plant with care as they were aware of its purgative effect. Perhaps a little safer was the plaster used to heal aching joints, made of 12 parts spurge oil and a little wax. In autumn the plant produces three-lobed fruit capsules, which burst open with a loud crack when ripe, throwing seeds over a wide area. Ants are attracted to the oil in the flesh enveloping the seeds and carry them off to eat. After the flesh has been consumed, the seeds are left to germinate, thus the plant spreads over a wide area.

BITING STONECROP *(Sedum acre)*

SIZE:	2.5–10 cm tall
HABITAT:	Dry walls, rocks and shingle in gardens, grassland and wasteland
IDENTIFICATION:	Thick, fleshy, yellowish-green leaves and creeping, mat-forming stems. Bright yellow flowers with five petals appear May to July
SIMILAR SPECIES:	English stonecrop, Reflexed stonecrop, Orpine

Also known as wall-pepper, the biting stonecrop is named for the sharp, peppery taste of the leaves. This is the smallest of the yellow stonecrop family. It was once used to ease ulcers, prevent fever and cure a variety of complaints. Biting stonecrop flourishes in dry places such as walls and it prefers limy soils. It used to be planted on the roofs of houses as it was said to ward off thunderstorms. English stonecrop prefers acid soils and is often seen on cliff-tops in western Britain. The upper leaves are tinged with crimson and the white flowers appear a little later, from June to September. Reflexed stonecrop was introduced from the Continent where it is found in Scandinavia and as far south as Sicily.

COMMON CHICKWEED

(Stellaria media)

SIZE:	5–35 cm
HABITAT:	Gardens, cultivated land and wasteland
IDENTIFICATION:	A weak, straggly plant with small white flowers throughout the year. A single line of hairs run the length of the stem. Flowers have five deeply divided petals
SIMILAR SPECIES:	Common mouse-ear, Field mouse-ear, Upright chickweed, Thyme-leaved sandwort, Greater stitchwort, Lesser stitchwort

Chickweed is so widespread throughout Britain that it has many local names, including chick wittles, cluckenweed, mischievous jack, murren, skirt buttons, white bird's eye and tongue grass. The weeds are fed to birds, hence the name, yet it is one of the tastiest wild vegetables. It can be eaten raw in salads or cooked like spinach. It should not be confused with the tougher, whiskery mouse-ear found in lawns. Herbalists make a tea or tisane and use it as an eye lotion for tired eyes, to relieve constipation or soothe an upset stomach. Its soothing and cooling properties also make it a popular ingredient of hand cream sold today. As a poultice, it was famed for curing abscesses and carbuncles.

HEDGE SPARROW/DUNNOCK
(Prunella modularis)

SIZE: 14–15 cm

HABITAT: Widespread in gardens, parks, scrub, wood, moors and coasts

IDENTIFICATION: Dull brown, grey head and chest, speckled flanks, thin beak. Song a high *tseep*

SIMILAR SPECIES: House sparrow

The hedge sparrow, or dunnock, is not a sparrow at all, but resembles a house sparrow. It is a common breeding bird throughout Britain and so has a variety of local names, one of which, hedge chanter, used in Yorkshire and Lancashire, betrays the bird's true family, the accentor songbirds. The dunnock is often the victim of the cuckoo's guile. There is something heartbreaking but touching about watching a couple of tiny dunnocks frantically searching out food for the ever-gaping maw of a huge and demanding cuckoo chick. This tolerance of the impostor's egg has also led the dunnock to be called foolish sparrow and blind dunnock. The cuckoo might choose the nest because it is quite substantial, made of twigs, stems, roots and moss and often hair-lined. The dunnock's own eggs are a wonderful deep blue and are usually in fours or fives.

HOUSE SPARROW (*Passer domesticus*)

SIZE:	15 cm
HABITAT:	Gardens, parks, fields and hedgerows
IDENTIFICATION:	Streaky brown back and wings. Stout bill. Male grey crown, black bib; female dull brown crown, no bib. Twitters and cheeps
SIMILAR SPECIES:	Hedge sparrow (Dunnock), Tree sparrow

The house sparrow, living alongside human beings since the Stone Age, has a reputation for being lustful, as it breeds so readily. The eggs were sold as aphrodisiacs in ancient Greece and the Romans kept sparrows as cage birds. The first century BC poet, Catullus, wrote: 'Come all ye loves and Cupids haste/To mourn, and all ye men of taste;/My lady's sparrow, O, he's sped,/The bird my lady loved is dead!' Whether this was literal or referred to his lady's spent passion is not clear. What is clear is that house sparrow numbers are falling rapidly in Britain. They are now a rare sight in many towns. Sparrows use martin and swallow nests, often barging out the rightful owners, and a folk tale says the displaced birds return to build over the nest entrance, walling in the squatters. The slightly smaller tree sparrow *(Passer montanus)*, rarer in the north and west, has an all-chestnut crown and a black cheek patch. It, too, has suffered huge losses in the past 30 years, with the number of farmland birds falling by almost 90%.

STARLING (*Sturnus vulgaris*)

SIZE:	21–22 cm
HABITAT:	Widespread and common
IDENTIFICATION:	Iridescent plumage of black, purple and green, duller and spotted in winter. Yellow bill. Mixed clicking, whistling song, often imitating birdsong and other sounds
SIMILAR SPECIES:	Vaguely like female blackbird

If the starling was not ubiquitous and numerous, it would be a treasured exotic. Its shining plumage, especially in country birds, is stunning; it is a brilliant mimic, a dashing flier and full of cocky character. It is only because it gathers in such huge numbers – sometimes flocks of hundreds of thousands – that we dismiss it as a nuisance. We also object to its bird-table manners as it struts round, pushing others out of the way and chucking food about. It is a bit of a yob, but it also performs useful service in eating pests like leatherjackets and wireworms and picking ticks off sheep. It will eat almost anything. The starling's nest, like its eating habits, is messy, often just a jumble of twigs and grass. The young are perhaps the most vociferously demanding of all baby birds, and can create real noise pollution in a quiet garden.

BLACKBIRD *(Turdus merula)*

SIZE: 25 cm

HABITAT: Widespread

IDENTIFICATION: Male all black with yellow eye ring, orange bill; female
                     brownish with indistinct spots on breast. Beautiful rich
                     song, delicate '*pink-pink*' when foraging, harsh, '*chowk-
                     chowk*' warning call

SIMILAR SPECIES: Ouzel, Starling (female blackbird only)

Known in times past as the ouzel cock or black ouzel, the blackbird
is one of the most common birds in Britain. Given a chance, it will
strip the berries from a fruit bush or the fruit from a tree and, with
a raucous shriek, sweep into the cover of a hedge when found out.
It is largely forgiven for its ravages because of its lovely song – a
sweeping mix of mellow notes sung from tree or rooftop, often at
dusk. The 18th century essayist, Joseph Addison, wrote: 'I value my
garden more for being full of blackbirds than of cherries, and very
frankly give them fruit for their songs'. They are omnivorous
survivors, and in the winter feed on hawthorn berries as well as
making shy visits to the bird table, where they tend to be
dominated by thrushes and starlings. They line their nests with
mud or similar and the eggs are blue–green with brown speckles.

SONG THRUSH *(Turdus philomelos)*

SIZE:	23 cm
HABITAT:	Widespread
IDENTIFICATION:	Brown back and head, conspicuously spotted, yellow flecked pale breast, white belly. Eggs blue with black spots
SIMILAR SPECIES:	Mistle thrush, Redwing, Fieldfare

Like a muezzin, the songthrush flings its mellifluous song across the neighbourhood, its minaret a tall tree, chimneypot or television aerial. Phrases are repeated several times over with slight variations and each bird's song becomes more complex and enjoyable as it grows older. Thomas Hardy in *The Darkling Thrush* referred to the bird's 'carolings of such ecstatic sound' and Browning's *Home-thoughts from Abroad* picked up on the song's phrasing: 'That's the wise thrush; he sings each song twice over,/Lest you should think he never could recapture/The first fine careless rapture!' but he always seems to. Thrushes are also known for smashing open snail shells on 'anvil' stones for the meat inside. They suffer in harsh winters and their numbers are in serious decline generally, with the blame shared between pesticides, birds of prey and domestic cats.

MISTLE THRUSH *(Turdus viscivorus)*

SIZE:	28 cm
HABITAT:	Widespread except in far north of Scotland
IDENTIFICATION:	Bigger than the song thrush and greyer on back and head. Large breast spots without yellow tinges. White flash under wing in flight. Eggs white with brown spots
SIMILAR SPECIES:	Song thrush, Fieldfare, Redwing

It is satisfying to be able to differentiate this thrush from the song thrush, but even more interesting to look at the derivation of its various names. The Latin *viscovorus* means mistletoe-eating, but, although we call it the mistle thrush, it is not known to favour the plant's berries in Britain. That is because they are white, and presumably less attractive, whereas in the Mediterranean there is red-berried mistletoe. In the 4th century BC, Aristotle recorded the bird's fondness for these berries and the name has stuck. Country folk here call it the hollin thrush, referring to its appetite for holly berries. It is also known for its carrying song: on the Isle of Wight it is the squawking thrush, in Derbyshire the screech. The names storm cock and storm thrush refer to its habit of singing before and during bad weather, when other birds have taken cover.

ROBIN *(Erithacus rubecula)*

SIZE:	14 cm
HABITAT:	Widespread
IDENTIFICATION:	Brown back and crown, red face and breast, white underside. Melodious song of trills and warbles with 'tic-tic-tic' alarm call
SIMILAR SPECIES:	Red-breasted fly catcher (no red on face)

Digging the garden for just a few minutes usually attracts a robin, which almost gets under your feet in its bold search for worms. It will even take worms from your hand. This willingness to be close to people is one of the reasons why it is so well loved, although, in bird terms, it is a pugnacious type, scrapping with intruders and defending its nest vigorously. On the Continent, however, where the robin is among many small birds that are eaten, it is understandably very shy and retiring. For a long time it was known simply as the redbreast, and it was only in 1952 that the alternative name of robin was officially accepted by the British Ornithologists' Union. The robin's popularity is reflected in folklore, which deems it extremely unlucky to kill one, and Blake spoke for many when he wrote: '… a robin redbreast in a cage, puts all heaven in a rage'.

NUTHATCH *(Sitta europaea)*

SIZE:	14 cm
HABITAT:	Large gardens, woods and parks. Frequent in England and Wales, thinning northwards. Absent from Scotland
IDENTIFICATION:	A plump, neat little bird, short tail, blue–grey upper parts, buff under parts and reddish flanks. Black eyestripe and strong, sharp bill
SIMILAR SPECIES:	None

This vigorous little bird skitters nimbly up and down trees as if held on by magnets. It is the only British bird that can run down a tree, and it was once thought that it roosted head down. Its original name was 'nut-hack', derived from the way it lodges hazelnuts and acorns in the bark of trees and hacks at them with its tough beak to get at the kernel. It is also known locally as the mud dabber or mud stopper because of its habit of adjusting the size of its nest opening with mud. It nests in trees or walls, and will readily occupy a nest box, where it covers the bottom with bark and dried leaves, which it then uses to cover the eggs. Nuthatches can occasionally be seen on bird tables. In the spring, the male sits in a treetop whistling so loudly that the sound carries for up to 100 metres, making it difficult to miss.

THE TIT FAMILY

The word tit is abbreviated from titmouse, the historical name for the species. Mouse, in this case, is a corruption of *'mase'*, an Old English word for a small bird. And 'tit' itself originated in the Icelandic word *'tittr'* meaning small – so titmouse, appropriately, means small, small bird.

If you still have milk delivered in bottles on the doorstep you have a good chance of spotting a **blue tit** *(Parus caeruleus)*, 12 cm, commonest of all tits, breaking through the foil cap to drink the cream. Although mainly a woodland bird, it is one of the most frequent visitors to the bird table, hanging from nut feeders or suspended coconut halves. It is a bustling little bird, activity which is well captured by John Clare who wrote that '…the bluecap tootles in its glee / Picking the flies from orchard apple tree'. Another observer noted that one pair of blue tits made about 1500 trips to their nest in a day to feed their young with apple blossom weevil and apple sawfly maggots.

The **great tit** *(Parus major)*, 14 cm, is the largest British tit, the size of a sparrow, with white cheeks, black head and a broad black bib down its yellow breast. It is common wherever there are trees. It is very vociferous with many calls, most with ringing, metallic notes, the most frequent being a repeated, double-noted 'tee-cher': if you hear a song you can't identify, it is probably a great tit. It eats buds, fruit, seeds, berries and household scraps. Like the blue tit, it is a regular visitor to the garden bird table and has been known to eat from the hand. It is found everywhere except in Orkney and Shetland.

Coniferous woodlands are the favoured haunt of the **coal tit** *(Parus ater)*, 11 cm, where it hangs acrobatically from cones to pick out seeds. It is the smallest British tit, feeding on insects, seeds, nut kernels and meat and suet from bird tables. Of all the tits it is probably the one that has flourished most in recent years and it can now be seen almost anywhere where there are conifers, whether in large woodlands or in parks and gardens.

great tit

blue tit

long-tailed tit

coal tit

The **long-tailed tit** *(Aegithalos caudatus)*, 14 cm, tail more than half this, has local names including jack-in-a-bottle, bottle tom and can bottle, but the container referred to isn't the milk bottle associated with its cousin the blue tit. The names echo its intricate oval nest made of moss, cobwebs and hair and lined with feathers (more than 2000 of which have been counted in one nest). Commonest in hedgerows and woodland edges, everywhere but the Outer Hebrides, it is rarely seen on its own but groups perch along branches or flit from bush to bush. It is very susceptible to severe weather, being small with a relatively large surface area, and harsh winters have been known to reduce the population by as much as 80 %.

Scotland, devoid of so many other tits, is the home of the **crested tit** *(Parus cristatus)*, 11–12 cm. It is only found in woodlands in small area of the Highlands around the Spey valley, although in winter it sometimes comes to rural gardens. It breeds throughout Europe, from France to Greece, from Spain to Scandinavia, so it is a puzzle why the only crested tits found in England are occasional continental visitors. This isolation might be due to the lack of suitable winter food, although the extensive conifer plantations of recent years throughout central and southern Britain ought to offer a perfect habitat.

Marsh tit and Willow tit are dealt with on other pages.

GARDEN WARBLER *(Sylvia borin)*

SIZE:	14 cm
HABITAT:	Widespread. Woodlands, copses, thickets and gardens with hedges and undergrowth. Rare in Highlands
IDENTIFICATION:	Nondescript small brown and buff bird. Short bill. Distinctive song
SIMILAR SPECIES:	Blackcap

The garden warbler is a fairly humdrum bird but makes up for its drab appearance with its song – a sweet collection of even, musical notes a little lower in pitch than that of the blackcap, which is very similar. The garden warbler knows the difference, though, and aggressively chases away blackcaps and any other warblers that come into its domain. The technique it uses, a moth-like fluttering of the wings along with spread tail feathers, is the same as that used by the male in his courtship display. Its local name in Surrey is juggler, possibly because of this behaviour. It visits in summer after a long haul from tropical or southern Africa. It is probably most noticeable towards the end of its stay, when it prepares for the journey back by eating as many berries as it can, often getting splattered with fruit juice in the process.

BLACKCAP *(Sylvia atricapilla)*

SIZE:	14 cm
HABITAT:	Overgrown gardens, tall hedgerows, woodlands. Unusual in northern Scotland
IDENTIFICATION:	Male has striking black cap, female a brown cap. Larger and longer billed than marsh and willow warblers
SIMILAR SPECIES:	Garden warbler, Marsh warbler, Willow warbler

Increasingly seen at bird tables in the winter, the blackcap spends its summer entertaining us with its wonderful, rich, deep-noted song. The refrain, which lasts several seconds, starts quietly and builds to end with a flourish. The beauty of the song has led to the blackcap being given the local name of mock (sometimes also March or northern) nightingale. The blackcap is more omnivorous than most warblers, taking ivy berries and fruit buds in the spring, cherries and pears in the autumn, although its staple diet is insects, spiders and snails. It is this willingness to vary their diet which sees those birds that do not return to tropical Africa, through the winter.

WREN *(Troglodytes troglodytes)*

SIZE: 9–10 cm

HABITAT: Widespread across range of habitats

IDENTIFICATION: Very small. Warm brown plumage, short upcocked tail. Loud song

SIMILAR SPECIES: Goldcrest roughly same size

This tiny bird has a song which belies its stature. Its familiar 5–6-second refrain can ring out across several gardens and, in the hills, the repeated phrase spills from the bird's rocky perch and can be heard from a hundred metres or more. The wren will take crumbs from a bird table, but it is usually seen out of the corner of the eye, flitting about the undergrowth, often mistaken for a mouse. It has been known as God's Bird or Our Lady's Hen, and harming it was unlucky and frowned upon. In a reversal of this protectiveness, many communities had ceremonies, usually held in mid-winter, which involved hunting and sometimes killing a wren. If the bird was killed, celebrators highlighted the disparity between its smallness and the huge reverence accorded to it, often pretending to stagger under its insignificant weight.

PIED WAGTAIL *(Motacilla alba yarrellii)*

SIZE: 18 cm

HABITAT: Widespread and varied

IDENTIFICATION: Black back, cap, bib and throat, white eye patches and under parts. Long black tail

SIMILAR SPECIES: Grey wagtail, Yellow wagtail, White (Continental) wagtail

Wherever there is some water, whether fast-flowing moorland stream or urban sewage settling tank, you are likely to find a wagtail of one sort or another. Of the three domestic species, the pied wagtail is the least restricted to watery environments but is still drawn to even temporary puddles, where it splashes and dips away with relish. It rewards the observer with its keen, alert manner, its sprightly, dashing gait interspersed with perky bobbings of the tail and its sudden lunges to snap up insects. When disturbed, it flies off with characteristic long swoops to land a little distance away and carry on its animated search for food. It is a regular visitor to the bird table, usually snapping up crumbs from the lawn beneath. Pied and grey wagtails are present all year, but the yellow wagtail is a summer visitor.

WAXWING *(Bombycilla garrulus)* ▶

SIZE: 18 cm

HABITAT: Winter visitor to E. and N.E. England and S. Scotland. Orchards, gardens and anywhere with berry-bearing plants

IDENTIFICATION: Velvety buff brown but with unmistakable crest and black eye mask, brightly coloured wings with waxy-looking red tips on flight feathers and yellow tip to tail

SIMILAR SPECIES: In flight, starlings have a similar shape.

Waxwings come here to eat. When poor weather or sheer numbers following a good breeding year, create food shortages in their homeland in the Arctic and sub-Arctic taiga forests, these strikingly coloured birds migrate south. They strip every berry they can from rowan trees, cotoneaster, pyracantha and hawthorn. They also eat apples and have been seen in the UK catching insects on the wing. The Dutch call them aptly pestvogel meaning invasion or plague bird. Belfast witnessed just such an invasion – or 'waxwing winter' – in 2001 when 500 spent 4 months in the city. Eating an estimated 500 berries each per day, they consumed 25 million berries during their visit. In the 'waxwing winter' of 1965–6 11,000 were recorded in the UK and one particularly large-scale invasion saw birds as far afield as Turkey. They have no fear of people but their indifference to traffic, however, leads to many casualties.

bullfinch

FINCH FAMILY

The finches are among our most familiar and widespread birds, making regular visits to the bird table and always being somewhere about in the hedges or trees, often flocking together to feed in the winter.

The **chaffinch** (*Fringilla coelebs*), 15 cm, has a distinct song of several downsweeping notes ending in a soprano flourish, but it is by dint of its alarm call that it earns its localised names such as chink-chink (Shropshire), pink-twink (Devon) and prink-prink (Inverness). It is recognisable by its pinky-brown undersides, grey cap and white wing bar and shoulder patch when in flight.

The prettiest finch, and absent only in the far north of Scotland, is the **goldfinch** (*Carduelis carduelis*), 12 cm. The Latin *carduus* means thistle and its preferred diet is seeds plucked from the head of a thistle or other annual weed. With its red face, black-and-white head, brown body, white rump, yellow-and-black wings and ringing song it is no wonder people used to keep it as a caged bird, gruesome though this practice is.

The chunky **bullfinch** (*Pyrrhula pyrrhula*), 15 cm, is also colourful, but its beauty does not cut much ice with fruit growers. It is a voracious eater of flower buds and can be so destructive that the growers are allowed to shoot or trap it. The male has red under parts, grey upper parts, a black cap and white rump with white wing bars in flight.

The **greenfinch** (*Carduelis chloris*), 14–15 cm, is the finch least shy of being near humans and therefore often at the bird table, which it comes to rely on for its winter foodstores. It has plainish olive green plumage with dashing yellow wing and tail flashes and a pleasant song.

Other finches include serin, siskin, twite, linnet and redpoll.

greenfinch

The **brambling** (*Fringilla montifringilla*), 14.5 cm, is really the northern equivalent of the chaffinch, visiting in winter and, on rare occasions, staying on to breed. You are most likely to spot a brambling in beechwoods, as the beech mast or nut is its favourite food. Numbers visiting the UK vary widely – anything from 50,000 to 2 million – depending on the weather and availability of food in its breeding grounds in Scandinavia and Russia.

If you have ever tried to crack open a cherry stone, you will appreciate just how powerful a jaw the **hawfinch** (*Coccothraustes coccothraustes*),18 cm, has. It is known as the cherry finch in Yorkshire and as the grossbeak there and elsewhere. It certainly does have a big bill for a small bird. Experiments by ornithologists using a device replicating the bill and jaw have shown that it takes a pressure of up to 43 kg (95 lb) to crack a cherry stone and 72 kg (159 lb) to crack an olive pip – a favourite with Mediterranean hawfinches. It likes deciduous or mixed woods and older parks and gardens where it can find a mix of seeds and kernels.

Just as impressive is the double-hooked beak of the **crossbill** (*Loxia curvirostra*) which allows it to pull seeds from the cones of pines and other conifers. The bill starts to cross 3 weeks after the bird leaves the nest and thereafter the bird looks and behaves more like a miniature parrot than a finch – juggling itself along branches, swinging and tumbling to get at its food. The male is particularly parrot-like with its orange–red plumage and dark eyepatch. Although present all year, it is not common and found mostly in Scottish pine forests and scattered along the south and east coasts of England.

goldfinch

chaffinch

SWALLOW *(Hirundo rustica)*

SIZE:	20 cm
HABITAT:	In and around towns and villages. Summer visitor
IDENTIFICATION:	Blue–black upper parts and band below throat, cream under parts. Male has russet throat, long tail streamers, female duller with shorter tail. Swerving, darting flight
SIMILAR SPECIES:	House martin

The swallow, harbinger of summer, migrates from South Africa every year, often returning to the same nest site, where it builds its familiar cup of mud and straw. It was once thought that swallows hibernated here, possibly even underwater or in mud beside rivers and ponds, as this is where large groups often gather before they 'disappear'. The first arrivals can be as early as March, hence the saying: 'One swallow doesn't make a summer'. Nevertheless, it is a sign that warmer days are coming and other weather lore is connected with it: that conditions will be good if it soars high, bad if it flies low. If swallows fly low or abandon a nest, it is bad luck and an even worse omen if one should fly between the legs of a domestic animal. Their flight, in which they catch insects and even scoop up water on the wing, is thrilling to watch.

HOUSE MARTIN *(Delichon urbica)*

SIZE:	12 cm
HABITAT:	Widespread except far north of Scotland. Towns and villages, also cliffs and bridges
IDENTIFICATION:	Black upper parts, white rump and under parts. Short forked tail and short beak
SIMILAR SPECIES:	Sand martin, Swift

It is thought lucky to have a martin's nest in the eaves of one's house. The nests are masterpieces of the potter's art, made from waterside mud dug out by the beakful and pressed into place. Sand martins, on the other hand, burrow tunnels into sandbanks or even railway cuttings. The house martin is happy to live alongside people and probably shared caves with mankind in the ancient past. Like the swallow and swift, the martin eats on the wing, snatching insects in darting, veering pursuit. On the Continent it is generally known, in translation, as the 'house swallow' but the name 'martin' seems to have come from the French word for a swift: *martinette*. The sand martin can be distinguished in flight by a brown band across its white breast.

REDSTART *(Phoenicurus phoenicurus)*

SIZE: 14 cm

HABITAT: Parkland, gardens, orchards and woodland. Widespread summer breeding visitor

IDENTIFICATION: Adult male rusty coloured tail, grey back, reddish chest, black throat, white forehead. Female brown above, pale below with dark centre to tail

SIMILAR SPECIES: Black redstart

Although the redstart is striking and distinctive with its flashy markings (named by the Anglo Saxons for its red steort or tail), its cousin, the protected black redstart *(P. ochruros)* is of far greater interest. With fewer than 100 breeding pairs, it is rarer than the golden eagle or osprey. It lives in the centre of our busiest urban centres and is threatened by regeneration plans for London and the Thames corridor, where up to 30% of the population live. This sooty–black bird with its red tail and pale wing patches even has its own conservation website (www.blackredstarts.org.uk), where planners, architects, councillors and regeneration agencies can get advice on how best to develop its favoured brownfield habitats of derelict buildings and industrial wasteland. Although concentrated in London and Birmingham, the black redstart has been recorded in Nottingham, Liverpool, Manchester and Ipswich, with the odd pair at cliff sites and power stations along the south coast between Suffolk and Dorset.

house fly

Two-Winged Flies

Sticky fly-papers, aerosols, and lamps to attract and electrocute have all been used to try to rid our houses of the **house fly** *(Musca domestica)*, 8 mm. But we are fighting a losing battle, as the female lays up to 150 eggs at a time which can produce new flies in a week. It breeds in the nastiest medium it can find, carrying bacteria to its next port of call – which might be your sugar bowl.

The really annoying fly, repeatedly circling the room with a loud buzzing, is probably the **bluebottle** or **blowfly** *(Calliphora erythrocephala)*, 11 mm. It can be seen during most months but is commonest in the summer. This metallic blue fly is another pest in the house as it looks for decaying animal matter such as uncovered meat on which to lay its eggs. If successful, a crawling mass of larvae (maggots) can be the result. In farmyards its other favourite place is the dung heap – ideal conditions for its larvae.

Another brightly coloured fly with unpleasant habits is the **greenbottle** *(Lucilia caesar)*, 10 mm, which also seeks carcasses in which to lay its eggs. Commonly found in gardens, woodland and waysides from April to October, it is a bright metallic green.

The fly that pesters beer drinkers, especially in the pub garden, is the **vinegar fly** or **fruit fly** *(Drosophila melanogaster)*, 3 mm. It is attracted to the smell of fruit juice, wine and vinegar as well as to beer and is well known to amateur wine makers. The male produces a 'love song' to attract its mate by rapid vibrations of its wings. This species has a practical use in that its larva's salivary glands have large chromosomes making them suitable for genetic research work.

bluebottle or blowfly

spotted crane fly

DADDY LONGLEGS *(Tipula paludosa)*

SIZE:	30 mm
HABITAT:	Gardens and grassland
IDENTIFICATION:	Thin body, narrow transparent wings and long, dangling fragile legs
SIMILAR SPECIES:	*Tipula maxima*

The dancing flight of the daddy long legs, or crane fly as it is also called, is a familiar sight in summer or autumn. It usually flies at night and, like moths, can be attracted by artificial light and come indoors through open windows. During the day it can be found on lawns or pastureland, where it will fly up and away when disturbed. Its larva, known as a leatherjacket, is considered a pest by farmers and gardeners. It hatches after 2 weeks and lives in the soil all winter, eating the roots and stems of a variety of plants. This can kill patches of lawn, and one old gardeners' solution is to flood the area, leave it covered with sacking overnight and, in the morning, sweep up the leatherjackets that have surfaced. The largest of our 291 species of crane fly is the less common *Tipula maxima*, frequently seen near water.

RINGED MOSQUITO

(Theobaldia annulata)

SIZE:	9 mm
HABITAT:	Hibernates in buildings in winter. Breeds by water in summer
IDENTIFICATION:	Dark spots on the wings and white rings on the legs
SIMILAR SPECIES:	Common gnat

Most mosquitoes are content to get their blood meal from birds or animals, but the ringed mosquito is one of our largest, and the female is fond of human blood. The mosquito mates in the autumn and the male dies soon afterwards, his objective in life achieved. The female hibernates in buildings or cellars, emerging on warmer winter days. In the spring she flies off to find stagnant water in which to lay her eggs. On hatching, the larva lives suspended just below the surface of the water, so that it can feed on tiny floating food particles. The common gnat, a similar species, is often swatted when found in houses even though it does not bite humans, being content instead to get its meal from birds. It is very abundant near stagnant water and its larva can often be seen jerking about in water butts.

BUFF-TAILED BUMBLE BEE

(Bombus terrestris)

SIZE:	25 mm
HABITAT:	Almost any well-vegetated habitat. Common and widespread except in N. Scotland
IDENTIFICATION:	Broad yellowish-orange band on abdomen and thorax. Buff or white tail but ginger on the queen
SIMILAR SPECIES:	Common carder bee and other bumble bees

A common and welcome sound of summer is the gentle buzzing of a bumble bee as it flies from flower to flower busily collecting nectar and pollen. It will stop from time to time to brush the pollen off its hairy body and into the pollen baskets on its hind legs. It has a relatively short tongue, so it sometimes uses its weight to open lipped flowers like snapdragons and reach down to the nectar. It has also learnt a shortcut and will occasionally bite out a hole in the flower tube so that its tongue can reach inside. There are 16 species of bumble bee in Britain, and the buff-tailed bumble bee is the largest and most common. It is a social bee, like the honey bee, often nesting in burrows made by a mouse or vole. It does not lay up a store of honey, and only the young fertilised queen survives the winter.

HONEY BEE *(Apis mellifera)*

SIZE:	12 mm
HABITAT:	Most habitats throughout the British Isles
IDENTIFICATION:	Brown hairy body with darker stripes
SIMILAR SPECIES:	Several species of mining bees and flower bees

Life in a honey bee colony is rather like a Shakespearean drama, with slaves, treason, favouritism, suicide, desertion and murder. The colony is ruled by a single queen, usually in a beehive, as only a few wild colonies exist, nestling in hollow trees. The male drones die after mating with the queen. The slaves, which are sterile female bees, work to build new cells and collect nectar and pollen, carrying it in 'baskets' on their hind legs. Enough food is stored to last the winter. Eggs to produce new queens are laid in larger cells and fed royal jelly, but when they are about to hatch, the old queen might leave the hive taking half the community with her. Such a swarm can sometimes be seen being chased across country by a beekeeper. Back at the hive, the first new queen emerges – and murders her rivals in their 'beds' by stinging them.

COMMON WASP *(Vespula vulgaris)*

SIZE: 120–180 mm

HABITAT: Common in most habitats and widespread throughout the British Isles

IDENTIFICATION: Black and yellow striped body with black anchor mark on the head. Wings fold longitudinally when at rest

SIMILAR SPECIES: German wasp, Tree wasp

The wasp's nasty sting is no less nasty for knowing that only the female inflicts it. However, it does not usually attack unless annoyed and is probably more interested in what you are having for your picnic. It is a social wasp, working as part of a colony for one queen. After hibernating, the queen starts to make a nest, perhaps underground but sometimes in attics or outhouses. Her first eggs hatch in 4 weeks and these are the workers, which take over all the work of building up the colony, leaving the queen free to lay more eggs. In late summer, the new generation of wasps mates and only the new queens survive the winter. The old queen, workers and males all die. A mossy red gall seen on wild roses is made by the grubs of the Robin's pincushion gall wasp. It is often invaded by other small wasps, who eat the gall or each other.

HOVERFLY *(Syrphus ribesli)*

SIZE: Body length 12 mm

HABITAT: Gardens, parks, hedgerows and woodlands throughout the British Isles

IDENTIFICATION: Yellow and black striped fly, similar to a wasp

SIMILAR SPECIES: Several similar hover flies with slightly different markings

The hoverfly pretends to be a wasp as a way of protecting itself from predators. A bird would hesitate to attack the wasp-patterned hoverfly in case it turned out to be the real thing, despite the fact that in flight it looks and sounds completely different from a wasp. The male seems to hover unmoving, sometimes making a humming or droning sound, unlike the buzzing of a wasp, before darting quickly away. The adult is seen on the wing from April to November, usually near flowers as it feeds on nectar and pollen. It has learnt a lazy shortcut to getting nectar from flowers, where it is normally out of reach, such as with common comfrey. The bumble bee, with its short tongue, has to bite a hole in the flower tube to reach the pollen and, when it has left, the hoverfly makes use of the convenient access.

COMMON EARWIG *(Forficula auricularia)*

SIZE:	10–15 mm long, excluding pincers
HABITAT:	House, garden and trees. Common throughout the British Isles
IDENTIFICATION:	Shiny chestnut brown body with pincers at the tail end, curved in the male. Short leathery forewings cover the folded hind wings
SIMILAR SPECIES:	Lesser earwig

The earwig is no more likely to crawl into a human ear than crawl into any other dark crevice, yet it is called *perce-oreille* (ear-piercer) in French and *ohrwurm* (ear-worm) in German. It is more likely to cause distress to humans by eating their dahlia leaves or spoiling home-grown soft fruit. In *A Miscellany of Garden Wisdom*, Bernard Schofield recommends suspending the hollow stems of elder or sunflowers in the bushes at night and, in the morning, blowing the insects out into a bottle of water. The earwig is omnivorous, and when seen in flowers might be pursuing other insects. The male only mates with one female, after which they both hibernate until early spring when the eggs are laid. These are guarded by the female before and after they are hatched. A family group with these nymphs might be found under flower pots in the garden.

HARVESTMAN

(Phalangium opilio)

SIZE:	3–6 mm
HABITAT:	Gardens, grassland, wayside verges
IDENTIFICATION:	Small globular body, eight very long legs, the second pair always the longest
SIMILAR SPECIES:	Other similar species in the harvestman group

The harvestman is only distantly related to the spider, despite the similarity in appearance. The globular body is the first noticeable difference, as it does not have the obvious divided body or 'waist' of the spider. Most species pass the whole winter as eggs and do not mature until late summer, harvest time, which is how it got its common name. It has no silk glands and so cannot spin a web but feeds on small invertebrates, dead or alive. It is often seen on walls and fences around the garden and in bushes or bramble patches in the countryside. The male can be differentiated from the female by its upward turning jaws which look like horns. The female has a long ovipositor with which she lays her eggs deep in the ground.

HOUSE SPIDER *(Tegenaria domestica)*

SIZE: 10–18 mm

HABITAT: Houses, sheds and out-buildings

IDENTIFICATION: Pale to dark brown body, mottled with black
                      and a pale chevron towards the rear. Long, slightly hairy
                      legs

SIMILAR SPECIES: Cardinal spider

The spider in your bath is most likely to be this one: it has climbed in looking for water and cannot climb out. If you cannot bear to pick it up to rescue it, leave the bathmat hanging over the side with one edge touching the floor of the bath so that it can escape. There is no point in killing it, as it does an excellent job of destroying flies. It spins a large web, up to 300 mm across, and waits in a tubular retreat in the corner. When it feels the vibrations of a trapped fly, it hurries out, poisons its victim and eats it at leisure. In Medieval times, a house spider was thought to be a good remedy for malaria, 'gently bruised and wrapped in a raisin or spread on bread and butter', and a butter-wrapped spider was thought to cure plague and leprosy. The larger Cardinal spider is supposed to have been named for frightening Cardinal Wolsey at Hampton Court.

GARDEN SPIDER *(Aranea diadematus)* ▲

SIZE: 12–15 mm

HABITAT: Gardens, hedgerows and other well vegetated habitats

IDENTIFICATION: Usually brown body, but can be orange or black with
                      paler, cross-shaped markings on the back. Shorter legs
                      than a house spider

SIMILAR SPECIES: *Araneus quadratus* (without a cross)

'Little Miss Muffet sat on a tuffet, eating her curds and whey. There came a great spider which sat down beside her and frightened Miss Muffet away.' As Miss Muffet was sitting on a tuft in this well-known nursery rhyme, it was probably the garden spider which frightened her. It really is harmless and it is fascinating to watch both the spider and its sophisticated web. The web is often almost vertical and the silk threads can be beautiful early on a summer morning with the sunlight catching clinging drops of dew. The garden spider might be sitting in the middle or, more likely, hiding in one corner. When an unfortunate flying insect becomes entangled in the web, the spider pounces, binds it in silk and takes it away to eat. The female dies soon after laying her 400–800 eggs in autumn. Protected by a silk cocoon, these hatch out in spring.

common red ant

GARDEN BLACK ANT *(Lasius niger)*

SIZE:	3 mm
HABITAT:	Gardens and parks, often nesting under paving stones
IDENTIFICATION:	Large black head and black waisted body
SIMILAR SPECIES:	Negro ant (black), Wood ant (black and brown), Common red ant (red)

In June or July these small creatures take off on their mating flights, sometimes in such huge numbers that clouds of them disrupt traffic in busy cities. These are not the worker ants, but the new generation of both sexes off to seek their fortune. The male dies after mating and the female, now a queen, will break off her wings and spend the rest of her 6–7 year life in the nest. Generally, the garden black ant is more likely to be seen outside the house but, for an unlucky few, it invades the kitchen or larder. The invaders will be the workers (wingless, imperfect females) foraging for food. Once one has found food, there will soon be a steady line of ants making a trail to and from it. The workers in the colony have designated tasks, apart from gathering food: some will care for the eggs and larvae, some will attend to the queen and others will become guards, maintenance personnel or dairymaids milking captured aphids.

garden black ant

STAG BEETLE *(Lucanus cervus)*

SIZE: Male 40 mm excluding horns; female 30 mm

HABITAT: Tree trunks and fences or tree stumps. Only in S. and central England

IDENTIFICATION: Brown body, black head and thorax. Extended jaws resembling antlers

SIMILAR SPECIES: Lesser stag beetle

This is one of our largest and most impressive beetles. When disturbed, the male rears up, raises his head and threatens his challenger by spreading his antler-like jaws. However, unless the newcomer is a rival for the affections of a female, the threat is a bluff and he is unlikely to inflict any harm. Although confined to the southern half of England, the stag beetle is common in London suburbs, where the larvae live for several years in rotting tree stumps, especially oak. The adult is seen from May to July, flying from dusk onwards. Sometimes it is attracted to artificial light, so it might fly in through open windows or doors. The female resembles the lesser stag beetle, being smaller and without horns. The black, lesser stag beetle is a little more widespread, but still most common in southern England.

HOUSE CRICKET *(Acheta domesticus)*

SIZE: 15–20 mm

HABITAT: Houses, bakeries and rubbish dumps, throughout England, more local in Wales and Scotland

IDENTIFICATION: Grey or yellowish-brown with darker markings. Tightly rolled hindwings project from rear like extra tails

SIMILAR SPECIES: Dark bush cricket

This cricket might have regretted its decision to emigrate from north Africa and south-west Asia. It is a warm weather creature and finds the British climate a little chilly. It has not ventured very far into the cooler areas of Wales and Scotland and is happiest in heated buildings. It used to be found in small local bakeries, but the modern stainless steel environment does not have the crevices to harbour the eggs. The adult can be seen throughout the year and flies in the open on hot summer evenings. The male produces a shrill 'song', usually heard at night, by rubbing a toothed rib in the left forewing against the right margin of the other. Several hundred eggs are laid by each female. They hatch 2 or 3 months later and the young nymphs take about 6 months to mature.

hawthorn shield bug

pied shield bug

HAWTHORN SHIELD BUG
(Acanthosoma haemorrhoidale)

SIZE: 15 mm

HABITAT: Garden hedges and shrubberies, parks and anywhere with hawthorn trees

IDENTIFICATION: Broad, flat beetle with shield shape behind the head. Triangular thorax with a red band at the rear

SIMILAR SPECIES: Common green shield bug, Pied shield bug, Birch shield bug

Hawthorn berries and leaves are the favourite food of this shield bug, but if they are not available it will move on to other trees like oak or whitebeam. It is common all over England and Wales but not found in Scotland. In autumn it can be seen on garden walls, basking in the sunshine before finding some leaf litter to hibernate in. The following spring the female will lay about 20 eggs at a time on the underside of leaves and abandon them to hatch 9 days later. The pied shieldbug makes a much better parent. The female guards the eggs, turning them from time to time with her beak. After hatching, she takes the young to their food and only leaves them when they start feeding. The broader, common green shield bug becomes a darker bronze colour in the autumn but after hibernating it reverts to bright green.

DEATHWATCH BEETLE *(Xestobium rufovillosum)*

SIZE:	8–10 mm long
HABITAT:	Old, usually damp timber in buildings
IDENTIFICATION:	Reddish brown with patches of short stiff yellow hairs. Often has dust from emergence hole sticking to it, obscuring red–brown colour
SIMILAR SPECIES:	None

You will hear the deathwatch beetle before you see it. Before the adult emerges from its pupal chamber, it makes a tapping noise. In former times when timber buildings were common, it was those keeping a long, quiet vigil beside sickbeds who were most likely to hear this sound – hence the common name. The beetle certainly can kill buildings. The larvae burrow into timber creating a labyrinth of channels and rendering it crumbly and fragile. In Britain infestations occur mostly in oak but also in elm, walnut, chestnut, elder and beech. The life cycle is similar to that of the common furniture beetle or woodworm *(Anobium punctatum)* but it can take up to 10 years. The hatched larvae wander over the timber before burrowing in. When fully grown the larva pupates and changes into the adult beetle, which emerges the following spring from a 3 mm hole. Keeping timber dry and well ventilated is the best defence.

BLACK BEAN APHID OR BLACKFLY *(Aphis fabae)*

SIZE:	2 mm
HABITAT:	Gardens throughout the British Isles, wherever there are suitable host plants
IDENTIFICATION:	Small, black or olive green aphids, with and without wings
SIMILAR SPECIES:	Other Black aphids, Rose aphid (greenfly), Woolly aphid

Anyone who has ever grown broad beans will be familiar with the dreaded blackfly, which settles in vast numbers on the soft growing tips. It causes a good deal of damage by sucking the sap, thus weakening the plant and distorting the leaves. If beans are not on the menu, it will attack spinach, beet, nasturtiums or docks. It has a curious life cycle, producing both winged and wingless aphids; the first generation female lays eggs and the second generation produces live young. The rose aphid or greenfly *(Macrosiphum rosae)*, is probably even better known, colonising roses in the spring and spreading to other plants by summer. The woolly aphid attacks apple trees and is seldom seen, as it is hidden by the mass of white, fluffy wax. There are many old methods of discouraging aphids, including spraying with an infusion of nettles or garlic.

GREEN LACEWING
(Chrysoperla septempunctata)

SIZE: 15 mm

HABITAT: Gardens, hedgerows and woods, most
                     common in S. England, absent from
                     Scotland

IDENTIFICATION: Transparent, well-veined green wings.
                     One black spot between the antennae

SIMILAR SPECIES: Several species of green lacewing with
                     similar or slightly different colouring

Far from being a foe, the lacewing is a friend of the
gardener, as its diet consists mainly of greenfly and
other aphids. A fragile, delicate creature, with
coloured veins on its transparent wings and a weak
flight, it is difficult to reconcile this image with
some of its more gruesome behaviour. The first
larva to hatch from a batch of eggs immediately
eats its unhatched siblings. It then preys on aphids
using its elongated mouthparts to pierce the body
of its victim and suck out the body contents. Not
one to waste anything, the larva uses the empty
skin of its prey to make itself a camouflaged home.
When it grows up, it does not seem to grow out of
its unsavoury habits: if threatened, it will produce
an evil-smelling substance from its stink glands.

CABBAGE WHITEFLY *(Aleyrodes brassicae)*

SIZE:	2 mm
HABITAT:	Gardens and fields throughout the British Isles
IDENTIFICATION:	White waxy wings resembling a small moth
SIMILAR SPECIES:	Greenhouse whitefly

Similar to aphids the cabbage whitefly leaves a horrible sticky mess on plants, much to the annoyance of the gardener, particularly when it spoils his food crop. They pierce and suck the juices of plants and expel excess sugars that they take in with the sap. This honeydew is eagerly sought by other insects and some, such as the ant, even capture the aphids and 'milk' it from them. The cabbage whitefly lives on the underside of cabbage leaves or other brassicas, often making them inedible by the coating of excess honeydew. It is sometimes called the 'snowfly' because, in late summer or autumn, the flies rise in a cloud when disturbed and settle back on the brassicas like snow. Similarly, huge numbers of greenhouse whitefly can infest tomatoes or houseplants, and gardeners usually resort to spraying them with insecticides.

VIOLET GROUND BEETLE

(Carabus violaceus)

SIZE:	20–30 mm
HABITAT:	Gardens, hedgerows, woods and waste ground
IDENTIFICATION:	Black beetle with violet, purple or reddish-blue edges to its wing cases. Five joints to all its feet
SIMILAR SPECIES:	Other black ground beetles including *Carabus granulatus*

There are several species of black ground beetle, many of which do not even have a common name. The violet ground beetle is quite distinctive because of its colouring. It cannot fly but has long powerful legs to run down its prey. It finds somewhere cool and dark to hide by day, sometimes under logs or stones and sometimes in a damp outhouse or shed. At night, it emerges to go hunting and does a good job of keeping down garden pests such as slugs. Around the garden pond or in marshy places a striking copper brown or metallic green ground beetle might be seen. This is *Carabus granulatus*, which can be identified by rows of large granules on each wing case.

BLACK VINE WEEVIL *(Otiorhynchus sulcatus)*

SIZE:	8–12 mm
HABITAT:	Gardens and parks, greenhouses and conservatories
IDENTIFICATION:	Brownish-black weevil with broad snout and jointed antennae which are usually folded back when at rest
SIMILAR SPECIES:	Several similar weevils including Nut weevil, Appleblossom weevil, Osier weevil, Nettle weevil, Sandy clover weevil and Figwort weevil

There are more than 500 species of weevil in Britain, many living exclusively on the plant they favour. The weevil differs from other beetles in having a long rostrum or snout, which varies in shape according to the species. Sometimes it is short and blunt as in the vine weevil, sometimes long and thin, or curving downwards. The adult vine weevil is a pest in the greenhouse or on pot plants: it eats the edges of leaves leaving semi-circular notches. It feeds at night and is difficult to detect, as it drops off and plays dead if the plant is disturbed. However, it is the larva that does the most harm, feeding on roots and tubers underground until the plant is unable to take up water and collapses. Commercial growers used the poison, aldrin, to control vine weevils, but this was withdrawn in 1990. Since then, numbers have increased dramatically.

COMMON CENTIPEDE *(Lithobius forficatus)*

SIZE:	Up to 30 mm long
HABITAT:	Almost everywhere, including houses and gardens
IDENTIFICATION:	Long, segmented, brown shiny body with 15 pairs of legs when adult
SIMILAR SPECIES:	Several other similar centipedes, many without a common name

It is not necessary to count all the legs to tell the difference between a centipede and a millipede, only those on one body segment. A centipede has one pair of legs on each segment and a millipede has two. In Britain we have several species of centipedes which are common throughout Europe and one species, *Lithobius variegatus,* which is exclusive to the British Isles. To avoid being dried out by the sun, the common centipede hides under stones or logs during the day, emerging at night to search for food. It is an aggressive hunter preying on slugs, worms or even on other centipedes. Once caught, the victim is instantly paralysed by the poison injected by the centipede's claws. When newly hatched, it has only 7 pairs of legs and adds to them each time it moults until it has the full quota of 15.

LADYBIRDS

Even the most hardened insect hater usually has a soft spot for the ladybird. Throughout Europe it is part of folklore and is reputed to bring good luck. It has a familiar, trusting way of landing on people and should not be brushed off, as it is supposed to bring good luck. It is also said to be a messenger to heaven, turning into an angel and reserving a place there for someone who has been kind to it.

The best known and most abundant is the **two-spot ladybird** *(Adalia bipunctata)*, 3–6 mm, but its colour pattern is variable. Usually red wing cases with 2 black spots, it can be black with red spots, sometimes with 4 spots instead of 2 and there is even a yellow form. The legs and underside are always black.

Another very common species with variable colours is the **ten-spot ladybird** *(A. 10-punctata)*, 3–5 mm. Generally yellow with 10 black spots, it can be black with yellow spots just to confuse us. The underside of this species is always brown and the legs are pale.

The main purpose of the bright colours is to give birds a warning that it is distasteful and, if touched, some species give off an acrid, staining fluid. In the north, the black form of the 2-spot ladybird is more common, as this background colour absorbs more heat in a cooler environment.

Less likely to vary its colour is the **seven-spot ladybird** *(Coccinella 7-punctata)*, although even on this one the wing cases can be orange instead of bright red.

There are more than 40 species of ladybird in Britain, some with up to 24 spots and some without any spots at all. Mostly they are welcomed by gardeners, as they eat aphids and mildew.

two-spot ladybird

Occasionally, ladybirds come into the house to hibernate, but central heating could cause their metabolism to continue and use up fat and water reserves.

fourteen-spot ladybird

SMALL TORTOISESHELL BUTTERFLY *(Aglais urticae)*

SIZE: Forewing 25 mm

HABITAT: Gardens and other flowery places. Probably the commonest garden butterfly

IDENTIFICATION: Upperside bright orange with black border containing blue spots, 3 rectangular black spots at front. Hindwing black at base. Underside mottled black and brown, faint blue spots near outer edge

SIMILAR SPECIES: Large tortoiseshell (extremely rare), Painted lady

The small tortoiseshell is found everywhere from city parks to mountain pastures up to 2750 m. In the garden it adds wonderful colour between May and October (as early as February in warm weather) and the caterpillar eats stinging nettles so is anything but a pest. The caterpillar is 22 mm long, brown or black, with branching spines and 2 yellow bands along each side. You might find one of the butterflies hibernating in a shed or even in the house. These hibernators are among the earliest spring butterflies. If you want more tortoiseshells in the garden grow aubrietia, buddleia, candytuft, common ragwort, common thistle, Michaelmas daisy and scabious – all favourite feeding plants. The large tortoiseshell is duller with little black dots on the hindwing and the painted lady paler with black dots on the hindwing.

LARGE WHITE BUTTERFLY
(Pieris brassicae)

SIZE:	Forewing 25–35 mm
HABITAT:	Gardens, cultivated land and other flowery places
IDENTIFICATION:	Upper side chalky white, blacks tips reaching half-way down edge of forewing. Male 1 spot on forewing. Underside of hindwing yellowish with dusting of black scales
SIMILAR SPECIES:	Small white butterfly, Moorland clouded yellow

The large white, or cabbage white, is a common sight in the garden between April and October, but it is no friend of the gardener. The dirty green caterpillars (40 mm) with their black and yellow markings are also a common sight in the vegetable garden, where they wreak havoc on cabbages and other brassicas. Farmers hate them as they can reduce a field of rape or kale to mere stalks in no time. The mustard oils in their food make all stages of the large white's lifecycle distasteful to predators. However, the tiny parasitic wasp *Apanteles glomeratus* lays its eggs in the caterpillar, which is eaten by the growing wasp grubs. They bore out and pupate in little yellow cocoons beside the corpse. Apanteles would have wiped out the large white were it not for Continental immigrants. The small white *(P. rapae)*, 15–30 mm, is similar but with paler markings.

WALL BROWN BUTTERFLY
(Lasiommata megera)

SIZE:	Forewing 17–25 mm
HABITAT:	Gardens, roadside verges, rough grassland
IDENTIFICATION:	Upper sides deep orange with brown borders and streaks. Prominent eye-spot near wing tip, 3–4 spots on hindwing. Underside of hindwing mottled brown or pearly with 6 eye-spots and golden sheen
SIMILAR SPECIES:	None in Britain

As its name suggests, the wall brown likes to settle on a wall or rock and soak up the sun. You will see it between March and October. Its 25 mm long, bluish-green hairy caterpillars, on the other hand, come out to feed at night or in milder weather on the tall, coarse grasses of the verge or rough meadowland. They have 2 short 'tails' and faint white stripes.

HOLLY BLUE BUTTERFLY *(Celastrina argiolus)*

SIZE:	Forewing 12–18 mm
HABITAT:	Gardens, parks, woodland margins and hedgerows. Absent from Scotland
IDENTIFICATION:	Male upper side bright violet with narrow black margins; female more sky blue with broader margins (very broad in late summer broods). Undersides powdery-blue with long black spots
SIMILAR SPECIES:	None in Britain

If you have a largish garden with a patch of brambles or an escallonia hedge, you might find the holly blue in among the foliage between April and September feeding on honeydew. Its name comes from the main food plant of the early-brood caterpillar, which also eats brambles, raspberries, hops and bell heather and many garden shrubs and herbaceous plants. The caterpillar, which consumes the flowers and developing fruit, is 12 mm long, bright green and slug shaped with a bumpy back and sometimes pink or purple stripes. Second-brood caterpillars usually feed on ivy, so this omnivorous creature can be a bit of a pest in the garden, but potential exterminators should dwell on William Blake's words: 'The caterpillar on the leaf/Repeats to thee thy mother's grief,/Kill not the moth nor butterfly/For the last judgement draweth nigh'.

RED ADMIRAL BUTTERFLY *(Vanessa atalanta)*

SIZE:	Forewing 30 mm
HABITAT:	Gardens and other flowery places
IDENTIFICATION:	Velvety black upper side, bold marks of red and white. Underside similar with mottled brown hindwing lacking red margin
SIMILAR SPECIES:	None in Britain

There is nothing like windfall apples to bring the red admiral into your garden. It loves to drink the sweet stickiness, sometimes over-indulging on fermenting juice and getting a little 'drunk'. It lays distinctive green, ribbed eggs on nettle leaves. When the caterpillar emerges it sews together a little tent of leaves with silk and begins feeding on nearby foliage. It lives there until the food runs out or until it grows too big for the tent. Then it moves to the next plant and builds a bigger home. This happens several times during its lifetime and you can find the tents around the edges of nettle beds, sometimes with a dark, spiky, white-speckled caterpillar, about 35 mm long with yellow spots along its sides, curled up inside. The butterfly hibernates, but few survive the British winter and almost all in the garden are European immigrants.

Painted Lady Butterfly
(Vanessa cardui)

SIZE:	Forewing 28 mm
HABITAT:	Gardens, roadsides and all other flowery places
IDENTIFICATION:	Upper side pale orange with black markings including broad triangle at wing-tip enclosing white spots. Forewing underside paler but similar, but hindwing underside mottled brown and grey with row of eye-spots near edge. Caterpillar largely black with branched spines and broken yellow line on each side
SIMILAR SPECIES:	None in Britain

The North African winter of 1995/6 was very wet. These conditions created what naturalists across Britain would remember as 'The Year of The Painted Lady'. Adult painted ladies migrate each summer throughout Europe to breed before returning to Africa. The exceptional wetness allowed a huge number to reach adulthood and, in 1996, they arrived in their millions. This is from a Forestry Commission report by an observer in Hamsterley Forest, Co. Durham: 'On 2nd June, I saw four painted ladies (during 1995 I saw four the whole year). Four days later I saw 16, a week later 50…something strange was happening. On 9th August [it] was there in hundreds. I have never seen anything like it before and probably never will again.' A rough count along one verge totalled 415. The caterpillars, which usually eat nettles, devastated fields of borage.

PEACOCK BUTTERFLY *(Inachis io)*

SIZE:	Forewing 30 mm
HABITAT:	Wide-ranging wherever there are nectar-rich flowers. Common in gardens and parks. Rarer in N. of Scotland
IDENTIFICATION:	Distinctive. Upper side rich chestnut or maroon, four large eye-spots, sooty brown margins. Dark brown underside almost black
SIMILAR SPECIES:	None

The peacock, one of the most eye-catching creatures in British wildlife, flits about all summer saying 'look at me'. Then comes the winter and, folding its wings, it performs a disappearing act. The intense dark brown of its underwings provides wonderful camouflage in the shadows of its favourite hibernation haunts – hollow trees, sheds and attics. When it emerges in the spring it lays its green eggs in clumps, often piled several deep to foil parasites, on the underside of nettle leaves. The caterpillar is also distinctive: 45 mm long, black and spiky, and covered in tiny white spots. It eats nettle leaves, elms and hops. The peacock butterfly, which can live for more than a year, will be attracted into your garden if you grow buddleia, common ragwort, common thistle, hemp agrimony or scabious, all of which it favours.

COMMA BUTTERFLY *(Polygonia c-album)*

SIZE:	Forewing 23 mm
HABITAT:	Wide ranging in gardens, orchards, hedgerows, clearings and woodland glades. Rare in Scotland
IDENTIFICATION:	Distinctive. Upper sides orange with sooty-brown markings and pale spots near deeply jagged margins. Undersides mottled brown, resembling dead leaves, with hindwing carrying white comma-shaped mark
SIMILAR SPECIES:	None in Britain

Habitat loss denied butterflies the chance to capitalise on increased average temperatures in the late 20th century. In the 25 years to 2001, springs and summers were 1–1.5 °C warmer and scientists expected butterflies, many at the limit of their ranges, to spread north. They did not, mainly because intensive agriculture had eroded 70% of semi-natural habitats since 1940. One of the few exceptions was the comma. Always a familiar and welcome sight in southern English gardens and countryside, it is moving north and adapting to new habitats. It is attracted to bramble blossom, buddleia and sedums like 'ice plant', and the later broods like blackberries and pears. The caterpillar is 35 mm long, brown with branched spines and, when mature, a large white rear patch. The butterfly hibernates in hedges, looking just like a dead leaf.

COMMON (OR WEBBING) CLOTHES MOTH
(Tineola bisselliella)

SIZE:	Forewing 4–5 mm
HABITAT:	Widespread in houses
IDENTIFICATION:	Body about 6.5 mm long with wings folded, golden-yellow with satiny sheen. Upright, reddish-gold tuft of hairs on head. Eggs oval, ivory, about 1 mm long. Larva shiny, creamy white with brown head, up to 13 mm long
SIMILAR SPECIES:	Brown house moth

If your clothes are dirty and shut up, unused, in a dark place, you are inviting the attentions of the clothes moth. Wearing clothes regularly and keeping them aired and clean works better than any of the many anti-moth tactics, which include using expensive cedar-lined closets or even deep-freezing your possessions. There are also many natural and artificial chemicals that deter the moth, but none is 100% effective. This is the most universal of the four common species of clothes moths. The webbing name comes from the silk-lined tubes made by the caterpillar in the material they are feeding on. If it becomes too dry or cold, the caterpillar can enter a dormant period until conditions improve. The female moth dies after laying about 50 eggs from which hatch tiny larvae that can sneak through any opening greater than 0.01 mm.

clothes moths

BROWN HOUSE MOTH
(Hofmannophila pseudospretella)

SIZE:	Length at rest 10 mm
HABITAT:	In and around buildings
IDENTIFICATION:	Bronze–brown, dark flecks on forewings. Male 8.5 mm long, female 14.5 mm. Larva 6 mm long, white with tan head
SIMILAR SPECIES:	Common (or Webbing) clothes moth

More destructive than those of the clothes moth, the larvae of the brown house moth (or false clothes moth) will eat upholstery, carpets, furs, stuffed animals, skins, birds' nests, dried flowers and fruit, books and even leather. The moth itself is a pest in warehouses, where it not only consumes spilt cereals and flour but will get into bagged commodities and bulk containers, as it will in the home if you allow it. It owes its success to its varied diet and its breeding rate. In favourable conditions the female can lay 500–600 eggs, which can take as little as 8 days to hatch into larvae, depending on temperature and humidity. The whole lifecycle usually takes 11–13 months. It can tolerate a wide range of conditions, but the larvae are susceptible to low humidity and if this is kept below 80% they cannot complete their development.

ELEPHANT HAWK-MOTH
(Deilephila elpenor)

SIZE: Forewing 31–36 mm

HABITAT: Widespread in gardens, parks, woodland margins and open country. Absent in N. Scotland

IDENTIFICATION: Distinctive. Upper forewing bronze-green with pink stripes; hindwing bright pink with black underside. Named for the trunk-like snout of the caterpillar

SIMILAR SPECIES: Small elephant hawk-moth

Research has shown that not only can this moth, like other nocturnal moths, see exceptionally well in the dark, it can also see in colour. On a moonless night, with light levels 100 million times dimmer than day, nocturnal moths fly agilely between flowers. The elephant hawk-moth has three spectral classes of photoreceptors, the same as in humans, and has been trained by researchers to associate a blue or yellow disk with sugar solution. The results show that it does see colours, even when it is too dark for humans to see at all. It feeds on honeysuckle and other tubular flowers. The caterpillar is 90 mm long, dark brown or green with 2 pairs of pink-and-black eye-spots behind its snout. When alarmed, it pulls in its 'trunk', swelling the eye-spots, and sways from side to side. It feeds on willowherb, bedstraw and fuchsias.

DEATH'S HEAD HAWK-MOTH
(Acherontia atropos)

SIZE: Forewing 51–66 mm

HABITAT: Gardens and potato fields

IDENTIFICATION: Distinctive. Upper side dark brown to reddish on forewing, yellow and brown on hindwing. Thick brown-and-yellow striped body, dark thorax with characteristic pale skull-shaped pattern

SIMILAR SPECIES: None

This huge and relatively rare moth loves honey and will sneak into the old-fashioned skep-type beehives or a wild bee colony in search of its favourite meal. Once in there, it displays another of its peculiarities, apart from its 'death's head' marking: it squeaks by blowing through its short proboscis. It has been said that this noise pacifies the bees, but as it makes it when handled it is probably a defence mechanism. The moth also eats tree sap and rarely visits flowers. It lays its eggs on potato plants, the main foodplant of the fearsome caterpillar – up to 125 mm long, yellow with seven purple diagonal stripes and a curly horn at the rear. The death's head is a summer visitor from Africa and a few pupae survive the winter. Both the caterpillars and the large, dark brown chrysalises are often dug up in potato fields, usually in the south.

HUMMINGBIRD HAWK-MOTH
(Macroglossum stellatarum)

SIZE: Forewing 25–29 mm

HABITAT: Gardens, parks and other flowery places. Continental resident spreading to most parts in summer

IDENTIFICATION: Forewing dull brown. Hindwing orange, although usually seen as a brownish blur as it hovers.

SIMILAR SPECIES: None

Hawk-moths are very fast fliers, recorded at speeds of up to 60 kph, but none beats its wings as rapidly as the hummingbird hawk-moth. Most European reports of hummingbirds are actually sightings of this moth, which hovers noisily by its chosen blossom, licking the nectar out with its long tongue. It is unusual in that, while preferring to fly in bright sunlight, it will also take wing at dawn, dusk or at night, in rain, or on cool, dull days. Very hot weather tends to make it lethargic, confining its activity to the relative cool of the morning and late afternoon. It is very strongly attracted to nectar-rich flowers like jasmine, buddleia, nicotiana, tulips, primula, viola, syringa, verbena, phlox and stachys. The caterpillar, up to 60 mm, is green or brown with a pale line on its sides and a yellow-tipped blue horn at the rear.

RED UNDERWING MOTH *(Catocala nupta)*

SIZE:	Forewing 35–45 mm
HABITAT:	Parkland, woodland and marshes. Common in S. and central England, scarce in S.W. England and W. Wales. Absent from Scotland
IDENTIFICATION:	Forewing marbled brown, hindwing brilliant crimson with black hoops and yellow margin
SIMILAR SPECIES:	Rosy underwing, Dark crimson underwing, Light crimson underwing

The bright hindwings actually help the big, beautiful red underwing escape predators. When disturbed, it flies off quickly, flashing vivid crimson. The enemy pursues this beacon, whereupon the moth just as quickly settles on a tree, closes its wings and merges with the background. The pursuer, still looking for something bright red, departs bewildered. The red underwing is one of the largest British moths and rests by day, usually high in a tree or on a post or wall. It flies after dark and is attracted to light or to sugar. The Latin name comes from the Greek *kato* (below) and *kalos* (beautiful) – referring to the hindwings – and *nupta* (marriage). This was possibly an oblique reference by Linnaeus, the Swedish naturalist who established the naming system, to gaudy underwear supposed to have been worn by Scandinavian brides.

HERALD MOTH *(Scoliopteryx libatrix)*

SIZE:	Length at rest 20 mm
HABITAT:	Gardens, commons, marshes and woodlands. Widespread and plentiful, especially in south. Thinly scattered in Scotland and Northern Isles
IDENTIFICATION:	Forewing rusty brown with reddish markings on the inner side, margins deeply notched. Hindwing uniform brown with lighter margin and paleness on inner side
SIMILAR SPECIES:	Lunar thorn

The wing shape of the herald moth sets it apart from other common moths, although some less usual moths, like the lunar thorn, resemble it. The notched wing margin and its colouring make the herald look exactly like a dry, shrivelled leaf when it is at rest during the day. This is also perfect camouflage for a moth which overwinters as an adult, usually in a barn or outhouse, although not particularly useful if it hibernates in a cave, as it is known to do in parts of America. It can sometimes be found in fairly large numbers hibernating in abandoned sheds and old army bunkers and pillboxes. It feeds on ivy blossom before hibernation and on sallow catkins when it emerges in the spring. The 55 mm long caterpillar, which spins a white cocoon in which to turn into a black pupa, feeds on sallow, willow, osier, poplar, aspen and rowan leaves.

SWALLOWTAILED MOTH
(Ourapteryx sambucaria)

SIZE:	Forewing 25–31 mm
HABITAT:	Widespread, moderately common in England and Wales, less so in S. Scotland. Gardens, woodlands and commons
IDENTIFICATION:	Both wings bright lemon–yellow at first, fading to cream or almost white. Distinctive short, pointed 'tail' on hindwings
SIMILAR SPECIES:	None

The swallowtail gives a lie to the idea that butterflies are more delicately beautiful than moths. There are plenty of moths which rival, and excel, butterflies for colour, but the swallowtail has a butterfly-like grace and fineness of line. It is not a strong flier but is on the wing from the end of June and throughout July. It is strongly attracted by light, so there is every chance of seeing it at the window at night. The scarlet-red eggs are laid mainly under the leaves of ivy, privet, oak and hawthorn, on which the caterpillars feed. The 50 mm caterpillar is a 'looper', lacking most of its prolegs and moving by looping and extending the whole body. This type is sometimes called an inchworm or measuring worm. After hibernating in a bark crevice, the caterpillar makes a flimsy cocoon, suspended under a leaf or twig, in which to pupate.

BUFF ERMINE MOTH *(Spilosoma lutea or luteum)*

SIZE:	Forewing 17–21 mm
HABITAT:	Widespread and common throughout Britain in gardens and open country
IDENTIFICATION:	Distinctive, silky creamy-yellow wings with extremely variable dark markings from a few spots to almost total coverage. Dense hairy mantle behind head and hairy legs. Brown caterpillar, 45 mm, heavily tufted, eats docks and dandelions
SIMILAR SPECIES:	White ermine moth

Before the *1955 Clean Air Act*, the buff ermine was a lot blacker – not because pollution dirtied it but because its colouration evolved to match the surfaces on which it rested. Before the Act, everything, particularly in the industrialised areas, was more grimy. The *New Naturalist Moths*, first published in 1955, shows two 'normal' buff ermines, collected in Oxford and Huntingdonshire, beside three blacker versions collected in Yorkshire. It is explained that the blacker versions got their colouring from their inheritance of particular genes. In polluted areas the normal versions, sitting on soot-blackened tree trunks, were easily spotted by predators, leading to an increase in the proportion of the better-camouflaged melanistic variety in the population. Nowadays, with cleaner air, darker versions are a rarity.

LARGE WHITE PLUME MOTH
(Pterophorus pentadactyla)

SIZE:	Forewing 12–15 mm
HABITAT:	Widespread and common in gardens, hedgerows and wasteground
IDENTIFICATION:	Forewing split into 2 feathery lobes, hindwing into 3, which gather at rest to form single 'limb' at right-angles to body. Thin body and long, spidery legs; hind legs have side 'spurs'. Flies in June and July.
SIMILAR SPECIES:	Several plume moths

The plume moths are distinctive, both at rest, when they adopt a cruciform shape, and in flight, when their many-lobed wings spread to look like feathers. The large white, which can be spotted during the day resting on long grass, is ghostly white all over, but others are brown. Some plume moths look like large mosquitoes or crane flies and have wings with as many as 10 lobes (many-plumed moth, *Alucita hexadactyla*). The large white plume's caterpillar feeds on bindweed until hibernating, then wakes in the spring to eat the young leaves and flowers. *A. hexadactyla* hibernates as a moth among ivy or in a barn and is commonly seen in spring on honeysuckle, the 12 mm long caterpillar's food plant. The triangle plume moth *(Platyptilia gonodactyla)* is common wherever there is coltsfoot, and all plume moths are readily attracted to light at night.

GARDEN TIGER MOTH *(Arctia caja)*

SIZE: Forewing 35–39 mm

HABITAT: Widespread and familiar in gardens as far north as Orkney

IDENTIFICATION: Patterned brown-and-white forewings, bright red hindwings with black spots. Highly variable colours. Female larger and stouter-bodied

SIMILAR SPECIES: Jersey tiger

Anyone who believes butterflies are more colourful than moths has not seen a garden tiger. Along with the scarlet and jersey tigers, the green silver-lines, the cinnabar and the rare crimson speckled, it proves how vivid a moth can be. The garden tiger's bright colours and its distinctive smell warn predators that it is unpleasant to eat. At rest, it usually 'tents' its wings over its body, but when disturbed it extends its antennae and exposes its bright hindwings and the fringe of red hairs behind its head. The very hairy, 60 mm long caterpillar, sometimes called a 'woolly bear', feeds mainly on dock, dandelion and nettle leaves and hibernates when still quite small, emerging in the spring to make a cocoon of silk mixed with its own hairs. The moth flies at night in July and August, and the male is frequently attracted by light.

CINNABAR MOTH *(Tyria jacobaeae)*

SIZE: Forewing 40 mm

HABITAT: Gardens, grassland, wasteland, heath. Where ragwort or groundsel grow

IDENTIFICATION: Upperside black with crimson stripe and two marginal spots. Hindwing entirely crimson. Underside crimson. Eggs spherical, yellow when fresh, darkening as they develop, laid in clusters on underside of leaves. Larvae (40–45 mm long) pale yellow with black heads at emergence, developing characteristic black and yellow banding around body

SIMILAR SPECIES: None

The probable cause of the plague of ragwort (see p.106), which struck the UK in the late 1990s was that this troublesome plant had been growing for years without control from its natural predator, the cinnabar moth caterpillar. One caterpillar can eat a ragwort flower in 3 minutes and a brood will eat a whole plant in a day and 30 plants during their life cycle. The larvae of a single moth eat nearly one million seeds. The plague had its origins in 1988, which was a boom year for the caterpillars. They ate not only all the flowering plants but also all the first-year rosettes. The following year millions of moths emerged but had nowhere to lay eggs. The population crashed. But ragwort seeds can grow after lying dormant for up to 20 years and, without cinnabars, the plant ran amok. Although some moths survived and others crossed from the continent, natural losses prevented the rebuilding of a population necessary to control ragwort. A company called Ragwort UK pioneered the re-introduction of pupae, eggs, caterpillars and even freshly emerged moths to help fight the plague and by 2003 these measures were having a noticeable effect.

PUSSMOTH *(Cerura vinula)*

SIZE:	Forewing 31–40 mm
HABITAT:	Widely distributed as far north as Orkney, moderately common, close to poplars, willows and sallows
IDENTIFICATION:	Upper sides of both wings pale grey and white with swirling dark markings. Female with darker hind wings. Abdomen grey and white hooped, furry-looking like a cat. Flies May–July
SIMILAR SPECIES:	None

The pussmoth is large and quite handsome but not really striking. Its caterpillar, on the other hand, is extraordinary. It is like a creature from a science fiction movie: a fat, green hunchbacked body with a white-bordered, purple 'saddle' and bulbous corrugations dotted with white-and-purple spots; a huge flat, red 'face' with big 'eye' markings and, most bizarre of all, a whiplash 'tail' of two red threads, which it slashes at attackers. If the intruder is not sent on its way, the 35 mm long caterpillar squirts it with a jet of strong formic acid. It spins a cocoon of silk and chewed wood which, when hardened, is perfect camouflage. In the spring, the emerging moth softens this hard casing with a secretion of caustic potash, then cuts its way out with a specially modified part of the pupa case that stays on its head until it is free.

MAGPIE MOTH *(Abraxas grossulariata)*

SIZE:	Wingspan 35–40 mm.
HABITAT:	Gardens, fruit farms. Once common in most of Britain, less so in Scotland, now in decline in many areas.
IDENTIFICATION:	Upperside, varied geometric patterns of black and yellow on a white background. Hindwing less densely marked.
SIMILAR SPECIES:	Small magpie moth

This very striking moth was once a great favourite with collectors because it could easily be bred to create forms with new and unusual colours and patterns. This great variation of marking has made the moth an ideal 'guinea pig' for genetic studies more recently. Of greater interest to the gardener, however, are its caterpillars, which can severely defoliate currant and gooseberry bushes. The white caterpillars, with black spots on their back and an orange–yellow stripe down each side, are found during May and June and should be picked off the bushes and destroyed. The moth flies in July and August and breeds on hawthorn, blackthorn and other hedgerow shrubs. Although day-active it is regularly attracted to light. The small magpie (Eurrhypara lancealis) is a common summer moth, flying from mid-July to the end of August. It likes woodland, hedgerows and gardens.

COMMON SNAIL *(Helix aspersa)*

SIZE:	3.5 cm high and 3.5 cm wide
HABITAT:	Gardens, woods and hedges, common throughout England, Wales and S. Scotland
IDENTIFICATION:	Brown spiral shell with tortoiseshell markings
SIMILAR SPECIES:	Copse snail, Roman snail

This is the 'common or garden' snail: the creature that brought the stock phrase for mundaneness into our everyday speech. It is, indeed, too common in most gardens, and gardeners go to great lengths to keep it away from their plants. Snails can be captured by placing a large rhubarb leaf upside down in the evening for them to crawl under at dawn. If you cannot bear to kill them, make sure you take them far enough away: snails marked with Tippex have been recorded returning home after being dumped two miles away. The snail is a favourite food of the song thrush, and the tapping of the thrush trying to break open the shell on an anvil stone is a familiar sound in gardens. Land snails exhibit an interesting Cupid-like behaviour: before mating, they drive chalky darts into their mate's body, which apparently act as an aphrodisiac stimulant.

BLACK SLUG *(Arion ater)*

SIZE:	Up to 12 cm long
HABITAT:	Gardens, woodland and hedgerows throughout the British Isles
IDENTIFICATION:	Shiny black or occasionally red body with two long and two short tentacles
SIMILAR SPECIES:	Common garden slug, Great grey slug

A walk through the garden after a heavy shower will probably astound you if you look closely at the lawn. These ideal conditions bring out more black slugs than you ever knew existed. Ridding the garden of the black slug and the common garden slug is a popular subject for gardening column writers. Slug pellets are largely frowned upon now, as the poison also kills slug eaters like birds and hedgehogs, so organic gardeners use old-fashioned methods. Salt, wood ash or soot sprinkled around precious plants act as deterrents, or the slugs can be lured and drowned by sinking a jam jar half-full of beer into the ground. In the south, an orange–red form of *Arion ater* is commonest, whereas in the north and in upland areas, the black form is prevalent. When threatened, the slug withdraws almost into a ball, making it more difficult to eat.

GREAT GREY SLUG *(Limax maximus)*

SIZE: Up to 20 cm long

HABITAT: Gardens and woods throughout the British Isles

IDENTIFICATION: Dark grey with white spots, raised ridge along the centre of the back

SIMILAR SPECIES: Black slug

The great grey slug is horribly large. It belongs to the keelback family: the keel being the raised ridge that runs about a third of the way along its back from the tail end. Another distinguishing feature is the fingerprint pattern of raised ridges on the mantle (the elevated part of the front of the body). Like all slugs, the great grey slug is slimy and leaves a trail as it moves along. Much as we might be disgusted by the slime, it is essential for the slug. It is used for suction (to travel upside down) and as a lubricant to allow it to squeeze into small crevices and avoid sunlight. The slug exudes a thick, unpleasant tasting mucus when threatened and contracts to a shorter, fatter shape. This makes it less attractive and more difficult for predators to eat.

COMMON EARTHWORM

(Lumbricus terrestris)

SIZE: Up to 30 cm long

HABITAT: Gardens and farmland throughout the British Isles

IDENTIFICATION: Soft pencil-like body with more than 100 segments

SIMILAR SPECIES: Other species of earthworm

The earthworm digs more of the garden than the average gardener. This valuable member of the community works the soil by aerating it, mixing in leaves and other organic matter, so improving germination and growth. Gardeners used to kill this 'pest' for leaving unsightly casts on manicured lawns. Nowadays, they use various methods to encourage the worm to the surface and then move it to where its efforts will be more appreciated. In Bernard Schofield's *A Miscellany of Garden Wisdom*, he recommends boiling 10 horse chestnuts in a quart (1.1 litres) of water for an hour and then spraying the cooled water on the lawn to bring the worms to the surface. The common earthworm, the fattest of our earthworms, has to keep the surface of its skin moist as, without respiratory organs, the entire body surface is used to exchange gas.

SLOW WORM *(Anguis fragilis)* ▲

SIZE: 30–50 cm

HABITAT: Gardens, hedgebanks, grassland and dry heaths, throughout Britain

IDENTIFICATION: Grey, bronze or light brown body, not tapering like a snake

SIMILAR SPECIES: Smooth snake, Grass snake, Adder

The slow worm is not a snake at all, it is a legless lizard. One difference is that the slow worm, like all lizards, has eyelids whereas snakes do not. Another is that a snake's body tapers down towards the tail but a slow worm's body is the same thickness all the way. It is certainly an unhurried creature and feeds on slow-moving prey such as slugs – a good reason not to ban it from your garden. Like snakes, it is protected under the Wildlife and Countryside Act, 1981, but you cannot tell that to cats which, unfortunately, often catch and kill slow worms. If it is caught by a predator, it can shed its tail to make its escape and the tail grows back to some extent. The slow worm's shiny body can vary in colour and, in coastal areas, it sometimes has blue spots.

Coral Spot Fungus *(Nectria cinnabarina)*

SIZE: Up to 2 mm across

HABITAT: Decaying wood in gardens or woodland

IDENTIFICATION: Orange–pink spots and red lumps

SIMILAR SPECIES: None

This distinctive fungus is often seen on twigs or fallen branches, looking like a particularly nasty case of German measles. It is widespread and very common in moist conditions, with the spots showing throughout the year. The cinnabar–red granular cushions burst through the bark forming raised clumps. At one stage in its life cycle, when the pink, powdery cushions are seen on the wood, the fungus is known as *Tubercularia vulgaris.* Canker in apple trees is caused by a related species, *Dialonectria galligena,* which cracks or destroys the bark. It is easily identified by gaping wounds and scars, killing the growth above it.

HYPOGYMNIA PHYSODES

SIZE:	Flat, spreading
HABITAT:	Gardens, parks, particularly on trees, fences and walls
IDENTIFICATION:	Irregular patches of smooth, grey, hollow tubes
SIMILAR SPECIES:	*Parmelia sulcata, Parmelia saxatilis*

This lichen is very common throughout Britain. As well as on trees it can be found on rocks, walls and well-weathered wooden structures. It is a similar colour to *Parmelia sulcata* and often grows with it, jostling for space. The underside of the thallus is securely attached to the bark or stone without the usual anchoring threads of the *Parmelia* species. On moors and heaths, the form *elegans* can be found growing on heather and other twigs giving them a lacy appearance. Lichens provide food and camouflage for a large number of creatures: larva of the scalloped hazel moth can change from the dark purple of a bare twig to the mottled bluish-green of one covered with lichen. Apart from the 28 rare species listed on Schedule 8 of the *Wildlife and Countryside Act 1981*, few lichens have acquired English names. The Latin name, *Parmelia sulcata*, means small, round, furrowed shield. This lichen is a familiar sight in parks and gardens, growing on the trunks of trees, with a penchant for apple trees. In polluted areas, it is only found near the base of the tree; the cleaner the air, the higher up it will grow. *P. sulcata*, is one of the commonest lichens chosen by birds to decorate their nests. Long-tailed tits, in particular, cover the outside of their nest with lichen using an ingenious 'Velcro' principle. One theory is that they try to make the nest blend in with the rest of the lichen-covered tree.

WOODLOUSE *(Oniscus asellus)*

SIZE:	14 mm long
HABITAT:	Gardens, woodland and hedgerows
IDENTIFICATION:	Dark grey segmented body with paler sides
SIMILAR SPECIES:	Pill woodlouse and other species of woodlouse

Turn over a stone in any garden and you are likely to see clusters of these creatures sheltering from the light. This is because the woodlouse easily becomes desiccated, especially in strong sunlight. Stones, crevices in rocks, behind loose pieces of bark, all make good hiding places for this nocturnal animal, and if its refuge starts to dry out it will leave in search of an alternative. A woodlouse matures at 2 years and a female can sometimes be seen carrying eggs in a pouch beneath her body. There are several similar species, but one with a different, interesting characteristic is the pill woodlouse. Its body is completely slate-grey without markings or spots and, when disturbed, it rolls itself into a small ball. Unscrupulous apothecaries were said to pass them off as pills, hence their common name.

HEDGEHOG *(Erinaceus europaeus)*

SIZE: Up to 27 cm

HABITAT: Gardens, parks, woodland, hedgerows. Common throughout the British Isles except for a few Scottish islands

IDENTIFICATION: Short legs, pointed snout and body covered with spines

SIMILAR SPECIES: None

In Britain we have a soft spot for the hedgehog, despite its prickly spines and fleas, perhaps conditioned as toddlers by Beatrix Potter's *Mrs Tiggywinkle*. We encourage it into the garden by leaving out a saucer of bread and milk, and children watch excitedly from windows as it snuffles and grunts its way up the path at night. It squeals when alarmed, and its usual defence is to roll up into a ball presenting a barrier of spines. Unfortunately, this is no protection against traffic, and road casualties are a common sight. The hedgehog is popular with gardeners because of its penchant for slugs and was introduced to the Outer Hebridean island of North Uist in 1974, with devastating results. It decided it preferred the easily accessible eggs of ground-nesting birds to slugs and has been blamed for reducing the dunlin population by 65%.

HOUSE MOUSE *(Mus domesticus)*

SIZE: 7–9 cm excluding tail

HABITAT: Houses, farms and outbuildings

IDENTIFICATION: Greyish-brown fur, paler underside.
Long scaly tail adds 5–7 cm to total length

SIMILAR SPECIES: Woodmouse,
Yellow-necked mouse

It is not just the tooth-marks in the cheese that make us want to get rid of this pest, it can also cause chaos by chewing through cables. Trains on the London to Cambridge line were stopped for 3 hours in 1981 after mice chewed through a 650-volt cable. The usual method these days is to poison them with Warfarin (an anti-coagulant), but some so-called 'supermice' are building up a resistance to it. The house mouse thrives around human habitation, easily getting everything it needs: warmth, food, water, soft fabric or paper for nesting material, and skirting boards to travel behind, safe from the family cat. It became extinct on the Hebridean island of St. Kilda after the evacuation in 1930, as it could not compete with the woodmouse on an uninhabited island.

MOLE *(Talpa europaea)*

SIZE: 15 cm

HABITAT: Gardens, orchards, grassland and woods throughout the British Isles

IDENTIFICATION: Black velvety furry head and body with pink nose, short tail and large forepaws

SIMILAR SPECIES: None

Seldom seen above ground, the presence of moles is usually announced by mole hills on the lawn. These are made of surplus loose earth pushed up to the surface as the mole digs. It burrows by bracing itself with its hind feet and using one forefoot at a time to loosen the earth ahead as it searches for worms. Three or four naked young are born in nests within the burrow. Countless methods of ridding the lawn of moles have been tried over the years, from placing mothballs in the tunnels to fixing a hose pipe to the car exhaust and trying to gas the poor creatures. In *A Miscellany of Garden Wisdom*, Bernard Schofield recommends sinking empty wine bottles into the ground with a couple of inches of neck protruding. Apparently, the moles cannot stand the sound of wind singing in the bottles and move off elsewhere.

Farmland, Hedgerows and Verges

*Spring will not wait the
   loiterer's time*

Who keeps so long away;

*So others wear the broom
   and climb*

*The hedgerows heaped
   with may*

A SHROPSHIRE LAD
A.E.HOUSMAN

CHESTNUTS

The **horse chestnut** *(Aesculus hippocastanum),* opposite, is the tree responsible for more bruised knuckles than any other. The introduction of the horse chestnut into Britain from the Balkans in the late 16th century brought the big artillery into the playground. Before the beautiful, glossy chestnuts became available, the game of conkers used to be played with smaller cobnuts or even snail shells – not nearly as satisfying for the bellicose schoolboy. Chestnuts were first used as conkers in the late 18th century but before that they were eaten by cattle, sheep and deer. The chestnut's other association with bodily injury is that the light, easily-shaped wood was formerly used to make artificial limbs. The Turks also fed the nuts to horses to cure them of the breathing disorder of 'broken wind'.

The impressive flower display makes the horse chestnut a favourite ornamental in parks, playing fields, estates and avenues. It is also often found in hedgerows and was once, before space was at such a premium and motor cars became dominant, a regular sight in village centres, where its vast span offered shade from the sun and shelter from the rain. The spreading chestnut tree under which Longfellow's village smithy stood was just such a specimen.

The horse chestnut, which grows to a height of 35 m, has bright green leaves of 5–7 stalkless, ovoid leaflets. The white flowers are in profuse upright 'candle' spikes ripening to a spiny green fruit enclosing the familiar shiny brown nuts. The bark is reddish or dark brown and scaly.

The **Indian horse chestnut** *(A. indica),* a native of the Himalayas, is similar in general appearance, but blooms about 6 weeks later, making it a boon for bees. The leaflets are more pointed and narrower and the outer husks of the fruits are thinner without spikes, looking more like unripe figs. The bark is grey–green or pinkish-green and smooth.

If you know where there is a **sweet chestnut** *(Castanea sativa)* tree, then start taking walks past it in October and keep a lookout for the fallen fruit husks. Breaking into these spiky balls reveals 1–3 nuts. Although the nuts seldom grow to an impressive size in Britain, they might still be worth taking home and roasting, either in a tray at the top of a hot oven or beside a

Sweet chestnut

blazing fire. Make a small cut on the flat side first or they will explode. When the outer skin starts to peel away they are done and both layers of skin can be pulled off and the nut eaten – preferably washed down with mulled wine.

If you can't find your own nuts, you might be lucky enough to have a hot chestnut vendor visit your local town at Christmas time, his glowing brazier giving a moment's warmth to passing shoppers and his wares wrapped in traditional paper cones. These nuts will almost certainly be grown commercially in Italy or the south of France. The Romans used to make a porridge, called pollenta, from dried and ground sweet chestnuts mixed with milk and we still use them for stuffing and treats such as

marrons glacé. Sweet chestnuts, with just 2–4% protein, 2–5% fat and up to 70% starch, are, unlike most commercial nuts, filling without being fattening.

The sweet chestnut, which is found in hedgerows, parks and playing fields, estates and gardens, grows to about 30–35 m. It has shiny, dark green, alternate leaves, shaped in narrow oblong ovals with toothed margins. The sparse, long, yellow catkins of male flowers have small green female flowers at their base, which ripen into the nuts. The brown bark has deep spiral fissures. The tough timber is split easily and makes excellent paling fences.

ENGLISH ELM *(Ulmus procera)*

SIZE: Up to 63 m tall

HABITAT: Lowland hedgerows and farmland in S. England

IDENTIFICATION: Dark green, alternate, oval leaves, toothed margins, asymmetrical bases. Small crimson flowers ripening into oval, winged fruits with seed in centre. Dark brown bark with long, deep fissures

SIMILAR SPECIES: Wych elm, Smooth-leaved elm, Dutch elm

English elms reigned for 300 years as monarchs of the lowland landscape. Although already present in small numbers, they exploded on to the scene when 17th century landowners decided that these stately trees were the perfect thing for their estates, planting them along hedgerows as boundary markers and scattering them around parkland, where they stood tall in isolated splendour. Then came Dutch elm disease in 1967. More than 12 million mature elms fell victim to this fungus, spread by the bark-burrowing scolytid beetle, and the English landscape lost what had become one of its key elements. The abundance of dead elm contributed to the rise in popularity of that classic fixture of the country home of the 1980s – the wood burning stove.

FIELD MAPLE *(Acer campestre)*

SIZE: Up to 26 m

HABITAT: Hedgerows, scrubland, chalky soils. S. England

IDENTIFICATION: Opposite leaves, 5-lobed, dark green but orange–yellow in autumn. Small, green flowers in upright clusters ripening to winged pairs of seeds. Bark grey or light brown, shallow fissures

SIMILAR SPECIES: Norway maple, Cappadocian maple

We usually only see this tree as a splintered victim of the hedgerow chain-flail or as a scrubland bush. This is a pity since as a mature tree it is most impressive and can grow very tall. Its orange and yellow leaves make a splash of autumnal colour but its wood is even more beautiful. 'Bird's eye maple', with its characteristic mottled pattern, was used for veneers and panelling and was produced by cutting across all the small knots along the trunk. However, there are no longer any field maples large enough to produce workable timber and most modern maple products come from other varieties. Maple wood also delights the ear, as it is used to make violins. The field maple's seed wings lie almost in a straight line rather than at an angle like those of other maples.

CRAB APPLE *(Malus sylvestris)*

SIZE: Up to 10 m tall

HABITAT: Hedgerows, woodlands and thickets. Commonest in S. and E. England, rare in Scotland

IDENTIFICATION: Softly hairy, toothed, oval leaves. Clusters of large, pinkish-white flowers ripening into small, hard, green apples. Brown bark with flaky patches

SIMILAR SPECIES: Cultivated apples

Pick a crab apple and bite into it and you will soon bear a crabby expression – puckered and frowning – as you struggle with the bitter flesh. Luckily for us, ancient man had tougher taste buds and devoured it willingly, leading to the cultivation nowadays of more than 3000 varieties of domestic apple, all sprung from the humble crab. American Indians buried crab apples in the autumn and dug them up in the spring when they had become less bitter. We can make them palatable by adding sugar to make crab apple jelly, jam and wine, or just by mashing them and leaving them to ferment into rough cider. Best of all, though, is 'lambs' wool', a drink made from hot ale, pulped roasted crab apples, sugar and spice. Crab apple wood carves beautifully and smells wonderful on an open fire.

WILD CHERRY *(Prunus avium)* ▶

SIZE: Up to 30 m but usually about 10 m tall

HABITAT: Hedgerows and field boundaries, beechwoods. Clay soil over chalk. Mostly in the south

IDENTIFICATION: Alternate, oval leaves with short-toothed margins. White, 5-petalled flowers in clusters ripening to dark red berries. Reddish-brown bark distinctively peeling in horizontal bands

SIMILAR SPECIES: Bird cherry and cultivated cherries

Just as crab apples begat all cultivated apples, so the sweet cherries we now enjoy in many different forms all sprang from the wild variety. As with apples, cultivated cherries are still propagated by grafting on to wild rootstock. In the spring you can spot wild cherry trees among other trees by their conspicuous white blossom which appears before the leaves. Wild cherry can grow big enough to provide timber which makes beautiful decorative panelling, furniture and veneers, and it is much sought after by wood-turners. It makes good firewood and gives off a lovely fragrance of blossom as it burns. The cherries themselves are palatable and can be sweet if they are very ripe, but the chances of getting to them before the birds do are very slim indeed.

HAWTHORN *(Crataegus monogyna)*

SIZE:	Up to 14 m as a tree but usually a trimmed bush
HABITAT:	Hedgerows. Widespread
IDENTIFICATION:	Shiny, rough, oval alternate leaves, deeply divided lobes with paired stipules at the base. Abundant white, scented flowers ripen to fleshy, dark red fruits (haws) each with a single seed. Bark scaly greyish-brown
SIMILAR SPECIES:	Midland hawthorn

As befits our most common hedge plant, there are many local names for the haw berry including aggle, shaw, halve, hippertyhaw, heethen-berry, hegpeg, pig berry and pixy-bear. You can eat haws straight off the bush. Some say they taste like sweet potato. Most hawthorn was planted during the land enclosures of the 16th and 18th centuries not for its berries but for its outstanding hedging qualities. When cut and laid by a good hedger it makes an ecologically sound, virtually impenetrable barrier. But erecting barbed wire fences takes fewer man–hours, so hawthorn now tends to be left to grow or is thrashed to within an inch of its life by flailing machines. Myth surrounds hawthorn, which is linked by its flowering time to the pagan festival of May Day. Bringing the blossom indoors is said to be unlucky.

BLACKTHORN, SLOE *(Prunus spinosa)* ▲

SIZE:	Up to 5 m tall
HABITAT:	Hedgerows and scrubland throughout Britain. Sometimes dense thickets
IDENTIFICATION:	Small, oval, dull green alternate leaves, hairy beneath. White blossom in clusters ripening to perfectly round, dark plum-coloured fruit (sloes) 10–15 mm diameter. Greyish-brown bark scrapes to reveal orange
SIMILAR SPECIES:	None

Tough blackthorn wood makes good walking sticks and the traditional Irish shillelagh or club, but it is the berries which are most valued. It is worth a few pricks from the large thorns to pick sloes, preferably after the first frosts of October but before the bloom has gone from the skins. Whatever you do, do not eat them raw: one bite will shrivel the inside of your mouth with bitterness. Sloes make excellent jelly and jam, being the wild precursors of cultivated plums and damsons, but few delights beat sloe gin. Prick about 750 g of berries all over with a skewer, mix them with an equal weight of sugar and half fill bottles with this mixture. Top up with gin, seal tightly and leave for a month or two, shaking occasionally. When Christmas comes drink the gin – and eat the berries.

DOGWOOD *(Cornus sanguinea)*

SIZE: Up to 4 m tall but often low bushes

HABITAT: Hedgerows, scrubland. Commonly in south, on chalk and limestone

IDENTIFICATION: Dark green, hairy, pointed, opposite oval leaves turn red in autumn. Distinctive reddish stems and shoots. Clusters of small flowers with unpleasant scent, ripening to small black berries. Ridged bark smells unpleasant when crushed

SIMILAR SPECIES: Privet and Elder have similar berries

This tree has played quite a large part in country life, quite apart from its glorious display of blood red branches and leaves in the autumn. Its common name comes from its use in making wooden skewers or 'dogs' which butchers used to hold meat in shape in the days before food hygiene regulations. The hard, white wood was also used to make charcoal, wheel spokes, bobbins, pestles and mill cogs. The berries were crushed to extract oil for lamps. The flowers smell horrible, but seem to attract insects including the green hairstreak butterfly, whose caterpillars feed on the leaves. The dogwood has also been known as the 'dogberry' or 'dog tree' but, confusingly, these names have also been used by some communities for the elder and rowan.

ELDER *(Sambucus nigra)*

SIZE: Up to 10 m tall but usually a shorter shrub

HABITAT: Widespread in hedgerows, field margins and neglected ground

IDENTIFICATION: Opposite leaves of 5–7 oval, toothed leaflets. Abundant creamy-white flowers in flat-topped clusters ripening to small black berries on reddish stalks. Bark deeply furrowed and spongy

SIMILAR SPECIES: Berries similar to Dogwood and Privet

With the rise in popularity of herbal infusions, more people are now enjoying the taste and benefits of elderflower tea. This was used as a cough remedy by country folk who also made a purgative from the bark. The flowers have been used in skin ointments and eye lotions and can even be munched straight off the branch. The berries make delicious wine and jam. The stinking leaves make green dye, the bark makes black and the flowers blue or lilac. Even the stems are useful: the soft pith inside can be hollowed out to make a peashooter. Using the berries as ammunition results in a satisfying splatter on the victim – the original paintball game. Elders are ubiquitous (except in mountains), the seeds being spread readily in bird droppings, but prefer nitrogen-rich soil near abandoned buildings or rabbit warrens.

IVY *(Hedera helix)*

SIZE:	Up to 30 m long
HABITAT:	Climbing through hedgerows, up trees, over walls or along the ground
IDENTIFICATION:	Evergreen, glossy, dark leaves with 3–5 lobes, fibrous stems. Inconspicuous green flowers in globular heads, black fruits
SIMILAR SPECIES:	None

Traditionally used as a Christmas decoration along with holly to guard against goblins, who were said to be at their worst at this time of the year. It is a familiar plant clinging to walls, trees, fences and old buildings, with its fine rootlets which grow from the stems. Cultivated varieties, which are more colourful and might be variegated, are often seen covering the walls of town houses. The pale, greenish flowers, attractive to wasps and flies, are followed by more distinctive black berries in the autumn. These provide food for birds while the leaves are eaten by caterpillars of the holly blue butterfly. Ground ivy *(Glechoma hederacea)* is part of the mint family. As the name suggests, it creeps along the ground, and the scented leaves are almost round, unlike true ivy.

HEDGE BINDWEED
(Calystegia sepium ssp *sepium)*

SIZE:	Up to 3 m long
HABITAT:	Hedgerows and fenland, mainly in S. England and the Midlands
IDENTIFICATION:	Heart-shaped leaves with prominent veins, large white, trumpet-shaped flowers from July to September
SIMILAR SPECIES:	Large bindweed, Field bindweed, Sea bindweed, Dodder

In the West Country, the flowers are known as 'morning glory', although they remain open into the night and can stay open until morning if there is bright moonlight. The distinctive flowers attract the convolvulus hawk moth which pollinates the plant while using its long tongue to extract the nectar. The flowers of large bindweed can be 6–7.5 cm across and are among the largest of British wild flowers. Field bindweed, with its pretty pink flowers, is disliked by farmers and gardeners, not only for the strong twining stems which strangle other plants, but also for the extensive root system. The stems revolve anti-clockwise as they twine around other plants and can complete a full circle in under 2 hours.

PRIMROSE *(Primula vulgaris)*

SIZE:	15 cm tall
HABITAT:	Hedgebanks, woods, sea cliffs and railway banks
IDENTIFICATION:	A rosette of large, wrinkled, toothed leaves which are hairy on the underside. The yellow flowers are borne singly on hairy stalks from the centre of the plant from March to May
SIMILAR SPECIES:	Bird's-eye primrose, Cowslip, False oxlip

One of the best loved wild flowers of Britain and the symbol of spring. Disraeli's birthday, 19th April, is called 'Primrose Day' after his favourite flower. It grows throughout Britain but numbers are dwindling, probably from over picking. In mild winters, the flowers can appear as early as January, whereas in the north they are sometimes seen in flower until August. The scented blooms were used to make drinks and as a dressing for roast veal, while the roots made an infusion for nervous headaches. The less common Bird's-eye primrose is found only in northern England. Its pink flowers are in clusters and smaller. In fairy folklore the primrose makes the invisible visible. It is said that if you touch a fairy rock with the correct number of primroses in a posy, fairy gifts befall you: the wrong number spells doom.

OLD MAN'S BEARD *(Clematis vitalba)*

SIZE:	Up to 30 m long
HABITAT:	Hedgerows, woodland edges and scrubland on chalky soil
IDENTIFICATION:	Distinctive seed heads in late summer, containing numerous feathery plumes. Leaves with 3–5 leaflets. Sprays of green or white flowers
SIMILAR SPECIES:	None

A woody climber with leaf stalks, which twine around other plants, can climb up trees, and the thick stems hang down from the tree-tops like jungle plants. The small flowers do not have petals but long, white or greenish sepals. They have a fragrance reminiscent of vanilla. The fluffy seed heads, resembling soft curly hair, are a common and impressive sight in southern England and Wales but rarer farther north. It is also known as 'Traveller's-joy' as named by John Gerard, the English botanist, because he found it 'decking and adorning ways and hedges where people travel'. 'Boy's bacca' is another old name for the plant, as young boys once smoked the dried stems of the plant.

COW PARSLEY *(Anthriscus sylvestris)*

SIZE: 60–120 cm tall

HABITAT: Verges, banks, hedges and wood edges. Very common throughout Britain except for the Scottish Highlands

IDENTIFICATION: Upright plant with hollow, furrowed stems and slightly downy, much-divided leaves. Lacy white flowers in May

SIMILAR SPECIES: Bur chervil, Sweet cicely, Fool's parsley, Hemlock, Hogweed and other members of the parsley family

The first common umbelliferate to flower in the spring, its frothy white flowers gave it the folk-name of Queen Anne's lace. Devil's parsley, gypsy laces, lady's needlework and cow chervil are among its other local common names. Country roads can be narrowed by the overhanging foliage during early summer. It is a relation of the garden herb chervil and is said to have a similar flavour. It should not be confused with fool's parsley or hemlock, which can cause serious poisoning. The hollow stems of both cow parsley and hogweed have been used by children to make pea-shooters, but it is inadvisable to use giant hogweed as it contains a substance which can cause blistering on contact with the skin.

COMMON VETCH *(Vicia sativa* ssp *sativa)*

SIZE: Climbing 15–120 cm tall

HABITAT: Hedges, arable land, grassland. Throughout Britain but rarer in N.W.

IDENTIFICATION: The tendrilled leaves have four to eight pairs of leaflets. Pink flowers usually in pairs, from May to September

SIMILAR SPECIES: Smooth tare, Tufted vetch, Bush vetch, Bitter vetch

Vetches are attractive plants with pea-like flowers in shades of pink, purple and blue. The common vetch has two black-blotched stipules at the base of each leaf, which distinguishes it from other vetches. The flowers are followed by pods of 4–12 seeds, which were used as pigeon food in the 18th century. The tufted vetch (*V. cracca*) is a taller plant, up to 200 cm and carries spikes of up to 40 bluish-purple flowers, followed by brown seed pods. Bush vetch (*V. sepium*) is also common throughout the British Isles, and can be fed to livestock. It has a smaller number of larger flowers than tufted vetch and the seed pods are black. Bitter vetch is not so widespread, but is common in Scotland. In the Hebrides it used to be grown as a subsistence crop for its edible tubers.

tufted vetch

common vetch

BRAMBLE *(Rubus fruticosus)*

SIZE:	Sprawling up to 5–6 m
HABITAT:	Hedgerows, heaths, waste ground and woods in England and Wales. Rarer in Scotland
IDENTIFICATION:	Prickly stems and leaves which turn reddish in autumn. White or pink flowers, May to September. Edible berries turn black when ripe
SIMILAR SPECIES:	Dewberry

Blackberrying is one of the urban dweller's ideas of country living. It provides a satisfying outing, some free food and a pie or some jam to look forward to. The berries form in clusters on older shoots, and the first to ripen is the lowest berry which is the sweetest and fattest. There is a saying that blackberries should not be eaten after Michaelmas because the Devil then spits on them. In fact it is the flesh fly that sucks up the juice of the berries after having dribbled on them. The sprawling, arched stems or canes start by growing erect but then curve down and touch the ground. Here they take root and a new clump of canes soon grows.

WHITE CLOVER *(Trifolium repens)*

SIZE:	50 cm tall
HABITAT:	Common in fields and grassy places throughout the British Isles
IDENTIFICATION:	Mid-green leaves with three leaflets, each having a whitish circular band at the base. White flower heads on long stems from June to September
SIMILAR SPECIES:	Red clover, Zigzag clover, Hare's-foot clover, Crimson clover

Much loved by bee-keepers, white clover contains abundant nectar available early in the season. The round clusters of flowers are held erect at first, but droop and fade to brown when pollination is complete. The stems creep along the ground taking root as they progress. It is a valuable addition to mixed lawn seed as the leaves remain lush and green if the grass is burnt in a dry summer. Red clover does not creep, but is widely grown as cattle fodder or ploughed back into the ground to enrich the soil. Bumble bees, butterflies and moths are attracted by the delicately scented flowers. Both red and white clover can be made into a country wine and clover tea can be used as a remedy for whooping cough.

COMMON FIELD SPEEDWELL
(Veronica persica)

SIZE: 10–30 cm

HABITAT: Arable farmland, verges

IDENTIFICATION: Sky blue flowers with a white lower lip, appearing throughout the year

SIMILAR SPECIES: Germander speedwell, Wall speedwell, Heath speedwell

Speedwells are well known for the azure blue of the flowers, which can appear all year round except during the hardest frosts. Common field speedwell, a native of Iran, is widespread on disturbed ground; other species prefer hedgebanks, woods and grassy places. The Germander speedwell (*V. chamaedrys*) is the largest and brightest of the British species, flowering from March to July. The speedwell is said to have got its name from the medicinal properties of the plant, although it has several other local names. The fruits are heart shaped, so break-your-mother's-heart is another old name. Heath speedwell (*V. officinalis*) has the alternative name of common speedwell, but is not as widespread as other speedwells, preferring dry soils and heaths.

heath speedwell

RAGWORT *(Senecia jacobaea)*

SIZE: 30–120 cm tall

HABITAT: Verges, neglected pastures and waste ground throughout Britain

IDENTIFICATION: Erect plant with deeply lobed leaves. Rosette of lower leaves dies back when flowering. Highly branched upper stem bears bright yellow daisy-like flowers June to October

SIMILAR SPECIES: Oxford ragwort, Hoary ragwort, Marsh ragwort, Groundsel

Tansy ragwort or common ragwort is one of the injurious weeds specified in the *Weeds Act 1959*, and occupiers of land on which it is growing may be required to prevent it spreading to agricultural land. It is highly toxic, particularly to horses, but is fairly unpalatable so usually avoided. The danger comes when it is cut, dried and fed unknowingly in bales of hay. The name refers to the ragged leaves, although in Scotland it is known as stinking Billy because of the smell of the leaves when crushed. Oxford ragwort is claimed to be the prettiest of British ragworts because of its bright yellow flowers. Originally only found in Oxford or Bideford, it spread along the line of the Great Western Railway in 1844, probably aided by turbulence from the trains.

SCARLET PIMPERNEL
(Anagallis arvensis)

SIZE:	Sprawling 5–30 cm
HABITAT:	Cultivated land, waste ground and sand dunes, throughout Britain
IDENTIFICATION:	Sprawling plant with shiny oval leaves, small, scarlet flowers with five petals, May to August
SIMILAR SPECIES:	Blue pimpernel, Bog pimpernel, Chaffweed, Yellow pimpernel, Creeping-jenny

The pimpernels are members of the primrose family, and the scarlet pimpernel is the most colourful. One of its local names is poor man's weatherglass, because the flowers close when the sun goes in. Baroness Orczy's novel of the French Revolution was called *The Scarlet Pimpernel*, as that was the undercover name chosen by the hero when rescuing aristocrats from the guillotine. The plant occasionally has pink, white or blue flowers, but the blue pimpernel is a subspecies with petals that do not overlap, and is found mainly in south and west England. Bog pimpernel is found in bogs, fens and damp grassy or mossy places, except in parts of southern Scotland. It has small, bell-like pink flowers from June to August.

COMMON BIRDSFOOT TREFOIL
(Lotus corniculatus)

SIZE:	10–40 cm tall
HABITAT:	Fields, verges, dry grasslands throughout Britain
IDENTIFICATION:	Leaves with five leaflets, three in one group and two close to the stem. Yellow or orange flowers from May to September
SIMILAR SPECIES:	Greater birdsfoot trefoil, Kidney vetch, Lesser trefoil, Horseshoe vetch

The trefoils are among the commonest of British grassland plants, which probably accounts for the fact that there are more than 70 local names. One of the most popular is bacon-and-eggs, referring to the colour of the pea-like flowers. Birdsfoot, or crow toes as it is sometimes known, refers to the seed pods which resemble a bird's claw. The pods twist as they open, releasing several seeds. Greater birdsfoot trefoil grows in damper grassland and has more flowers in each head. Dry grassland, especially by the coast, is favoured by kidney vetch where its yellow flowers, tinged with brown as they fade, are a common sight. After flowering, the seed pods are enclosed by soft woolly sepals.

kidney vetch

birdfoot trefoil

RED CAMPION *(Silene dioica)* ▶

SIZE: 30–90 cm tall

HABITAT: Hedgerows, wood borders and sea cliffs throughout most of Britain

IDENTIFICATION: Upright plant with distinctive flowers with inflated calyces. Red or deep pink flowers with deeply divided petals are borne mainly in May and June

SIMILAR SPECIES: White campion, Sea campion, Bladder campion, Ragged robin

The campions are members of the pink family and are easily identified by the calyx at the base of the flower where the sepals are joined to form a sticky tube. The red campion is the most colourful and takes its Latin name from Silenus, the merry god of the woodlands in Greek mythology. Male and female flowers are on different plants, so two plants are needed to make seeds. Bladder campion (*S. vulgaris*) has an even larger calyx, inflated like a balloon, hence its common name. Bumble bees have discovered that the easiest way to reach the nectar, which can be half an inch below the top of the petals, is to bite through the base of the flower.

welsh poppy

COMMON POPPY *(Papaver rhoeas)*

SIZE:	20–60 cm tall
HABITAT:	Verges and edges of cornfields, throughout Britain except for N. Scotland
IDENTIFICATION:	Tall plant with stalkless, three-lobed leaves and hairy stem. Deep scarlet , single flowers often with a black patch at the base, May to October
SIMILAR SPECIES:	Long-headed poppy, Prickly poppy, Welsh poppy

Once a familiar sight covering cornfields, the poppy is becoming rarer because of herbicides and treated corn seed. The Roman corn goddess Ceres was depicted with a bundle of poppies in one hand and today the flowers are sometimes known as corn poppies or corn roses. After the battles of the First World War the fields of Flanders were covered in poppies and it has now become the symbol of Remembrance Day. The flower sheds its petals after one day and is followed by a seed head with a ring of pores near the flat top. These heads can be gathered and the grey seeds used for baking. No part of the common poppy is narcotic and the opium poppy *(P. somniferum)* is seldom found growing wild in Britain.

Archaeologists have found remains of poppies in prehistoric settlements in southern England and other parts of Europe. The plant might have been grown for its oil or seeds or the opium poppy for its medicinal properties. This was used as a cough remedy, painkiller and sedative and believed to be a powerful aphrodisiac. Opium has been widely used since ancient times and was a vital ingredient in laudanum – developed by the English doctor Thomas Sydenham. Laudanum was taken by ladies to calm the nerves and aid sleep. However, it was overprescribed for agitated children leading to opium addiction in later life.

SPEAR THISTLE *(Cirsium vulgare)*

SIZE:	Up to 3 m tall
HABITAT:	Fields, verges and waste ground throughout the British Isles
IDENTIFICATION:	Sharp spiny leaves, large, lilac–purple flower heads surrounded by spine-tipped bracts from May to September
SIMILAR SPECIES:	Creeping thistle, Marsh thistle, Welted thistle, Cotton thistle, Common knapweed and many others of the Composite family

The biennial spear thistle is the tallest of the British thistles and the most difficult to handle because of its sharp spines. The colourful flowers are attractive to butterflies and can be as much as 40 mm across. This plant became Scotland's heraldic emblem in 1503 when *The Thistle and the Rose* was written to celebrate the marriage of James IV to Princess Margaret of England. Clouds of butterflies can be seen feeding from the creeping thistle (*C. arvense)* in summer. This perennial thistle is a common and troublesome weed, as its creeping roots send up new plants to add to those grown from seeds. Others are fussier about where they grow: the marsh thistle is found in fens and other, damp grassy places, the welted thistle prefers drier places and hedge banks.

COMMON KNAPWEED *(Centaurea nigra)*

SIZE:	30–60 cm tall
HABITAT:	Verges, grasslands and waysides throughout Britain
IDENTIFICATION:	Grooved stems, narrow leaves, black globular flower heads with purple florets from June to September
SIMILAR SPECIES:	Greater Knapweed

Roadside verges, especially in chalky areas, support many colourful wild flowers and common knapweed is one of the most widespread. Its purple, thistle-like flowers are borne at the top of branched stems, usually carried above surrounding foliage. Girls used to pick them to see whether they would soon meet their future husband: after pulling off the expanded florets, a maiden would keep the flower heads in her blouse for an hour then check whether the remainder had bloomed – a sign that she would not be single for long. The hard, knob-like buds have also given this plant the alternative name of hardhead. Greater knapweed is mostly seen on dry grasslands in southern and eastern England. The medicinal properties of the plant were known by herbalists and were used to treat wounds, bruises and sore throats.

DOG ROSE *(Rosa canina)*

SIZE: 90–270 cm tall

HABITAT: Hedges and scrubland throughout England and Wales, rarer in Scotland

IDENTIFICATION: Tall, sturdy shrub with hooked prickles, toothed leaves and large pink, 5-petalled, flat flowers during June and July

SIMILAR SPECIES: Field rose, Harsh downy rose, Soft downy rose, Burnet rose

The wild rose is less showy than the garden variety, and the delicate, fragrant flowers have been a favourite since Roman times, when petals were showered down from the ceiling at banquets. Generations of children were brought up on rose-hip syrup, rich in vitamin C. Nowadays, the bright red fruits are more likely to be made into a country wine. Rose petals are used for flavouring jams, jellies and confectionery, especially Turkish delight. The ancient Greeks believed that the roots could cure a man bitten by a mad dog, hence the name dog rose. It was Henry VII who adopted it as the Tudor rose, his official emblem, and it is still a symbol of British monarchy.

DEVIL'S BIT SCABIOUS *(Succisa pratensis)*

SIZE:	15–100 cm tall
HABITAT:	Damp grassland, fens and heaths
IDENTIFICATION:	Slender, hairy stem with few, narrow leaves
SIMILAR SPECIES:	Field scabious, Small scabious, Sheep's scabious

Legend tells us that the devil bit away part of the root of this plant to try to destroy it because he envied the good it might do to the human race. The plant survived, but with a stumped root and a curious name. The devil also failed to destroy its healing capabilities and the dried herb is still used in remedies today. The herbalist, Nicholas Culpepper, said 'it helpeth also all that are inwardly bruised or outwardly by falls or blows, dissolving the clotted blood'. His uses included fighting the plague, curing tonsillitis and acting as an antidote to bites from 'venomous creatures'. Like Devil's bit scabious, the small scabious and the field scabious were once used to cure skin conditions such as scabies, which is how they got their name.

CHICORY *(Cichorium intybus)*

SIZE:	30–120 cm tall
HABITAT:	Fields and verges on chalky soils
IDENTIFICATION:	Branching stems with divided leaves and bright blue flowers from June to September
SIMILAR SPECIES:	None

Common only in southern England and rare in Scotland, this tall, distinguished plant can be a real head-turner when its startling cornflower-blue flowers come into bloom on roadside verges. It is Britain's only blue-flowered dandelion-like plant, with the blooms staying open only during sunny mornings. The roots are roasted and ground to make a substitute for coffee or as an addition to strengthen the flavour. The name chicory comes from the Arabic *chicouryeh*: the Arabs are fond of the roots as a boiled vegetable. On the continent, the leaves are used in salads in a similar way to those of the dandelion, and the plant is sometimes grown as animal fodder.

SILVERWEED *(Potentilla anserina)*

SIZE:	Creeping, 5–25 cm tall
HABITAT:	Damp grassy places, verges and gardens
IDENTIFICATION:	Fern-like silvery leaves, flat, gold 5-petalled flowers from May to August
SIMILAR SPECIES:	Creeping cinquefoil, Tormentil

If silverweed were not so invasive, its handsome foliage would make it a welcome addition to any garden border. The silvery leaves, with a long tapering mid-rib and pairs of serrated leaflets on each side, turn to red in the autumn, making them ideal for flower arrangements. The pale gold flowers look like strawberry blossoms or miniature wild roses. The whole plant has an ancient history of medicinal and culinary uses, and foot soldiers would rest by the wayside and fill their boots with the cooling leaves. The roots were cultivated in the Hebrides and in other upland areas until the introduction of the potato. As a vegetable, they have been likened to parsnips when boiled or baked. The dried and ground roots were also used like flour to make bread or gruel.

WILD PANSY *(Viola tricolor)*

SIZE:	Up to 30 cm tall
HABITAT:	Arable land, short grassland, waste ground and dunes
IDENTIFICATION:	Branching stems with oval leaves and leaf-like stipules, deeply lobed. Purple and/or yellow flowers appear April to September
SIMILAR SPECIES:	Field pansy, Mountain pansy, Seaside pansy, Sweet violet and others of the violet family

'Fetch me that flower, the herb I showed thee once,' says Oberon, king of the fairies, in Shakespeare's *A Midsummer Night's Dream*, explaining: 'The juice of it, on sleeping eyelids laid,/Will make a man or woman madly dote/Upon the next live creature that it sees'. He called for the wild pansy to make Titania fall in love with Bottom. According to Shakespeare 'maidens call it love-in-idleness'. It is perhaps more commonly known today as heartsease. The field pansy is widespread and common on cultivated land, its flowers are smaller than those of the wild pansy and usually white or creamy-yellow. In the north of England and Scotland, the mountain pansy is common on upland areas. Different colours dominate in different areas, purple is seen more frequently than yellow in Scotland.

HEDGE WOUNDWORT *(Stachys sylvatica)*

SIZE:	30–100 cm tall
HABITAT:	Hedges, woods and shady places throughout the British Isles
IDENTIFICATION:	Upright plant with hairy stem. Large stem leaves and smaller leaves below the flowers. Red, snapdragon-like flowers in July and August
SIMILAR SPECIES:	Betony, Marsh woundwort, Field woundwort

The antiseptic qualities of this strong-smelling plant have been known for over 2000 years. The soft downy leaves were made into poultices, infusions and ointments to treat wounds and stem bleeding. The beetroot-red flowers with a white-marked lip were also made into conserves. They are popular with smaller bees and are planted in wildlife gardens to encourage them. Betony has paler flowers, is less hairy and has fewer stem leaves. It can be found growing around old churchyards and monastery gardens, where it used to be cultivated by herbalists. Marsh woundwort prefers damp conditions and is common in ditches and marshy ground. Its medicinal properties are similar to the hedge woundwort and were used by the herbalist, John Gerard, to treat people wounded in tavern brawls.

COMMON TOADFLAX *(Linaria vulgaris)*

SIZE:	25–75 cm
HABITAT:	Cultivated land, verges, railway embankments. Throughout England, rarer in the north
IDENTIFICATION:	Leafy stems bearing many-flowered racemes of snapdragon-like flowers, pale yellow with an orange palate, from June to October
SIMILAR SPECIES:	Pale toadflax, Small toadflax

These snapdragon-like flowers have two lips, which close preventing access to the nectar at the tip of the spur. Only insects that are heavy enough can use their weight to open the palate and reach their prize. The plants flourish on richer soils, and the wild seed can be purchased from specialist suppliers for those wanting to encourage bees into their garden. Children open the flowers by squeezing the sides and this has led to many folk names such as squeeze jaw, weasel-snouts and lion's mouth. The grey–green leaves are narrow and arranged in spirals up the stems, similar to those of flax. Pale toadflax has lilac-coloured flowers and is less showy. The petal tube of the small toadflax is not completely closed by the palate; its botanical name, *Chaenorhinum minus,* comes from the Greek meaning 'gaping snout'.

RIBWORT PLANTAIN *(Plantago lanceolata)*

SIZE:	Up to 45 cm tall
HABITAT:	Pastureland, verges, lawns and bare places on alkaline soil
IDENTIFICATION:	Thin, oval, hairy leaves with 3–5 veins, single, blackish-brown flower heads with prominent stamens
SIMILAR SPECIES:	Greater plantain, Hoary plantain

Despite grazing by stock or mowing by gardeners, this plant survives because most of the new growth comes from the base of the rosette of leaves. Pollen found preserved in lakes and peat beds shows that it has been around since the Stone Age. Children still use it as a toy weapon, looping the stalk around the flower head and flicking it off. Greater, or ratstail, plantain thrives wherever the ground is well trodden such as on footpaths and lawns. The North American Indians called it 'English man's foot' as the rosettes of leaves seemed to follow where the white man had trodden. The longer flower heads of the greater plantain, which prompted its alternative name of ratstail, produce many seeds valuable for caged birds.

OX-EYE DAISY *(Leucanthemum vulgare)*

SIZE: 20–60 cm tall

HABITAT: Verges and grassland, common in England especially on limy soils, more scarce in Scotland

IDENTIFICATION: Deeply divided leaves clasping the upright stems. Single daisy flowers, white with yellow centres, borne from May to September

SIMILAR SPECIES: Sea mayweed, Corn chamomile

The striking white and gold flowers, up to 5 cm in diameter, are held above the foliage and surrounding grass, transforming grassy banks and meadows. It often grows among other flowering plants, liking the same short grassland, creating nature's own mixed bouquet. The cultivated varieties of marguerite or shasta daisy are popular with florists in the same way. Today's trend of sowing an organic wildlife meadow will ensure the wild variety survives despite declining numbers in intensely farmed pastures. The ancient Greeks thought the flower heads reminded them of the eyes of their oxen and thus gave it its common name. Eyes were once treated with a juice from the stems, said to stop them from running.

YARROW *(Achillea millefolium)*

SIZE:	15–50 cm tall
HABITAT:	Hedges, grassland, verges and dunes throughout Britain
IDENTIFICATION:	Strongly divided feathery leaves. Clusters of pinkish-white florets form a flat head from June to August
SIMILAR SPECIES:	Sneezewort

One of our most ancient herbs, Yarrow is also known as soldier's woundwort as the Greek warrior, Achilles, supposedly used it to treat wounds. English soldiers are reported to have carried it into battle either to heal their wounds or to ward off evil spirits. It was also used as part of a garland of protective herbs hung in the church or the home on Midsummer's Eve when the spirits were believed to be most potent. Herbalists recommend a tea made from the dried flowers to act as a stimulant and ease a head cold. Snuff was made from sneezewort (*A. ptarmica*), as its application caused sneezing and was valued as an antidote for headaches. The slightly bitter leaves also have a culinary use as an addition to salads or boiled as a vegetable.

COMMON SORREL *(Rumex acetosa)*

SIZE:	Up to 100 cm
HABITAT:	Grassland, verges, and heaths throughout the British Isles
IDENTIFICATION:	Sturdy upright plant with arrow-shaped, green leaves turning crimson in late summer. Spikes of small red and green flowers from May to August
SIMILAR SPECIES:	Sheep's sorrel, Curled dock

Prized in France as a vegetable and a herb, the sharp-tasting leaves of sorrel are one of the first green plants to appear in early spring. The leaves can be picked and used young in salads from February until November. Henry VIII was said to have been particularly fond of it, and the sharpness was used in the same way as we use lemons or limes today to flavour many dishes. Housewives have also used the leaves as a polish and to remove ink stains. A cloth soaked in a solution from boiling the leaves is said to be good for cleaning wicker furniture and for polishing silver. The slightly shorter sheep's sorrel is also common and widespread, but is seldom seen on chalky soil.

GROUNDSEL *(Senecio vulgaris)*

SIZE:	7–30 cm
HABITAT:	Arable land, waste land and gardens throughout Britain
IDENTIFICATION:	Irregular branched stems with soft, bright green, lobed leaves. Small, yellow dandelion-like flowers January to December
SIMILAR SPECIES:	Heath groundsel, Sticky groundsel

The compact flower heads have been likened to shaving brushes because of the mass of stiff white hairs surrounding the seeds. The generic name *Senecio*, is from the Latin *senex*, meaning 'old man' and, as a Tudor herbalist describes it, 'the flower of this herb hath white hair, and when the winde bloweth it away, then it appeareth like a bald-headed man'. As it flowers all year round there is a constant supply of tiny seeds to be carried from garden to garden on even the slightest breeze. It is a greedy weed, disliked everywhere, but was once grown as a crop for pigs and poultry. Children gather it today and pet shops sell it for tame rabbits and canaries.

COWSLIP *(Primula veris)* ▶

SIZE:	10–30 cm tall
HABITAT:	Meadows, mostly on chalky or limestone grassland. Rarer in Scotland
IDENTIFICATION:	Wrinkled, toothed leaves form rosettes similar to primroses. The flower heads comprise up to 30 yellow flowers in April and May
SIMILAR SPECIES:	False oxlip, Primrose

A fairy in *A Midsummer Night's Dream* says to Puck: 'I must go seek some dew drops here,/And hang a pearl in every cowslip's ear'. He must have known the pleasure of coming across these delightful flowers on an early morning walk in the summer when little drops of dew gather in the cowslip's petals. This familiar flower was once widespread, but has suffered from over-picking probably more than any other meadow flower. Not only was it picked for the jam jar arrangement on the kitchen table, but was used in vast quantities to make a potent country wine. Izaak Walton used cowslip and primrose blossoms to flavour a coating for fried minnows. Rather more appetising is the Wiltshire dish 'paigle fry', where you add a quarter cup of cowslip blossoms to a cup of pancake batter before cooking the pancakes and sprinkling them with sugar.

COMMON MALLOW *(Malva sylvestris)*

SIZE: 50–100 cm

HABITAT: Verges, waste ground, meadows and embankments. Grows abundantly in coastal areas, less common in Scotland

IDENTIFICATION: Bushy, sometimes straggly plant with rounded or ivy-shaped leaves having 3–7 blunt lobes. Large pink flowers with darker veins from June to October

SIMILAR SPECIES: Musk mallow

The leaves, flowers and fruits of the common mallow are all edible and have been valued as both food and medicine since before Roman times. It was reputed to cure hangovers and to act as an anti-aphrodisiac. Herbalists, recognising its astringent and demulcent qualities, use the leaves and flowers today as a poultice for bruises, stings and insect bites. Mallow leaves are rather glutinous when cooked but are useful to make into soup. One of Egypt's national peasant dishes, 'melokhia' is made from the leaves of a similar species and Richard Mabey in his *Food for Free* suggests using mallow leaves with chicken stock, garlic, coriander and cayenne to make a British version. The flowers, up to 50 mm across, are the most striking part of this plant, the purplish-pink petals are deeply notched and it comes as no surprise to learn that it belongs to the same family as the hollyhock.

SWEET VIOLET *(Viola odorata)*

SIZE:	3–10 cm
HABITAT:	Hedgerows and woodland throughout Britain
IDENTIFICATION:	Heart-shaped, evergreen leaves with slightly serrated edges forming a basal rosette. Blue-violet, occasionally white, scented flowers with five petals are borne on long stalks from February to May.
SIMILAR SPECIES:	Common dog violet

There is an old country saying that, if violets bloom at autumn time, whose soil they grow on will surely die. Fortunately they usually bloom in the spring and their sweet scent has more associations with the goddess of love than with death. Baskets of fragrant bunches were offered by flower sellers on the street corners of London in the days before florists. The perfume industry still uses the oils from the flowers and leaves and the flavouring is well known as a breath freshener. The attractive flowers can be used in salads or preserved for use as edible cake decorations. To make crystallised violets, mix 3 teaspoons gum Arabic crystals with 3 tablespoons rosewater in a screwtop jar and leave, shaking occasionally, for 3 days. Paint the flowers with this mixture using a soft brush, lightly coating all surfaces. Sprinkle with a blend of two parts caster sugar to one part granulated sugar before leaving them to dry for up to a week.

BLACK BRYONY *(Tamus communis)*

SIZE:	Climbing up to 4 m
HABITAT:	Hedgerows, woodland edges and scrubland. Common in central and southern England
IDENTIFICATION:	Twining stems with heart-shaped leaves, small greenish flowers followed by bright red berries
SIMILAR SPECIES:	White bryony

In late autumn and early winter, when deciduous hedgerows lose their greenery, the black bryony provides stunning colour, none of it black. The herbalist Gerard thought this plant was named for its black berries but it is the root that is black. The shiny, pea-sized berries ripen to a bright red. The large, heart-shaped leaves turn purple or bright yellow in autumn, adding to the colourful show provided by the berries. It is part of the yam family but the berries and roots are poisonous, although the tubers can be boiled to reduce toxicity. Too acrid to be eaten for food, the roots were once squeezed and the juice mixed with honey to take as an asthma remedy. In the Middle Ages, parts of the plant were used externally for gout, chilblains, rheumatism and to remove bruises. White Bryony also has red berries but there the similarity ends. It belongs to the cucumber family and has different leaves and flowers.

LADY'S MANTLE *(Alchemilla vulgaris)*

SIZE:	Up to 45 cm high
HABITAT:	Grassland and verges, especially in upland areas
IDENTIFICATION:	Large, rounded leaves with 7–11 lobes. Clusters of tiny, yellowish green flowers appear from May to September.
SIMILAR SPECIES:	Alpine lady's mantle

Lady's mantle is not one plant but a name given to several species with only slight variations. It is dedicated to the Virgin Mary, hence its name, and was once used to cure women's ailments and even to restore sagging breasts. Along with bistort and nettles, lady's mantle leaves are traditionally used to mix with butter and eggs to make 'Easter pudding', a popular Yorkshire dish eaten with veal. In humid conditions water is forced out of tiny holes in the large leaves of lady's mantle, forming large drops of dew when surrounding plants are dry. This was collected by medieval alchemists who called it 'celestial water'. The clusters of tiny petal-free flowers are prized by flower arrangers for their bright yellow stamens. In the Scottish highlands and the Lake District, the smaller alpine lady's mantle is common and can be distinguished by its silvery leaves divided to the base.

COMMON ST JOHN'S WORT
(Hypericum perforatum)

SIZE:	40–90 cm
HABITAT:	Dry grassland, hedgerows, verges and open woodland
IDENTIFICATION:	Erect plant with oval, unstalked leaves spotted with translucent dots. Yellow flowers appear from June to September. They have five petals with black dots at the edge and bunches of prominent stamens.
SIMILAR SPECIES:	Square-stalked St John's wort, Marsh St John's wort, Trailing St John's wort

The pressure and pace of modern living mean more and more people suffer from stress or anxiety-related illnesses. Rather than taking prescribed antidepressants, people are turning to alternative medicine, and extract of St John's wort is one of the most popular herbal remedies. It can, however, interact with other medication including some taken for asthma or migraine so should be used with care. It is named after John the Baptist and one of the legends refers to John's beheading saying the black–red dots on the petals represent his drops of blood. The translucent spots on the leaves were said to be the tears shed over his death. The flowers first appear around the time of St John's Tide and, according to medieval folklore, sleeping with a sprig under your pillow on St John's Eve would cause the saint to bless you in your dreams and prevent you from dying during the coming year.

MAGPIE *(Pica pica)*

SIZE: 45 cm

HABITAT: Widespread. Woodlands, hedgerows, parks and gardens. Numbers increasing in towns. Not in Scottish Highlands

IDENTIFICATION: Easily recognised by black and white markings, tinged with iridescent green, and long tail

SIMILAR SPECIES: None

The magpie is earning itself a reputation as a real pest, with camps divided as to how much of a villain it really is. Numbers are soaring at a time when songbirds and garden regulars are disappearing, and some believe the magpie is largely responsible for the slaughter. It certainly takes eggs and nestlings as well as eating carrion and whatever else it comes across. Its hoarse, mocking, cackling call does not endear it, and it has long been associated with evil. Traditionally it is unlucky to see one on its own; if this does happen, the 'victims' must either cross themselves, spit three times over their right shoulder, raise their hats or chant 'Devil, devil I defy thee' – or preferably all these things. The old rhyme 'One for sorrow, two for joy…' comes in many different variants.

JACKDAW *(Corvus monedula)*

SIZE:	33 cm
HABITAT:	Widespread. Open woodland, farmland, parks
IDENTIFICATION:	Black plumage with conspicuous slate grey nape
SIMILAR SPECIES:	Carrion crow, Rook

The jackdaw is smaller than the carrion crow and the rook and this might explain the first part of its name. 'Jack' was traditionally used to denote something smaller than the norm, as in jack snipe. Another possible origin is that 'jack' was once used to refer to a knave or thief, and the jackdaw has a reputation for flying off with bright, shiny objects that take its fancy. The 19th century humorist, the Rev. Richard Barham, author of *Babes in the Wood*, wrote a poem called *The Jackdaw of Rheims* in which the bird stole the ring of the Archbishop and was duly enthroned. The 'daw' part of the name is probably alliterative of the bird's call; it is known as the caw or caw-daw in some parts of Britain. It can be a pest for those with open fires, blocking up chimneys with nests of sticks and twigs.

CARRION CROW *(Corvus corone corone)*

SIZE:	47 cm
HABITAT:	Widespread (except in Scottish Highlands, replaced by Hooded crow). Farmland, moorland and urban areas
IDENTIFICATION:	Glossy black plumage, heavy bill
SIMILAR SPECIES:	Raven, Rook, Hooded crow, Jackdaw

Lewis Carroll had Tweedledee and Tweedledum alarmed by a 'monstrous crow, as black as a tar-barrel', and this macabre image is one which recurs in literary references to the bird. Ted Hughes, in his story-poems *Crow*, cast the bird as a demonic figure creating a nightmare world: 'Then heaven and earth creaked at the joint/Which became gangrenous and stank –/A horror beyond redemption…/Crow/Grinned/Crying:/ "This is my Creation,"/Flying the black flag of himself'. It has always been persecuted for eating crops and stealing eggs and chicks, and its cunning, just-out-of-reach, manner provokes dislike. Crows and rooks look similar from a distance, but the crow is smaller. Also, if you see a big black bird in the company of others, it is probably a rook; if it is on its own, it is most likely a crow.

ROOK *(Corvus frugilegus)*

SIZE:	45 cm
HABITAT:	Widespread in woodland and farmland. Absent in far north-west Scotland
IDENTIFICATION:	Black plumage with pale face patch. Stout, long, pale bill. Stockier and larger than carrion crow
SIMILAR SPECIES:	Carrion crow, Raven, Hooded crow

Ralph Hodgson describes in his poem *The Song of Honour* how, as light fell, the 'rooks came home in scramble sort,/and filled the trees and flapped and fought'. This captures perfectly the mass, straggling nightly return to the rookeries of these gregarious, but sometimes bickering, birds. Rooks breed very early in the season, so their large, twiggy nests are easily spotted high in the bare branches, where hundreds or even thousands of pairs may congregate. When they have gathered, they do not settle immediately, erupting now and then in a circling mob, cawing and screeching, before finally settling back among the branches for the night. Similar communal flying displays are seen during the day. Although once sentenced to eradication in Scotland for eating corn, the rook is a farmer's friend, devouring pests like leatherjackets and wireworms.

LAPWING *(Vanellus vanellus)* ▲

SIZE:	30 cm
HABITAT:	Widespread on farmland and pasture, seashore and mudflats
IDENTIFICATION:	Distinctive. Iridescent green upper parts tinged with purple; white under parts with chestnut under-tail; white head with black face patch, black cap and long crest
SIMILAR SPECIES:	None

Even when it is not windy, a lapwing in flight looks as though it is being battered and swept along by a swirling breeze. If it was not already distinctive enough in appearance, its 'floppety' flying and its 'pee-weet' call make it easy to identify. Country folk call it peewit after its call, but 'lapwing' comes from the Old English *hleapewince* meaning a leap with a wink in it – a perfect description of its flight as it wheels and turns, showing first its shimmering green back then its white underside. In a big flock, moving in unison, this flashing display is extremely impressive. Lapwing chicks are renowned for being able to run about within moments of hatching, often with bits of shell still stuck to them, if disturbed. Lapwings and their eggs used to be a popular delicacy.

PHEASANT *(Phasianus colchicus)* ▶

SIZE:	Male 75–90 cm, female 50–65 cm
HABITAT:	Widespread except north-east Scotland. Parkland, farmland, woods, plantations
IDENTIFICATION:	Male distinctive with flecked russet plumage, red face, dark green head and long pointed tail. Female mottle buff
SIMILAR SPECIES:	Female similar to female Black grouse but with pointed tail

The pheasant is an established part of our countryside and rural traditions, having been introduced from Asia as a foodsource, possibly early in the 11th century. Many a country walk is punctuated by the clattering explosion of a startled pheasant from almost beneath the feet, followed by its long, low glide to the safety of a thicket or hedgerow. They prefer to run away rather than fly, which presents a problem for those out to shoot them – hence the need for gangs of beaters to get the birds to rise from the undergrowth. The pheasant shooting industry has brought many benefits, including the establishment of woods and copses where other species can flourish. One disadvantage has been the persecution of pheasant predators such as foxes and birds of prey. There are several ornamental species of pheasant that have escaped to breed in the wild.

REDWING *(Turdus iliacus)*

SIZE: 21 cm

HABITAT: Widespread winter visitor, some breeding in northern
                Scotland. Farmland, heaths, moors and gardens

IDENTIFICATION: Like a Song thrush: brown back and pale
                     mottled breast, but with pale eye stripe,
                     red patches on flanks and under wings

SIMILAR SPECIES: Song thrush, Mistle thrush, Fieldfare

Although it spends its time in the fields and woods, the redwing is probably seen by most people as it flits beside the road. It has a habit of 'following ahead' along the verge or hedgerow as you walk or drive. Quite large groups will do this, giving the observer ample opportunity to spot the distinctive red patch beneath the wings. If on foot, you will also hear the redwing's characteristic twittering chatter. The redwing arrives from its summer breeding grounds in Europe in October and gorges on the berries of hedgerow and woodland. It also eats small invertebrates and, in a hard winter, will either carry on flying south or stay on to be fed at bird tables. A few pairs breed in northern Scotland, where the dense woodlands and highland gullies offer sufficient shelter.

FIELDFARE *(Turdus pilaris)*

SIZE:	25 cm
HABITAT:	Widespread winter visitor on farmland, pastures and moors
IDENTIFICATION:	Like a Song thrush but with grey head and rump, light eye stripe and black tail
SIMILAR SPECIES:	Song thrush, Redwing, Mistle thrush

If the fieldfare is here, then so is winter. Chaucer, in *The Parlement of Foules*, described it as 'the frosty feldefare' and some country folk call it the snowbird. It arrives in October and stays until late April, with just a few pairs staying on to nest in Scotland. Large flocks can be seen hopping about on pastures, often mixing with other thrushes or plovers, rooting out seeds and insects or dodging around in the woods and hedgerows looking for their favourite rosehips, hawthorn and rowan berries. The fieldfare is like all thrushes in that it is particularly partial to fruit, so if you want to see one in the garden then leave an old core or two on the lawn when the snow is lying and hope the other birds do not finish them off first.

QUAIL *(Coternix coternix)*

SIZE:	18 cm
HABITAT:	Southern England and parts of Scotland. Farmland, particularly cornfields and grassland. Summer visitor
IDENTIFICATION:	Squat rounded body like small partridge. Brown, streaked back and ruddy under parts. Head, neck and throat patterned with black and white streaks. Female drabber without head markings
SIMILAR SPECIES:	Partridge

The closest most people come to a quail is its tiny eggs, which were once something of a delicacy but are now readily available in large grocery stores. Each female can produce 10 or more of these creamy-coloured, brown-splotched eggs, although a nest might contain upwards of 20, as the males often take more than one partner. The bird itself is also a regular in the butcher's shop. In the wild, the elusive quail is hard to spot but you might hear its distinctive call. These three short notes have given rise to many of the quail's local names: wet-my-lip, wet-my-feet, but-for-but and quick-me-dick, being just a selection. Hearing the call will not help you track it down, however, as it 'throws' its voice like a ventriloquist. Quail numbers always fluctuate hugely, from almost total absence to migratory flocks of thousands.

red-legged partridge

PARTRIDGE *(Perdix perdix)*

SIZE: 30 cm

HABITAT: Widespread except in N.W. Scotland. Farmland, among crops, in scrubland and copses

IDENTIFICATION: Brownish upper parts, greyish neck and breast, orange–brown face with dark crown. Male has distinctive brown horseshoe mark on breast

SIMILAR SPECIES: Red-legged partridge, Quail

The name partridge is derived from the Greek *perdesthai* which means 'to make explosive noises'. This is quite appropriate nowadays, as a sighting of a partridge is likely to be accompanied by the blast of a shotgun. Originally the name derived from the brash clattering and loud grating it makes as it bursts from undergrowth when disturbed. The introduced red-legged partridge will usually skulk away, but the indigenous common or grey partridge makes a relatively easy target for the shooters, not only taking flight but staying together in a group: two birds with one shot is not uncommon. Shooting begins in September when the birds gather in coveys, or family groups, and the surviving birds pair off in February. Partridges lay a lot of eggs: 10 to 20 per female and 40 or more in a clutch, as males often take more than one partner.

SPOTTED FLYCATCHER
(Muscicapa striata)

SIZE:	14 cm
HABITAT:	Widespread summer visitor. Open woodland
IDENTIFICATION:	Grey–brown above, pale below with flecks and streaks on the crown and breast. Tiny whiskers either side of bill
SIMILAR SPECIES:	Pied flycatcher

The sound of a squeaky cartwheel making two or three turns betrays the spotted flycatcher as it sits on its vantage point waiting to swoop down on a passing insect. The song is really quite realistic – and eerie when you know there are not any wheels about. The birds arrive from central Africa in May and spread throughout Britain, making their nests in a wide variety of sheltered places, readily using nestboxes and cosy crannies in sheds or outhouses. The nest is a neat little cup of twigs, roots, grass and moss, lined with feathers and hair. If you are lucky enough to witness a flycatcher taking a flying insect, you will probably hear its bill snap shut like a trap. It usually does its hunting from the vantage point of a branch: it flies out, snaps up the insect, then flies back to its perch.

YELLOWHAMMER *(Emberiza citrinella)*

SIZE:	16.5 cm
HABITAT:	Widespread except in very far N.W. Scotland
IDENTIFICATION:	Bright yellow head and breast, light chestnut upper parts, white tail feathers show in flight
SIMILAR SPECIES:	Cirl bunting

You cannot mistake a yellowhammer. Bright yellow and with a loud, insistent song, this bird is seen almost everywhere out in the open, from the hedgerow and common to the allotment and meadow. It usually chooses a high perch from which to deliver its carrying song consisting of the repetition of one note. Dynamic though the song is, it takes quite a leap of imagination to interpret the 'chiz-iz-iz-iz-iz-zee' sound as 'a-little-bit-of-bread-and-no-cheese', as country folk call the yellowhammer. In Scotland, the phrase is taken to be the even more improbable 'may-the-devil-take-you' and it used to be believed that it drank a drop of the devil's blood every May morning. Because of this superstition it was persecuted in many northern parts. The cirl bunting *(Emberiza cirlus)* is scarce and is restricted to the far south and west of England.

STOCK DOVE *(Columba oenas)*

SIZE:	33 cm
HABITAT:	Widespread except in N.W. Scotland where replaced by Rock dove. Woodland, parkland, farmland and cliffs, coastal and inland
IDENTIFICATION:	Grey plumage. Smaller than Wood pigeon. Each wing with two short bars on upper side in flight
SIMILAR SPECIES:	Rock dove, Wood pigeon, Collared dove

The stock dove is often mistaken for a wood pigeon, but seen together the differences are obvious. The stock dove is smaller and without the white neck patch or pinkish breast. The name has been said to derive from the belief that all pigeons came from this stock, but they actually descend from the rock dove *(Columba livia)*, which replaces the stock dove in the north of Scotland and Ireland. Stock doves take little trouble over their nests, which are often reclaimed rabbit burrows or holes in trees or cliffs without any lining material whatsoever. The chicks are fed on 'pigeon's milk', a secretion from the parents' crops which they take from deep in the adults' throats. A group of stock or rock doves will often fly in formation, making a looping, hovering display before dropping to the ground.

COLLARED DOVE *(Streptopelia decaocto)*

SIZE:	32 cm
HABITAT:	Widespread on farms and common in towns
IDENTIFICATION:	Uniform grey upper parts and underside with darker wings and distinct black half-collar on nape
SIMILAR SPECIES:	Turtle dove, Stock dove, Rock dove

The collared dove was once known only in the Balkans, from which it began to spread in the 1930s. Since 1955, when it was first recorded as breeding in Britain, its numbers here have rocketed, and estimates have been put at up to a quarter of a million breeding pairs. Its 'invasion' began in the farmyard, where it clears up any fallen grain or animal feed, and spread to mills, docks and eventually to town and city centres. It has a pretty little cooing song of three syllables with the stress on the middle one and a little blip at the end – coo-*coooo*-coo*hik* – but it can become grating when you have heard dozens of birds repeating it non-stop for what seems like forever. It makes a different sound during its ritual courting flight, when it climbs high then descends in a glide, uttering a sort of growl.

SKYLARK *(Alauda arvensis)*

SIZE:	15 cm
HABITAT:	Widespread. Meadows, grassland, cultivated land, downland, moors
IDENTIFICATION:	Nondescript small brown bird. Slight crest, whitish outer tail feathers. Distinctive flight and song
SIMILAR SPECIES:	Woodlark, Shorelark

The skylark is embedded into our language, arts and sensitivities to an extent that might puzzle a stranger surveying British birds today. It has disappeared from huge tracts of countryside and generally become a rare sight. The reasons are not clear, but pesticides and changes in farmland management have certainly contributed. Between 1972 and 1992 three million larks were lost – one in four of the population. The lark spirals high above the summer fields, twittering its insistent yet pleasant song, then hovers, warbling, for several minutes before fluttering down into the long grass. Poets have written movingly about the lark (see George Meredith's *Lark Ascending*), yet it was once a regular item on the menu and caged larks were blinded 'to improve their song'. The woodlark *(Lullula arborea)*, restricted to southern Britain, is apparently on the increase.

MEADOW PIPIT *(Anthus pratensis)*

SIZE:	14.5 cm
HABITAT:	Widespread in farmland and open grassland from sea level to high altitudes
IDENTIFICATION:	Small brown bird with streaked breast, light eye stripe. Long hind claws. Distinctive song and flight
SIMILAR SPECIES:	Tree pipit, Rock pipit

Among the most undistinguished of 'small brown birds', the meadow pipit makes up for its boring appearance with its charming song and display flight. It climbs more vertically than the lark but nowhere near so high. As it ascends, its piping 'phweet' notes become faster until it reaches its zenith. Then, dramatically, it 'parachutes' back to earth, wings held stiffly up and tail spread to halt its fall, and as it drops it warbles an ever lowering, ever softer, ever slower refrain. After the dunnock, the meadow pipit is the most likely host to the cuckoo's egg, with an estimated 20% of nests doing the honour. The tiny pipit, in feeding the huge cuckoo, looks as if it might fall into its mouth and an Irish folk tale says that, should it happen, it would spell the end of the earth.

tawny owl

OWLS

Owls, with their humanoid faces, silent flight and eerie calls, are deeply ingrained in our superstitious consciences. No bird is more closely associated with magic, and any depiction of a wizard's den is bound to include one of these poised hunters.

The **barn owl** (*Tyto alba*), 34 cm, used to be a common evening sight, a white ghost of a bird, gliding soundlessly across farmland and hedgerows in search of small animals. It is widespread except in the far N.W. of Scotland, but is now on the decline and is protected. Its numbers fell initially as a result of persecution and yet it is not a pest. It was trapped and killed simply because people thought it an evil bird, the bringer of death and the stealer of souls. The witches in *Macbeth* used owls and bits of them in their brews, and Shakespeare frequently used the bird as a symbol of doom. But the owl and its eggs were also put into everyday medicinal concoctions. Owl broth was thought to cure whooping cough, and powdered, dried owl egg, it was said, improved eyesight. It was only fairly recently that the practice died away of nailing a dead owl to a barn door to keep away the 'evil eye'. The barn owl is also known as the screech owl because of its spine-chilling scream. Numbers continue to decline from the effects of pesticide, loss of nest sites, its prime hunting grounds and of field headlands, hedgerows and ditches.

The **little owl** (*Athene noctua*), 22 cm, has a far more pleasant call, a gentle mewing interspersed with a little yelp. This bird was introduced in 1842 from America and others were later brought over from Holland. Since then it has flourished and breeds as far north as the Scottish border. Although mostly found in agricultural settings, it will also make its homes in parkland and cliffs, either inland or by the sea. It is unusual among the owls in being largely diurnal. Although it will take very small mammals, its diet is mostly insects, worms and molluscs. The little owl was, in Greek mythology, the sacred bird of Pallas Athene, goddess of wisdom, and this is where we get our idea of the 'wise owl'. The Ancient Greeks regarded the owl as the embodiment of calm and moderation, and they too used it in recipes to cure alcoholism, madness, gout and epilepsy.

The owl that makes the classic owlish 'to-whit-to-whoooo' noise is the **tawny owl** (*Strix aluco*), 38 cm. This is the most widespread of the owls, being everywhere except the outer isles and the very far N.W. of Scotland. Its call is usually restricted to 'to-whit' and the second part is added during the mating season. As well as taking mice and other small mammals, the tawny owl will eat fish, frogs and even other birds. It is a superb hunter with, like the other owls, wonderful eyesight and hearing and huge, sharp talons.

little owl

People used to say that if you walked round and round a **long-eared owl** *(Asio otus)*, 34 cm, it would keep watching you and wind its head in a circle until it throttled itself. Of course, it will not, but the bird has a reputation for being simple. Common mostly in the eastern half of Britain, this tree-nester does not really have long ears but tufts of feathers that look like ears. Its call is a low drawn-out 'ooooo', which it repeats three times and which can carry a great distance. It is more likely to hunt small birds than other owls and it hunts at night.If, over a treeless moor, you see what looks like a giant moth flapping about a few feet off the ground in apparently random flight, it is probably a **short-eared owl** *(Asio flammeus)*, 38 cm.

Its flight is one of its prime characteristics, along with its almost horizontal stance when perching. It has small 'ear tufts', but its actual ears are perhaps the sharpest of all the owls, as it hunts by listening out for rustles of movement on the ground. It can be seen during the day or early evening and is found mostly in Scotland, the Pennines and upland Wales. It nests and roosts on the ground.

short-eared owl

CUCKOO *(Cuculus canorus)*

SIZE:	33 cm
HABITAT:	Widespread in hedgerows, woodland and copses, gardens, heaths and moors
IDENTIFICATION:	Distinctive. Grey upper parts, lighter and barred below. Long, rounded tail. Scythe-shaped wings in flight. Unique song
SIMILAR SPECIES:	In level flight similar to Kestrel or Sparrowhawk

No two notes have achieved such instant worldwide recognition as those uttered by the cuckoo. Threaded by musicians into numberless works, these notes herald the spring: the arrival from Africa of the first cuckoo in any locality is a significant event. Accordingly, the cuckoo is laden with folklore and is the subject of numerous country sayings and rhymes. On 'cuckoo day' (varying from March 21 in southern France to April 21 in Yorkshire), you can make a wish or turn over a coin to improve your finances. Counting the number of 'cuckoos' will tell you, according to circumstances, how many years will pass before you marry, have children or die. The cuckoo lays its eggs in other birds' nests, and its chick ejects the rightful eggs to get all the food the duped parents bring (see Hedge sparrow p.26). It is on the decrease, probably due to loss of habitat and food, and colder, wetter springs and summers.

KESTREL *(Falco tinnunculus)*

SIZE:	Wingspan 65–80 cm
HABITAT:	Widespread over farmland, open ground, motorway verges and urban areas
IDENTIFICATION:	Flecked grey underside, chestnut back. Upper wings chestnut with dark tips. Grey tail with black band. Distinctive hover
SIMILAR SPECIES:	In level flight similar to Sparrowhawk and Cuckoo

The kestrel is known in the south-west as the windhover, in Berkshire and Buckinghamshire as the hoverhawk, and in Kent as the windsucker – all names accurately singling it out from the other small birds of prey through its distinctive hunting technique. Most people have seen a kestrel hovering above a motorway verge, waiting to pounce on small mammals as they hesitate in confusion on reaching the tarmac and the thundering traffic. It attacks in stages, making its final dive from just a few metres. In the open, the kestrel 'quarters' its hunting ground, hovering for a while, flying a short way, rising and hovering again, wings working, tail spread, but head absolutely still. A birdwatching surveyor is reported as having focused his theodolite on the head of a hovering kestrel and noted that it did not move more than 1 centimetre in 28 seconds.

GEESE

No one sings 'Christmas is coming, the turkey is getting fat'. It is a mystery why this foreign species has usurped the native goose as the traditional Christmas dish. There is more meat on a turkey but how tasteless and dry it is by comparison. Geese are still eaten at Christmas, but seldom wild ones. It is illegal to sell a dead wild goose and wildfowlers tend to keep their hard-earned quarry to themselves. Canada (*Branta canadensis*) and greylag (*Anser anser*) may be shot throughout the UK during the open season, pink-footed (A. brachyrhynchus) and white-fronted (*A. albifrons*) in England and Wales only. Paradoxically, on Christmas day it is forbidden to shoot a goose.

Of course, not everyone is happy about geese being killed. There is a strong lobby to protect Canada geese, in particular, as these tame birds, introduced in 1665, have become something of a pest, especially in town parks where people feed them and encourage over-population. Local authorities often carry out culls and 156 birds were killed in Hyde Park in 1994.

If you do eat a wild goose at Christmas, you can use the breastbone to foretell the weather. Remove the bone, clean it and let it dry. Watch it as winter progresses: if it turns dark, a cold winter is just ahead; a white bone predicts a mild winter; a thin and transparent breastbone means a mild winter; if it is thick and opaque, expect a hard winter; reddish or red-spotted means cold but little snow; and some believe a very white bone means heavy snow to come. The scientific explanation is that, in preparing for a severe winter, geese absorb more natural oils to protect themselves against the cold. When dried, the oil-rich breastbone either turns dark or retains its original light colour according to its oil content. How the goose 'knows' the coming weather remains a mystery.

Geese feature strongly in much other ancient weather lore and many folk tales. The childhood Mother Goose was originally a

Canada goose

brent geese

northern European heathen goddess known as Frau Holt and the goose she rides on was believed to be able to cross over into the 'Otherworld'.

The **greylag**, our only indigenous species and the ancestor of most farmyard geese, once bred as far south as the Fens. Agriculture pushed it out and real wild greylags are now found only in Scotland, mostly in the Outer Hebrides where there are up to 700 pairs and a post-breeding population of 3000. The UK feral population is about 20,000 and winter figures reach about 100,000. An anonymous rhyme at the time of the 18th century Enclosures Acts bemoaned this ousting of the greylag as follows: The law doth punish man or woman/That steals the goose from off the common,/But lets the greater felon loose,/That steals the common from the goose. The greylag is larger (76–89 cm) and lighter grey than similar geese and has an orange bill and pink legs.

The widespread **Canada** (90–100 cm) is by far the largest of the

'black' geese – those with solid black areas of plumage. It has a black head and neck with a broad white chin strap. The rest of the body is mostly brown.

The **pink-footed** geese (60–76 cm) which breed in Greenland and Iceland migrate to Scotland and northern England in winter. They are very susceptible to disruption and populations declined during the first half of the 20th century due to increased disturbance and wildfowling but increased significantly in areas which became nature reserves. They have grey backs and the juvenile bird has yellow legs and feet.

The **brent goose** (*Branta bernicla*) is small (55–60 cm) and dark with a white neck patch. It winters along the south and east coasts of England and almost died out in the 1930s when its main food, eelgrass, was devastated by disease. Brent geese fly low in long, wavering lines.

Barnacle geese (*Branta leucopsis*) grow on trees. Or so people

barnacle goose

thought until their breeding grounds in the Arctic were discovered. In 'The Herball' of 1597 John Gerard described the barnacle or goose tree on which grew shells containing tiny living creatures (the goose barnacles we find on marine timber). These shells ripened and out came creatures which 'falling into the water do become fowles'. Because of this belief, barnacle geese were for a long time classified as seafood and eaten on fast days. Barnacle geese (58–68 cm) have a black head and neck with a white face and dark legs and feet. The upper parts are grey and the belly is light. They winter in the Inner Hebrides, notably Islay, and the Solway Firth.

Almost all Greenland **white-fronted geese** (almost 14,000 birds) winter in Britain along with about 6000 from Russia although up to 13,000 have come from the continent during particularly severe weather. The white-fronted (66–76 cm) likes wet grassland, saltmarshes and estuaries. It has an orange bill and legs and, with its white forehead and black-barred belly markings, is easily distinguished from other grey geese.

CORNCRAKE *(Crex crex)*

SIZE:	27 cm
HABITAT:	Restricted to small areas of Western Scotland and Northern Ireland
IDENTIFICATION:	Partridge shaped but, being a rail, with longer neck, long legs and narrow body. Streaked brown upper parts, paler under parts. Red–brown wing patches in flight. Distinctive call
SIMILAR SPECIES:	Spotted crake (rare visitor), Water rail

The corncrake is of enormous interest to bird watchers because it is not only rare but, even when within a few metres, extremely difficult to see. In one of its last remaining strongholds, the Outer Hebrides, the male can often be heard making its unmistakable rasping 'craak-craak' call from the cover of rushes or long grass, but lucky is the enthusiast who succeeds in spotting one, let alone gets a decent photograph. Also known as the landrail, it arrives from Africa each spring to breed and was once widespread throughout Britain, being heard on London commons just a century or so ago. Mechanised farming swept it away. When fields were reaped by hand, the mother and her young had time to scuttle away to safety. Combine harvesters and mechanical scythes, working from the outside inwards, gave the birds no escape route and moved faster than they could. Corncrakes simply got mown down. They survive now only where crofters and farmers employ the old methods and where grassland is left to be cut later in the year.

HORSE FLY *(Tabanus bovinus)*

SIZE: 12 mm

HABITAT: Farmland, usually near cattle or horses

IDENTIFICATION: Large 2-winged fly with yellowish-brown and black
                   markings. Iridescent eyes

SIMILAR SPECIES: Cleg and other horse flies

Perhaps the only thing to be said in its favour is that this particular biting horse fly does give fair warning of its approach by making a high-pitched humming. It is most common in southern England, flying from June to August, the female looking for a horse, cow or human to obtain its blood meal. A bite from one of these can make a hole big enough to see a drop of blood. The cleg is greyish-brown and does not have the same rules of fair play. The first time you notice it is when you have been bitten, as the female attacks silently. The species *Haematopata pluvialis* is commoner in the south and has many local names such as breeze fly, whame fly or dun fly. In the north, the cleg is more likely to be *Haematopata crassicornis*. It is on the wing from May to September, but its bite is mostly experienced in close, thundery weather in July.

NON-BITING MIDGE
(Chironomus plumosus)

SIZE: 8 mm

HABITAT: Farmyards, gardens, woods, ponds and ditches

IDENTIFICATION: Dark, slender body with transparent wings.
                   Bright red larva

SIMILAR SPECIES: Many other species of biting and non-biting midge

It is difficult to distinguish between the 380 or so species of non-biting midge, but you can tell a midge from a gnat by its humped back. Midges are common throughout Britain and the males can often be seen in large clouds, dancing up and down. This attracts the females and mating takes place in the air. The wriggling larva moves around the muddy bottom of its ditch by making a figure-of-eight and its bright red colour gives it the common name bloodworm. The biting midges are particularly well known to anyone who has visited Scotland in August. On a still day a cloud of thousands will bite any mammal or bird they can find. Disliking bright sunlight, they are most troublesome early in the morning or at dusk, and their attentions are enough to drive the strongest man to tears. Only females bite, needing a blood meal to fuel their egg-laying.

MEADOW ANT *(Lasius flavus)*

SIZE:	3–5 mm
HABITAT:	Pastureland and orchards
IDENTIFICATION:	Yellowish-brown body with single abdominal waist
SIMILAR SPECIES:	Common red ant (red), Garden ant (black), Negro ant (black), Wood ant (black and brown)

Taking a welcome rest on a grassy tussock could be a bad move for the walker. The grass-covered mounds often seen in uncultivated fields are the nests of the meadow ant, sometimes shared with the common red ant *(Myrmica ruginodis)*. Both species are dairying ants which milk aphids for their honeydew, but they are also likely to give an intruder a nasty nip. The meadow ant spends most of its time in the nest, a simple series of burrowed chambers. The ant does not make special cells for the eggs in the same way as bees or wasps, so if the nest is disturbed, the eggs, larvae and pupae must be carried to a new site. Different species of ant often have similar lifestyles but favour different habitats for their colonies. The garden ant and the negro ant form nests under stones or in gardens; the wood ant prefers open scrubland or forest floors.

MONEY SPIDER *(Linyphia hortensis)*

SIZE:	3–5 mm
HABITAT:	Fields, woods, downs and heaths
IDENTIFICATION:	Small spider with black body and brownish legs
SIMILAR SPECIES:	Several small black spiders of the genus *Linyphiidae* are known as money spiders

There is a saying that, if a money spider walks across your palm, it will bring good luck in money matters. According to *The Mascot Book* by Elizabeth Villiers, the Romans carried little spiders of gold or silver to bring good luck in trade. So these tiny spiders usually manage to escape the fate of their larger brethren when they cross the path of a human being. The money spider is widespread and can be extremely abundant. One Sussex field was estimated to contain over a million of them. On a dewy autumn morning the hammock-like webs are conspicuous on grassland. The spider spins its web in the morning and, as the day warms up, the webs are carried up by rising air currents. Towards evening, cooler air brings them floating down in clouds, sometimes up to 100 miles away from where they started.

SMALL COPPER BUTTERFLY
(Lycaena phlaeas)

SIZE: Forewing 10–17 mm

HABITAT: Gardens, parks, wasteland, heaths, rough grassland

IDENTIFICATION: Upperside of forewing shiny orange–copper, brown margin, scattered black spots. Upper hindwing brown with orange border, sometimes few blue spots, underside brown

SIMILAR SPECIES: Sooty copper (female)

Dock or sorrel leaves that have translucent patches in them, like little windows, have probably been providing food for the caterpillars of the small copper butterfly. This stripping of lower surface leaf tissue is usual with copper caterpillars and the small copper is extremely common – at the moment. Although still one of the most widespread European grassland butterflies, numbers are falling as meadows, woodland and moors go under the plough. A report in 2001, showed that 75% of species declined over the previous 30 years, the small copper among them. This is despite it being very prolific, with up to four broods between February and November. The caterpillar is green and slug-like, often with pink stripes, and grows to 15 mm. The small copper hibernates as a caterpillar, which will sometimes wake to feed on mild days.

GATEKEEPER BUTTERFLY ▶
(Pyronia tithonus)

SIZE: Forewing 17–25 mm

HABITAT: Woodland margins, hedgerows, scrubby grassland. Absent from Scotland

IDENTIFICATION: Upper sides rich orange, broad brown borders, large twin-pupilled eye spot near wingtip. Male with brown streak near centre of forewing. Underside similar but hindwing largely brown with yellow patches in outer half

SIMILAR SPECIES: None in Britain

The gatekeeper butterfly, also known as the hedge brown, is very keen on bramble flowers and is often seen in scrubland where blackberries grow. Other favourites among the many flowers it feeds on are marjoram and ragwort, so it is also seen in rural gardens with nearby hedgerows, and orchards or shrubberies where there is plenty of long grass. Grasses are the feedplants for the caterpillar, and the butterfly scatters its eggs among them as it flies. The young caterpillar is green with a grey–brown head and pale stripes along its sides but when fully grown (25 mm) the green turns grey–brown. The gatekeeper's wings are a rich deep colour and it is easy to spot as it flits down forest rides or through clearings. It is fairly widespread in the south of Britain but rare in the north and absent from Scotland.

COMMON FROGHOPPER
(Philaenus spumarius)

SIZE:	6–8 mm
HABITAT:	Gardens, hedgerows and any well-vegetated habitat. Common throughout the British Isles
IDENTIFICATION:	Either dark brown with lighter patches or light brown with darker patches. Wings carried 'roofed' when at rest
SIMILAR SPECIES:	Alder froghopper and other leaf hoppers

The white, frothy substance seen on grass stems and other plants, which is commonly called 'cuckoo spit', is not spit at all but a foam produced by the nymph of the froghopper, also known as the cuckoo spit insect. It is most likely to be seen on hawthorn or sorrel and appears in the spring, at the same time as we hear the first cuckoo. The adult female lays 50–100 eggs in the crevices of dead stems during the autumn. An egg hatches in spring and the nymph climbs to a suitable plant and sucks the sap, usually from around the axil of a leaf. A secretion from its abdomen is bubbled up by air and this forms a frothy coating to protect it from predators and to keep off the sun. The foam remains after the fully grown insect has hopped away.
The adult, which looks like a tiny frog, can leap a terrific distance for its size.

COCKCHAFER *(Melolontha melolontha)*

SIZE:	25–30 mm
HABITAT:	Hedgerows, woodland margins, parks and gardens
IDENTIFICATION:	Hairy, reddish-brown wingcases, sharp-tipped abdomen
SIMILAR SPECIES:	Garden chafer, Summer chafer

A large and ungainly insect thumping its hard body against the window pane on an early summer's evening is likely to be the cockchafer, or May-bug. It flies from May to June and sometimes comes indoors through an open door or window, humming loudly as it flies around the room crashing into things. It can appear in swarms around deciduous trees when feeding on the leaves. The curved, white larva spends three years in the soil, feeding on the roots of grass, herbaceous plants or even trees, occasionally in sufficient numbers to cause considerable damage. The smaller garden chafer varies in colour but often has a metallic green head and thorax. It appears later than the cockchafer and one of its common names is June bug. Other common names vary locally, often thought up by anglers who use the cockchafer as bait for trout.

GREAT GREEN BUSH CRICKET
(Tettigonia viridissima)

SIZE: 40–50 mm

HABITAT: Hedges, bushes and other coarse vegetation. Common in England and Wales, absent from Scotland

IDENTIFICATION: Yellowish-green body, legs and feet. Long thin antennae

SIMILAR SPECIES: Oak bush cricket

On warm August evenings the song of crickets is a typical sound of an English summer. The male produces the grating noise by rubbing a toothed rib in his left forewing against the hind edge of the other. To the trained ear, or to other crickets, there are three different songs. The first attracts a mate, the second is the intimate courtship song and the third is produced if another male tries to cut in on the romance. The great green bush cricket is the largest of our bush crickets and only the rare field cricket has a louder song. Unlike most crickets, the great green also sings by day but spends most of its time in thick vegetation hunting insects. The female has a sword-shaped ovipositor with which she deposits eggs into the soil, leaving them to overwinter. The smaller, oak bush cricket is the only British bush cricket to live in trees.

COMMON FIELD GRASSHOPPER
(Chorthippus brunneus)

SIZE:	18–24 mm
HABITAT:	Fields, open woodlands, dunes and grassy places. Widespread through the British mainland but less common in Scotland
IDENTIFICATION:	Colouring varies in shades of brown and green, hairy underside, indented side keels on the thorax. Long forewings reach beyond the hind knees when at rest
SIMILAR SPECIES:	Meadow grasshopper

In Aesop's fable a starving grasshopper begged food from the ants on a winter's day. On being asked why he had not stored up food during the summer, the grasshopper replied: 'I had not leisure enough. I passed the days in singing.' Singing is how we think of the grasshopper on warm summer days as the male tries to attract its mate. Sometimes it is answered by the female. The 'song' is made by rubbing little pegs on the hind legs against thickened veins on the forewing. This process is known as stridulating, and can be heard from June until November. The meadow grasshopper is equally widespread and is common in Scotland. It cannot fly and can be differentiated from other species by its shortened forewings.

ROMAN SNAIL *(Helix pomatia)*

roman snail

SIZE:	Shell 50 mm diameter
HABITAT:	Chalky soils, downland or woodland, mainly in S. England
IDENTIFICATION:	Cream or buff-coloured shell with dark spiral bands
SIMILAR SPECIES:	Common or Garden snail

This is the *escargot* eaten in France (and in Britain by the gastronomically adventurous), so it is sometimes called the edible snail. Although most snails are edible, some are more appetising than others and this one is said to have the best flavour. It is sometimes called the apple snail, but whether it tastes of apples is debatable. Some say this snail was introduced to Britain by the Romans and others say that it was here already. It certainly seems that the Romans were keen on them: apparently they kept them in nurseries and fed them on bran soaked in wine, which probably improved their flavour. In southern England, where it is most common, it prefers chalky soil and, where there is considerable chalk on the surface, the snail loses its outer layer of shell, appearing almost completely white and adding to its camouflage.

The **grove snail** is often used to illustrate the theory of natural selection because it can appear in many different shell colours depending on the 'background colour' of its environment. The theory is that birds, thrushes in particular, attack the most conspicuous snails, and the camouflaged ones remain untouched to continue their line. However, researchers have found that climate is also involved, and differences in microclimate on the scale of a few inches can alter the behaviour and survival of snails of different pattern. The shell colour of the grove snail is often yellow, but can also be pink, brown or various shades between. The lip is almost always brown and its other common name is the brown-lipped snail. A smaller but similarly coloured snail is the white-lipped banded snail, distinguished unsurprisingly by its lip colour.

GRASS SNAKE *(Natrix natrix)*

SIZE: 70–150 cm

HABITAT: Grassland, especially close to water and heaths, widespread throughout England and Wales

IDENTIFICATION: Vertical bars mark the sides of the greenish body and a yellow collar behind the head

SIMILAR SPECIES: Slow worm, Smooth snake (rare), Adder

This harmless snake was once very common in England and Wales, but since about 1950 numbers have dwindled and it is becoming increasingly rare. A strong swimmer, it often lives near water, as frogs feature largely in its diet. It also eats tadpoles, newts and small fish. Like all reptiles, the grass snake derives its body heat from external sources, so it needs to lie and bask in the sun. This is the best chance to spot one – as it is lying on a rock or at the base of a south-facing wall in summer. The grass snake hibernates from October until March and mates during April or May. It looks for somewhere warm to lay its clutch of 4–10 eggs; a compost or manure heap is ideal. The young hatch in late summer and, if they can avoid cats, have an extraordinarily long lifespan of up to 25 years.

BROWN HARE *(Lepus capensis)*

SIZE:	60–70 cm
HABITAT:	Grassland, woods, heaths and dunes. Widespread but rare in W. Scotland
IDENTIFICATION:	Brown furry body, long hind legs, long ears tipped with black. Short tail, black on top, paler underside
SIMILAR SPECIES:	Mountain hare, Rabbit

The hare has always been renowned for its speed, despite not winning the race against the tortoise in Aesop's well known fable. Not only is it fast, but it will swerve and change direction quickly to outwit its hunter. In the spring, the males chase each other and fight spectacularly – each hare rearing up and boxing with its front paws. The female will also box to rebuff an over-attentive male. The brown hare is a solitary animal, spending the day resting in its form (lair) and foraging at night for plants, berries or mushrooms, gnawing bark when food is scarce. The doe has three or four litters a year, each with up to five leverets which suckle for 3 weeks before making their own way in the world. When hares were more abundant, jugged hare was a popular dish; the rich casserole was flavoured with port and bacon, then thickened with the blood of the hare.

RABBIT *(Oryctolagus cuniculus)* ▶

SIZE:	42–60 cm
HABITAT:	Cultivated land, woods, scrubland and dunes
IDENTIFICATION:	Grey fur, long hind legs, long ears and short white tail
SIMILAR SPECIES:	Brown hare, Mountain hare

Domesticated rabbits are popular cuddly pets, but the wild rabbit is seen as a pest by farmers and gardeners. It crops closely when grazing and scrapes away soil to reach root crops, so large numbers can do considerable damage. In 1950, it was estimated that there were about 100 million wild rabbits in Great Britain, but the myxomatosis disease which reached Great Britain in 1953 destroyed 99% of them in 3 years. This had a knock-on effect, reducing species such as the buzzard and other birds of prey which depend on them. By the year 2000, the rabbit population had recovered to about 15 million, despite periodic outbreaks of the virus. The rabbit lives in large groups, burrowing to form complex warrens with living chambers. Planting a thick row of foxgloves round the vegetable garden is supposed to deter rabbits.

COMMON SHREW *(Sorex ananeus)*

SIZE:	7.5–8.5 cm excluding tail
HABITAT:	Hedgerows, grassland, scrub, marshes and woods
IDENTIFICATION:	Dark brown fur, greyish-white underside. Long pointed mobile snout, short ears and very small eyes
SIMILAR SPECIES:	Pygmy shrew, Water shrew

The long, flexible snout extending beyond its red-tipped teeth is the best way to tell shrews from mice or voles. The common shrew twitters as it searches for beetles, worms and slugs in the undergrowth, so it is more likely to be heard than seen. It is strongly territorial and will squeak as it chases away intruders. The female makes a tight nest on the ground using grass stems and leaves. If disturbed while suckling, she will rush off with the young tightly clasped to her nipples, removing them to safety in one go. At 6 cm long, the pygmy shrew *(S. minutus)* is our smallest mammal. Like the common shrew it is widespread in mainland Britain and on some islands, but less abundant. The dark coat of the water shrew *(Neomys fodiens)* appears silvery when it swims because of air bubbles trapped in its fur, and it leaves a trail of bubbles when it dives.

BROWN RAT *(Rattus norvegicus)*

SIZE:	35–45 cm including tail
HABITAT:	Farm buildings, towns, villages and river banks
IDENTIFICATION:	Greyish-brown fur with a greasy appearance. Long, scaly tail is shorter than the body
SIMILAR SPECIES:	None

The story of the Pied Piper of Hamelin tells how the piper played his magic flute to entice a plague of rats out to sea to drown. In the tale he was never paid (with dire consequences for the town's children), but he would make his fortune today, as we would pay a lot to rid ourselves of this unpopular mammal. It is a serious pest for farmers, eating grain and spoiling what it does not eat with its urine and droppings. Living in rubbish dumps and sewers does nothing for its reputation, and it is a well-known carrier of disease, including salmonella and Weil's disease. The brown rat digs tunnels up to 50 cm deep and builds a nest with passages or bolt-holes reaching almost to the surface, so that it can break through in an emergency. It is very prolific, with one pair multiplying to 200 in a year. Thankfully, it only lives one year.

WOOD MOUSE *(Apodemus sylvaticus)*

SIZE: 8–11 cm excluding tail

HABITAT: Fields, hedgerows, woods and gardens

IDENTIFICATION: Dark brown fur with greyish-white underside, large
                    ears and a long tail

SIMILAR SPECIES: Yellow-necked mouse

This is most likely to be the villain digging up the peas just planted in the vegetable patch. A generation ago, gardeners would roll their seeds in red lead powder, but this is not to be recommended. Another ingenious deterrent was to wash the cat and sprinkle the bath-water over the soil: the mice were deterred by the scent. The wood mouse is Britain's commonest and most widespread mouse. It has colonised on many offshore islands, and some different forms have developed, larger than their mainland cousins. Usually a solitary animal, it is active all year, particularly at dawn and dusk. Although this agile climber is abundant in deciduous woods, it is found in most habitats, even venturing indoors. The female has two to four litters a year nesting in any suitable site: a corner of the garden shed is a popular place and an old boot is not unknown.

HARVEST MOUSE *(Micromys minutus)*

SIZE:	5–7 cm excluding tail
HABITAT:	Grassland, hedgerows and deciduous woods
IDENTIFICATION:	Russet orange fur with paler underside, darker in winter. Very long tail
SIMILAR SPECIES:	Woodmouse

A nest the size of a cricket ball built among the stems of cereals or in hedgerows indicates the presence of the harvest mouse. This is the breeding nest, woven by the female in late pregnancy and supported by tall grasses or reeds. She might have two or three litters, each with up to eight young, but only uses the breeding nest once. At the base of tussocks, or under some cover at ground level, is the non-breeding nest, which is used in winter for sleeping and storing food. The harvest mouse is Britain's smallest rodent and is rarely found north of Yorkshire or in Wales. Its slender, prehensile tail is about the same length as its body and used to climb up the taller plants.

YELLOW-NECKED MOUSE
(Apodemus flavicollis)

SIZE:	9–13 cm
HABITAT:	Hedgerows, arable land, woods and scrubland
IDENTIFICATION:	Sandy brown fur with a yellow collar, white underside
SIMILAR SPECIES:	Wood mouse

Perhaps it was a yellow-necked mouse that prompted the nursery rhyme about three blind mice having their tails cut off with a carving knife. If a predator catches one by the tail, the skin pulls off easily, allowing the mouse to escape with bare vertebrae. It is not blind except, like all mice, when it is born. It is also naked when born, but soon grows grey fur, and the yellow collar becomes apparent after 2 weeks. The yellow-necked mouse is found mainly in southern England and Wales, in the same habitat as the wood mouse. It can be confused with the wood mouse but it is larger and more brightly coloured. It is a vigorous climber, foraging in hedges and trees, and sometimes using holes in trees as a site for its nest. In autumn it is occasionally heard indoors as it clambers noisily about in the attic.

BANK VOLE *(Clethrionomys glareolus)*

SIZE:	9–11 cm excluding tail
HABITAT:	Hedgerows, woodland and scrub
IDENTIFICATION:	Chestnut brown fur, creamy white underside, rounded muzzle with ears just showing above the fur and long tail
SIMILAR SPECIES:	Field vole, Water vole

The bank vole is the smallest vole in Britain: the largest, the water vole, is in long-term decline. There is one bank vole as large as a water vole, and that more placid creature lives only on Skomer Island, off the coast of Wales. On mainland Britain, the small bank vole is active day and night, making extensive surface runways that lead to the entrance of its burrows. It travels up to 50 m to feed and will mark its territory with urine. A nimble climber, it clambers into bushes to search for berries or buds. Chopped vegetable matter and nuts are stored in its burrows or under stones ready for the winter. A nest is made below ground using dead leaves, moss, grass and perhaps feathers. The young are born naked, blind and helpless. At 8 days old the velvety juvenile fur appears and the eyes open 4 days later.

SHORT-TAILED VOLE *(Microtus agrestis)*

SIZE:	11–13 cm
HABITAT:	Grassland, hedgerows, woodland, dunes and moorland
IDENTIFICATION:	Grey–brown fur, creamy-grey underside, short tail
SIMILAR SPECIES:	Bank vole

So many birds and carnivorous animals depend on the short-tailed vole (or field vole as it is also called) that it is thought to be the most important small mammal in Britain. Fortunately, it is widespread and abundant, absent only from a few islands. It makes burrows and surface runways through long grass, marking the runways with an unpleasant scent. The nest of shredded grass is usually formed in the base of a grass tussock, but another popular place is under an abandoned sheet of corrugated iron. The short-tailed vole is fiercely territorial and will become aggressive to an intruding vole, fighting it if squeaking does not frighten it away. The ultraviolet radiation it emits can be detected by birds of prey. It can be differentiated from the bank vole by its shorter tail and smaller ears barely visible through its shaggy fur.

skomer vole

WEASEL *(Mustela nivalis)*

SIZE: 20–23 cm excluding tail

HABITAT: Almost universal

IDENTIFICATION: Small, slender body, reddish-brown fur with white underside. Short tail without a black tip

SIMILAR SPECIES: Stoat

The weasel is renowned for being a relentless hunter, one reason being that it needs to eat a third of its body weight each day just to stay alive. Mice and voles make up the largest part of its diet, although it will prey on young rabbits which are larger than itself. Its head is the widest part of its body and the overall streamlined shape means it can follow its prey down into the burrow from which there is no escape. It kills with a swift bite to the back of the neck. The weasel can be found on mainland Britain wherever there is suitable prey. It needs very little cover and can sometimes be spotted up on its hind legs sniffing the air before dashing off again. The female has one or two litters a year, each with four to six young.

BATS

Bats are not lovely-looking creatures and they are usually full of fleas, but they keep themselves to themselves and none of the British species will sink its fangs into you and drink your blood (they all eat insects). The bat's appearance and nocturnal habits have always associated it with evil and witchcraft, and the poor thing has been chopped up and used in 'magic' potions since time immemorial. The Chinese consider it very lucky to have bats in the house, but whether we think so is immaterial: all 16 British species are protected and we are not allowed to make them homeless if we find them in our loft or attic. They all hibernate, sometimes in quite large colonies.

The **common pipistrelle** (*Pipistrellus pipistrellus*), wingspan 19–25 cm, total length 5 cm, is the one you are most likely to find in your roof space. It likes modern, relatively flat-roofed buildings and also roosts behind cladding tiles. It is our smallest and most common bat and most likely seen in woods and farmland just after sunset almost anywhere in Britain.

Daubenton's bat (*Myotis daubentonii*), wingspan 23–27 cm, total length 9.5 cm, is also common and sometimes known as the water bat, as it often feeds over ponds, lakes and slow rivers. It will roost in lofts but also in trees and tunnel entrances. It is not present in the far north of Scotland.

The other bat you might find in your home is the **brown long-eared bat** (*Plecotus auritus*), wingspan 23–28 cm, total length 11 cm. It is easy to identify by its huge ears, which it uses to locate flying insects. It flies at night and sometimes during the day, occasionally hovering to pick off an insect from a leaf. It is widespread as far as north and central Scotland.

The large, golden-brown and high-flying **noctule** (*Nyctalus noctula*), wingspan 32–39 cm, total length 14 cm, is classed as vulnerable. It usually hunts over woodland, sometimes in the day, and roosts in hollow trees and in old woodpecker holes. It has been known to migrate up to 930 km to its hibernation site. It is absent from the north of Scotland.

Natterer's bat (*Myotis nattereri*), wingspan 25–30 cm, total length 10 cm, is also officially vulnerable, although fairly widespread as far as southern Scotland. It is paler in flight than most others and has a hairy edge to its tail, although bats flicker about so swiftly that this fine point is hard to make out. It likes hunting in well-wooded areas, and when hibernating it squeezes itself into the tightest little cracks in the coldest part of the cave.

One of our largest bats, the **serotine** (*Eptesicus serotinus*), wingspan 36–38 cm, total length 14 cm, covers comparatively big distances of several kilometres between its roosting place and hunting grounds. It, too, will roost in houses, but its range is restricted to the south and east of England. It is vulnerable and its numbers are falling, partly due to the treatment of roof

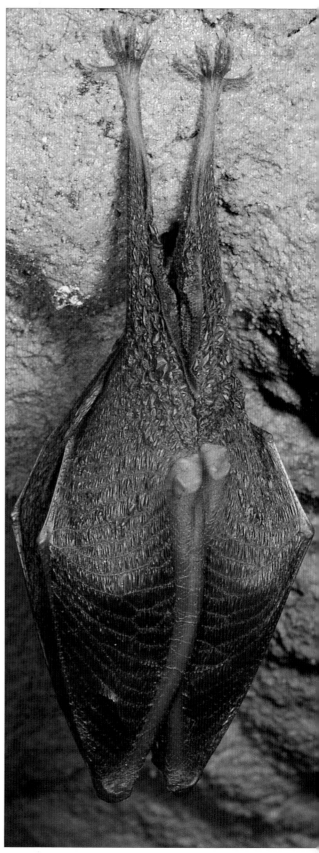

lesser horseshoe bat

greater horseshoe bat

timbers with insecticides which are toxic to bats.
The **lesser horseshoe** *(Rhinolophus hipposideros)* left, wingspan 22–25 cm, total length 8.5 cm, and **greater horseshoe** *(Rhinolophus ferrumequinum)* above, wingspan 34–39 cm, total length 11 cm, are both endangered species. They are easily distinguished from other British bats by their horseshoe-shaped 'nose leaves' – fleshy growths protruding from the sides of the

nose. They also lack a tragus – the pointed growth in the inner ear. Both like wooded areas, often near water. Both have shown a marked decline, particularly in western Europe. The lesser horseshoe is restricted to Wales and west and south-west England, and the greater horseshoe to south Wales and south-west England.

Field Mushroom *(Agaricus campestris)*

Size:	5–10 cm tall, up to 15 cm diameter
Habitat:	Grazed meadows and pastures
Identification:	White cap and stem, pink gills becoming darker with age
Similar species:	Wood mushroom, Horse mushroom

On misty mornings in late summer or autumn, country men and women can be seen from dawn onwards with baskets on their arms or bulging carrier bags as they return from mushrooming before breakfast. If you ask where they found their bounty you will get a vague reply or the more direct: 'A countryman never tells.' Field mushrooms are the most popular edible fungi in Britain and their sites are jealously guarded. The young button mushrooms appear overnight and the cap opens as it grows, leaving a narrow ring on the stem. The pink gills become dark brown and finally purple–black as they age. It advisable to learn how to distinguish edible mushrooms from those that, even if not dangerously poisonous, can cause severe digestive upsets.

Shaggy Inkcap *(Coprinus comatus)*

Size:	5–15 cm tall
Habitat:	Verges, fields, footpaths, playing fields and rubbish tips
Identification:	Cylindrical white cap with shaggy scales
Similar species:	Ink cap (*C. atramentarius*)

The shaggy cap is egg-shaped when young and looks a bit like a white busby. It grows into the more distinctive cylindrical shape and finally opens out to resemble a limp umbrella. For culinary use, it should be gathered while the cap is still closed and eaten as soon as possible or made into ketchup. The pleasant, mild flavour is brought out by casseroling it slowly with cream and seasoning. As the cap ages, or soon after it has been picked, it dissolves into an inky fluid. The only similar fungi is the ink cap (*C. atramentarius*), which is also edible, but which produces a nauseous feeling if eaten with alcohol. Interestingly, this substance (*bis*-diethyl-thiocarbomoyl-disulphide) has been used as an aversion cure for alcoholism.

Woods and Forests

I know a bank whereon the
wild thyme blows,

Where oxlips and the nodding
violet grows;

Quite over-canopied with
luscious woodbine,

With sweet musk-roses, and
with eglantine

A MIDSUMMER NIGHT'S DREAM
WILLIAM SHAKESPEARE

DOUGLAS FIR *(Pseudotsuga mentziesii)*

SIZE: Up to 55 m tall in Britain (100 m+ in USA)

HABITAT: Forestry plantations, woodland, large estates

IDENTIFICATION: Needles 25–30 mm long, soft, dark green, pointed, two white bands on underside.
Small yellow male flowers, red tasselled female flowers producing hanging, light brown cones with 3-pronged protruding bracts. Thick, corky bark ages to purple–brown

SIMILAR SPECIES: Coast redwood, Colorado white fir, Noble fir

To the unpractised eye many fir trees look the same, but one thing makes the Douglas fir stand out from the crowd – sheer size. Although not quite as tall in its native USA as its cousin the coast redwood, it grows higher in Britain. If you are still in doubt, look for the distinctive cones: hanging down with protruding bracts. It is named after the plant collector, David Douglas, who sent seeds home from America's west coast in 1827. It grows quickly and became an instant hit with big landowners in Scotland, adding grandeur to their estates. The commercial value of its durable, heavy timber is now exploited in plantations. Its only failing is that it blows over easily when in shallow soil, but it makes up for this by readily sprouting new trees from the branches of the fallen trunk.

NORWAY SPRUCE *(Picea abies)*

SIZE: Up to 60 m tall

HABITAT: Forestry plantations, woods

IDENTIFICATION: Short, prickly light green needles. Branches distinctly curved upwards. Yellow male flowers, reddish female flowers becoming long cylindrical cones with rounded scales. Smooth, light brown bark

SIMILAR SPECIES: Other *Piceas*, in particular Sitka spruce and Tiger tail spruce, look similar from a distance

Queen Victoria's husband, Prince Albert, probably feeling homesick during the festive season, brought a Norway spruce to Windsor Castle from Coburg in Germany one Christmas. The rest is history. Vast acreages are now planted in Britain just to supply the Christmas market, most of the trees never getting beyond 3 m tall. Left to grow in forestry plantations, however, Norway spruce provides excellent timber for a variety of uses from paper to pit props. It is probably the most important commercial conifer in Europe and, for this reason, the European Forest Genetic Resources Programme established the Norway Spruce Network in 1995 with the aim of maintaining a broad genetic variation in the species to ensure its evolutionary adaptability to changes in the environment. The scope of the Network has since increased to include all European conifers.

EUROPEAN LARCH *(Larix decidua)*

SIZE: Up to 35 m tall

HABITAT: A mountain species but widely planted on large estates

IDENTIFICATION: Soft, light-green needles, clustered on long shoots, single on short shoots, dropped in winter after turning yellow. Flowers yellow (male) and reddish (female). Egg-shaped cones. Grey–brown, cracking bark

SIMILAR SPECIES: Japanese larch, Hybrid larch

If you want to see European larches in their full glory, take a drive along the A9 north of Perth. Beside the main road and along side roads are tracts of the sprawling Tummel Forest Park, mostly planted by successive Dukes of Atholl in the late 18th and early 19th centuries. They put in some 14 million larches and, as they are very fast growers, these have multiplied manyfold. Larch makes a good forest. It does not cast much shadow, and sheds its needles each winter so other plants thrive beneath it, providing forage for large animals and shelter for smaller ones. Best of all is its display of golden yellow in the autumn when it is just about to shed its needles. The similar Japanese larch is used to create tiny bonsai trees.

Scots Pine *(Pinus sylvestris)*

Size:	Up to 35 m tall
Habitat:	Native to Scottish forests but widely planted
Identification:	Paired, bluish-green needles. Bare lower branches. Male cones yellow, female green when young maturing to grey–brown. Cracked bark, brown at the base, orange–brown higher up
Similar species:	Corsican pine

A Scots pine stands like a gnarled old warrior surveying a landscape it conquered 10,000 years ago. After the Ice Age this lone large native conifer crossed the land bridge before the English channel opened up. It is a survivor, yet its usefulness almost drove it to extinction. It has provided first-class timber, tar, resin, turpentine and charcoal. Superstition used to proscribe felling it for shipbuilding when the moon was waning as the resin content was believed to fall during this time. This 'old wives' tale' has now been confirmed by science. It can also cure a hangover: add chopped, crushed needles to boiling water, bring back to the boil, steep for 20 minutes, strain and serve hot or cold, sweetened or spiced. In America, Indians used pine needles to relieve stomach cramps and settlers made Vitamin C-rich pine tea to treat scurvy.

Grand Fir *(Abies grandis)* ▲

Size:	Up to 55 m tall. Spreading lower branches
Habitat:	Scottish estates and parks, plantations and forests
Identification:	Shiny green leaves projecting horizontally from twig. Small purplish male flowers, green female ripening into brown, upright, egg-shaped cone. Smooth, grey–brown bark. Cones and bark ooze resin
Similar species:	Common silver fir, Noble fir, Colorado white fir

Another import of the Scottish tree collector, David Douglas, the grand fir proved a huge success with both estate owners and plantation growers. At first it was planted as an ornamental, but its commercial value was quickly recognised as it grew so rapidly and is disease resistant. Douglas found the tree in 1852 in British Columbia, where Indians used the bark to make dyes, tonics, treatments for internal injuries and even canoes. Their shamans wove the branches into costumes and head-dresses and used them for scrubbing in purification rites. The dried, crushed needles were made into baby powder and the pitch of the young trees was mixed with oil and rubbed on the scalp to prevent balding. Nowadays, we use the soft, weak timber for more prosaic goods like boxes and packaging.

WESTERN HEMLOCK *(Tsuga heterophylla)*

SIZE:	Up to 35 m tall
HABITAT:	Woodland, plantations, large estates. Widespread except on chalk
IDENTIFICATION:	Dark green, variable-length needles with two white bands below. Characteristic drooping leading shoot. Male cones bright purple, female reddish-brown, hanging spheres. Purple–brown, flaky bark
SIMILAR SPECIES:	None

Hemlock is another good timber provider, but a very pretty one with its feathery, drooping branches, low to the ground, neat conical shape and daintily limp leading shoot. Its attractiveness made it a popular ornamental tree when it was introduced to Britain from America by the plant collector, David Douglas in the mid-19th century. It likes a moist soil so thrives on anything except chalk and is widely grown for its abundant timber crop, much of which is used for boxes. In its homeland, the American Indians used it, as they used nearly all their trees, for sustenance and medicine. Some ate the inner bark and one tribe used it to dye their fishing nets to make them invisible to the salmon, which were also attracted by the scent of the dye.

ASPEN *(Populus tremula)*

SIZE:	Up to 20 m tall
HABITAT:	Damp ground in southern, mixed broadleaved woodlands and Scottish hills
IDENTIFICATION:	Rounded leaves on whippy stalks, pale undersides. Pale purple, silky male catkins; green female. Silver–green bark becomes furrowed
SIMILAR SPECIES:	Grey poplar, Italian poplar

There is no mistaking the aspen when there is even the slightest hint of a breeze. The leaves flutter, making the crown of the tree into a whispering shimmer of light and dark green. In autumn, this display turns into golds and yellows. Aspen is a good reproducer and readily spreads either by suckers or by the windblown, woolly seeds shed by the female catkins. Aspen was once used to cure the ague, a disease characterised by constant shaking. The cure was based on the 17th-century Doctrine of Signatures, which proposed that plants physically resemble the body parts they are destined to cure. One widespread folk belief is that the aspen trembles because its wood was used to make Jesus's cross. The cheese industry uses aspen containers because the wood does not affect the smell or taste of cheese.

SILVER BIRCH *(Betula pendula)*

SIZE: Up to 30 m tall

HABITAT: Woods on light, dry soil. Widespread

IDENTIFICATION: Pointed, oval leaves with toothed margins. Long, drooping yellow–green male catkins, inconspicuous green female catkins shedding copious winged seeds. Conspicuous silver bark slashed with diamond-shaped bosses

SIMILAR SPECIES: Downy birch

Symbolically connected with rebirth and new beginnings, the silver birch is one of the first trees to recolonise an area after a mature forest is cut. Birchwoods are airy, mystical places, where it is easy to imagine the presence of gnomes and sprites. The tall, pale trunks rise like cathedral columns and the higher branches form a delicate interlacing archwork. The birchwood floor is rich in leaf mould and, as little shade is cast, many other plants thrive, including grass, heather and bilberry and saplings of oak and beech. Young birches make good grazing for deer and rabbits, while tits and redpolls gorge on the plentiful birch seeds. Fungi such as fly agaric also abound in the lushness and on rotting trunks – providing plenty of resting places for the goblins.

HORNBEAM *(Carpinus betulus)*

SIZE:	Up to 30 m tall
HABITAT:	Woodland with oaks, mainly S.E. England but planted elsewhere, sometimes as hedging
IDENTIFICATION:	Leaves toothed, pointed ovals with prominent veins. Male catkins green, feathery, female short and green ripening to long cluster of 3-lobed, winged nutlets. Smooth, pale grey bark with deep clefts
SIMILAR SPECIES:	Superficially resembling Beech

A beautiful, spreading, oval-crowned tree with a characteristically twisted trunk when left to grow, which is seldom. It used to be coppiced (cut down to almost ground level) to persuade new shoots to spring from the base. These were used for fire fuel, charcoal and beansticks. Sometimes it was pollarded (chopped off at head level) so the new shoots were out of grazing reach. It makes a very good hedge. The white wood is extremely hard (the name means wood which is as hard as horn) and close grained. In the past it was used for cogwheels, mallets and butchers' chopping blocks but it is very hard to work and it blunts carpenters' tools. Hornbeam nutlets provide food for the birds, but those that fall lie dormant for up to 18 months before sprouting.

COMMON HAZEL *(Corylus avellana)* ▲

SIZE:	Up to 12 m tall but usually coppiced to a few metres
HABITAT:	Widespread except on acid soils, often as understorey in oak woodlands
IDENTIFICATION:	Leaves alternate, circular, double-toothed margins. Male catkins hang long and yellow, female flowers small and red producing nuts in leafy husks. Light brown, scaly bark
SIMILAR SPECIES:	Turkish hazel (in all but tree shape), Filbert

An extremely useful tree for the country dweller, both human and animal, with a wealth of folklore surrounding it. A hazel rod was said to protect against evil spirits and was the best twig or 'witching wand' for water divining or 'dousing'. In medieval England hazel was a symbol of fertility, often used in marriage ceremonies. The nuts were said to have mystic powers, and people used to carry them to ward off rheumatism and burn them as offerings to the gods. The nuts are eaten by large birds, squirrels and mice, and are important for the survival of the native dormouse, although grey squirrels now take many before they ripen. Hazel was, and in many cases still is, used for fencing, hurdles, barrel hoops, walking sticks, fishing rods, whip handles, ties for fastening thatch, pegs, fuel for ovens, faggots and charcoal for gunpowder, domestic fires and ovens.

COMMON ASH *(Fraxinus excelsior)*

SIZE: Up to 40 m tall

HABITAT: Widespread but prefers lime-rich soil

IDENTIFICATION: Leaves opposite with 6–14 paired leaflets on flexible stalk. Small bunched purplish male and female flowers. Single seeds in oblong wings. Grey–green bark fissuring with age

SIMILAR SPECIES: Manna ash

The common ash is a major tree of lowland forests in much of Europe. Ash was and is an important timber tree, and is a traditional material for the handle of a besom. Having a good deal of folklore attached to it, it is also a popular wood for wizards' wands. The tree was worshipped by early Scandinavians and, in Norse myth, the giant ash Yggdrasil overshadowed the world, its roots in hell and its crown in heaven. It was said that burning ash logs would drive out evil, and a sick child, passed through the branches, would be cured. The pale creamy wood is strong and elastic and used for hockey sticks, oars, paddles, rudders, billiard cues, cricket stumps, polo sticks and policemen's truncheons. It is also used for veneer and furniture. One useful trait of ash is that, with a low water content of 30–35%, it burns well when green.

BEECH *(Fagus sylvatica)*

SIZE: Up to 40 m tall

HABITAT: South of England and Wales, single-species woodlands on
                         chalky soils but tolerant of wide range of soils

IDENTIFICATION: Alternate, silky green, oval leaves with parallel veins,
                         turning yellow–brown in autumn. Drooping, yellow,
                         long-stalked male flowers, small green females becoming
                         paired nuts (mast) in spiky fruit husk. Smooth, grey bark

SIMILAR SPECIES: Roble beech, Raoul (both 'false' beeches)

Beechwoods, with their towering, snaggle-rooted giants, are
perfect places for a stroll at any time of year. In spring the sun
filters down through a canopy of light green leaves and there are
little oceans of drooping-headed bluebells, dotted with star-like
wood anemones; in summer the leaf cover thickens and keeps
the walker wonderfully cool; in autumn squirrels and mice
skitter about among the fungi gathering their hoards of beech
nuts, and the carpet of fallen leaves is kicked through with
childish glee; in winter animal trails can be followed through the
snow and dark flashes of muntjac or even fallow deer might be
half-seen, ghosting through the grey pillars. Beech also makes a
good thick hedge and the fine-grained, knot-free wood has been
used for centuries for furniture and turned ware.

SESSILE OAK *(Quercus petraea)*

SIZE: Up to 40 m tall

HABITAT: Widespread in woodland, commonest in west

IDENTIFICATION: Leaves less lobed than English oak and have longer stalks. Acorns rounder with no stalks (*sessile* = unstalked). Grey–green, fissured bark

SIMILAR SPECIES: English oak, Turkey oak

Of our two native oaks, the sessile grows faster and in poorer conditions. It prefers acid upland soils and lighter well-drained areas as it is not as tolerant of flooding as the English oak. It was the sessile oak which provided the iron smelting furnaces of the north with their charcoal in the 16th century but, although faster growing than *Q. robur* (English Oak), it could not keep up with demand and disappeared from huge areas of the countryside. The sessile oak is less susceptible to epicormic growth than *Q. robur*, so has fewer knots in it. Depending on size and quality, its hard, pale brown wood is used for sawn timber, veneer, building timber, hardwood pulp, poles, fencing and firewood. In the past, sessile oaks were coppiced to produce stakes, tannin was produced from the bark for tanning leather, and the acorns were fed to pigs.

ENGLISH OAK *(Quercus robur)* ▶

SIZE: Up to 35 m tall

HABITAT: Widespread in mixed woodland

IDENTIFICATION: Deeply lobed leaves on short stalks. Drooping yellow male catkins, small green female flowers ripening into familiar acorns on long stalks. Smooth young bark becoming deeply fissured

SIMILAR SPECIES: Sessile oak, Hungarian oak

Probably the most common tree in Britain and the basis of more folklore and history than any other, the regal oak plays a big part in our collective culture. Until the advent of iron tools, the vast, tough oak resisted all attempts to fell it and was adopted as a symbol of British steadfastness and stoutness of heart. Once man did start chopping it down, however, its sheer usefulness led to its virtual eradication. It became the principal house and boat-building material and was used for panelling, furniture, barrels, sea defences and a great deal more. The only thing it does not do well is burn on an open fire. The tree had to be protected from overharvesting in Elizabethan times, and huge numbers were planted to supply timber for the navy. As the oak can live for 1000 years or more, many of these trees are still with us.

BRACKEN *(Pteridium aquilinum)*

SIZE: Up to 2.5 m tall

HABITAT: Heaths and woodlands throughout the British Isles

IDENTIFICATION: Tough stalks with mid-green, compact, curled tipped fronds

SIMILAR SPECIES: Broad buckler fern, Hay-scented fern, Lady fern

Woodlands and hillsides with light, acid soils can be carpeted with this common and widespread fern as the fronds appear in spring. It is a pest on grassland with its extensive root system making it difficult to eradicate. It can be hard work walking through bracken, as the stems are tough and sometimes grow above head height. The pretty, young fronds are covered with brown scales and soft hairs, which fall off as the fronds uncurl. As the plants age, glands at the base of the main branches secrete a sugary liquid, attracting ants and other insects. After the bracken has died and turned brown, it is sometimes cut and gathered by gardeners to use as a mulch to protect tender plants against frost. A few leaves included in the planting hole encourage stronger blooms on fuchsias.

FOXGLOVE *(Digitalis purpurea)*

SIZE: 60–150 cm tall

HABITAT: Woodlands, moors, sea cliffs throughout the British Isles

IDENTIFICATION: Soft, downy, oval leaves; tall flower spikes with pink or purple tubular flowers from June to August

SIMILAR SPECIES: None

This bold and stately plant is one of the tallest and most conspicuous of British wild flowers. The pink or purple flowers have dark patches ringed with white on the inside of the petal tube. They appear during the second year, as the plant is biennial or sometimes perennial. In 1785, it was discovered that foxgloves could be used to treat heart complaints and the drug digitalis, originally derived from the plant but now created chemically, is still in use today. Gardeners grow foxgloves near other plants as they are said to stimulate growth and encourage resistance to disease. In Ireland and parts of the West country, the flowers are known as fairy bells, which is easier to imagine than foxes wearing them as gloves.

HONEYSUCKLE *(Lonicera periclymenum)*

IZE: Climbing up to 6 m

HABITAT: Woodland and hedgerows throughout the British Isles

DENTIFICATION: Twining stems, early leaves, whorls of yellow or pinkish-cream trumpet-shaped flowers from June to September

IMILAR SPECIES: None

Walking or cycling down a country lane or even travelling in an open-topped car at dusk on a summer's evening, you will always know when you have passed a clump of honeysuckle, even if it is too dark to see it. The perfume is unmistakable and has been an inspiration for poets over the ages. The fragrance attracts many of the more spectacular moths, and the bright red berries provide food for birds in the autumn. Honeysuckle twines itself round shrubs and trees, sometimes so tightly that it deforms the host into a barley-sugar shape. The leaves are among the first of the year to appear, sometimes in January, when the remainder of the deciduous wood is still bare bark.

BLUEBELL *(Hyacinthoides non-scripta)*

SIZE:	25–50 cm tall
HABITAT:	Woodlands, occasionally hedgerows and scrubland
IDENTIFICATION:	Long, narrow, basal leaves, bell-shaped blue flowers in spikes from April to June
SIMILAR SPECIES:	Spring squill

One of the glories of the British countryside is the sight of a bluebell wood in full flower in May. Sadly, the hazy blue sight of bluebells *en masse* is becoming increasingly rare. Over the past 60 years, ancient bluebell woods have been reduced by 50%. It is now illegal to dig up the bulbs, but a lot of plants are destroyed by crushing or trampling down the leaves. The flowers appear on only one side of the stalk, and the upright stems bend over slightly when in full flower. A small proportion of plants have white or pink flowers instead of blue. In Scotland, this plant is known as wild hyacinth and the name bluebell is given to the harebell *(Campanula rotundifolia)*.

LESSER CELANDINE *(Ranunculus ficaria)*

SIZE:	5–15 cm tall
HABITAT:	Woodland and hedgerows
IDENTIFICATION:	Dark green, heart-shaped leaves with light blotches. Bright yellow flowers with 6–8 petals appear from February to May
SIMILAR SPECIES:	Creeping buttercup, Lesser spearwort

The lesser celandine is part of the buttercup family, but comes into flower before any of its relations. The clumps of golden flowers are a welcome sight on woodland floors as winter gives way to spring and William Wordsworth wrote passionately about them. It prefers damp, shady places and is common in hedge bottoms where conditions are favourable. The flowers close in dull or wet weather. The lesser celandine is no relation to the greater celandine, which is a member of the poppy family. The creeping buttercup and lesser spearwort have similar flowers, but can be distinguished by their leafy stems, in contrast to the separate leaves of the lesser celandine.

HERB ROBERT *(Geranium robertianum)*

SIZE:	10–50 cm tall
HABITAT:	Woodland, hedgebanks, rocks or walls throughout Britain
IDENTIFICATION:	Straggling plant with hairy fern-like leaves, pink, 5-petalled flowers from April to October
SIMILAR SPECIES:	Dove's-foot crane's-bill, Shining crane's-bill, Cut-leaved crane's-bill

The crane's-bills owe their name to their pointed fruits and herb robert is one of the most widespread. It is an attractive plant with deeply divided leaves with 5–7 narrow lobes. In the autumn, or where the plant is growing on shingle, the leaves become suffused with red. The leaves are also characterised by their strong smell and the plant is sometimes known as stinking Bob. *Gymnocarpium robertianum* is a limestone fern, which owes its name to the fact that its fronds have a similar smell when crushed. Dove's-foot crane's-bill has similar flowers but is found in fields and wasteland rather than woods. It was used by herbalists in the Middle Ages: one recipe required the dried plant to be mixed with nine powdered, oven-dried slugs before being added to claret and drunk.

DEADLY NIGHTSHADE

(Atropa belladonna)

SIZE:	Up to 150 cm tall
HABITAT:	Woodland and hedges, mostly in S. or E. England
IDENTIFICATION:	Tall plant with large, oval leaves. Soft, purple, bell-shape flowers from June to September. Black berries
SIMILAR SPECIES:	Black nightshade, Woody nightshade

Fortunately, the deadly nightshade is fairly rare, only found on chalk or limestone soils. All parts of the plant are poisonous, although it is the cherry-sized, shiny fruits that are the most deadly. The alkaloid poisons attack the nervous system and were favoured by witches to aid flight and, for their victims, to bring on hallucinations or death. Italian ladies were said to improve their beauty by dilating their pupils with the juice of the berries, thereby giving it the name *belladonna*. The more common black nightshade with its white flowers and dull, black berries can be found throughout England but it avoids limy soils. Both the black nightshade and the climbing woody nightshade contain the toxic alkaloid solanine, although not in deadly quantities.

RAMSONS *(Allium ursinum)*

SIZE: Up to 45 cm tall

HABITAT: Woodland and shady places, throughout Britain

IDENTIFICATION: Large, bright-green ridged leaves, clusters of starry white
                  flowers from April to July

SIMILAR SPECIES: Field garlic, Wild onion

An enchanting plant with delicate flowers and lily-of-the-valley leaves, but its charm dwindles when the plant is picked or bruised, and the strong garlic smell is overpowering. Dairy farmers fence off woodland where ramsons grow to prevent cattle grazing on this herb as their milk would be tainted and useless. The leaves can be used as a culinary herb and impart only a mild garlic flavour to the dish, as cooking reduces the pungency. According to John Gerard in *The Herbal*, a sauce made from the leaves may 'very well be eaten in April and May with butter, of such as are of strong constitution'. The field garlic and wild onion, or crow garlic as it is sometimes called, are less common. Rarely seen in Scotland, these similarly pungent plants favour grassy banks in the south and east.

GREATER STITCHWORT
(Stellaria holostea)

SIZE:	15–60 cm tall
HABITAT:	Woods and hedgerows, common throughout the British mainland
IDENTIFICATION:	Long narrow leaves on straggly stems. White flowers with 5 divided petals appear from April to June
SIMILAR SPECIES:	Lesser Stitchwort, Common chickweed

Until the flowers appear, this plant might be overlooked, as the weak stems straggle among other foliage for support. The botanical name *Stellaria* means 'little star', referring to the numerous pretty white flowers which show their heads on the longest stems from April onwards. Early herbalists used the plants mixed with acorns to make a remedy for a 'stitch', which led to its common name of stitchwort. Lesser stitchwort, *S. graminea,* has flowers less than half the size of its greater cousin, and their petals are divided for more than half their length. It is more commonly seen on heaths and acid grasslands. Stitchwort's starry flowers are similar to those of the chickweed, but the leaves differ, as chickweed's are shorter and broader.

WOOD ANEMONE *(Anemone nemorosa)*

SIZE:	5–30 cm tall
HABITAT:	Woodlands throughout mainland Britain
IDENTIFICATION:	Clumps of plants with deeply divided leaves forming a ring part way up the stem. Single white flowers from March to May
SIMILAR SPECIES:	None

Deciduous woodlands, especially when regularly coppiced, often produce a stunning carpet of wild flowers in the spring. Although not as colourful as the bluebell or primrose, the wood anemone's delicate flowers add their own special charm to this scene. In cloudy weather or towards dusk, the flowers start to close and hang their heads showing their lilac sepals on the underside of the petals. Folklore says this is the wood fairy curling up inside and drawing the petals around itself. According to Greek mythology, the wood nymph, Anemone, was banned from court by the jealous queen of flowers. Zephyr, the wind god, having lost the object of his attentions, turned her into a flower he could caress, which is why it is known today as the windflower.

LORDS AND LADIES *(Arum maculatum)*

SIZE: 30–45 cm tall

HABITAT: Woods and hedgerows, common in
                   S. Britain, scarcer in N. Britain

IDENTIFICATION: Arrow-shaped leaves, sometimes spotted,
                   club-shaped flower enclosed by spathe or cowl
                   during April and May

SIMILAR SPECIES: None

From an early age, country children are taught to leave this plant well alone, and fortunately it is very easy to identify. The flower head comprises a rod-like purplish-brown spadix surrounded by tiny clusters of male and female flowers. This is shrouded by a pale green spathe or cowl, which withers in the autumn leaving a spike of highly poisonous red berries. All parts of the plant produce a serious irritant, yet it is harmless once baked and the roots were once ground and used as a substitute for arrowroot. Adam and Eve, cuckoo-pint, and sweethearts are among its many local names. The black spots generally seen on the leaves recall the days when the rich wore artificial beauty spots to cover pimples, so endowing the common name, lords and ladies.

EARLY PURPLE ORCHID
(Orchis mascula)

SIZE:	15–60 cm tall
HABITAT:	Woodland, scrub and grassland
IDENTIFICATION:	Lance shaped with spotted leaves, dense spike of purple or pink flowers from April to June
SIMILAR SPECIES:	Green-winged orchid, Pyramidal orchid, Fragrant orchid

Widespread on limy soils, this common orchid has long been associated with love and assumed to have magical properties. Known as the enticing plant in Scotland, one piece of folklore tells us how the roots can be pulled before sunrise, while facing south, and placed in spring water to determine luck in love. A maiden would select the larger root to represent the man she loves and, if it sank, he would become her husband. The plant is also known as Adam and Eve (but see lords and ladies), as the smaller root represents women. The tubers contain a nutritious substance called bassorine, which was made into drinks in Victorian times as a sustaining beverage for manual workers. The dark spots on the leaves are said to be from the blood of Christ, as these orchids grew beneath the Cross.

LESSER PERIWINKLE *(Vinca minor)*

SIZE:	30–60 cm
HABITAT:	Woodland and hedgerows
IDENTIFICATION:	Low-lying evergreen plant with long sprawling stems, oval hairless leaves in pairs, purple–blue flowers from March to May
SIMILAR SPECIES:	Greater periwinkle

The ancient mystical powers of the periwinkle led to its old name 'Sorcerer's violet'. It was used as a love charm by being sprinkled under the bed and the leaves were eaten as a fertility aid. Also seen as a symbol of immortality, the flowers were made into garlands worn by people about to be executed and woven into funeral wreaths for children, to help them on their way. Both the greater and lesser periwinkle have been valued by herbalists for many years and it is still used as an astringent. Another relative, the Madagascar periwinkle, has recently been found to contain two drugs used to treat cancer. The bright, sweetly scented flowers are a welcome sight in spring. They are borne on short upright stems, the five petals forming a funnel with a white star in the centre.

MISTLETOE *(Viscum album)*

SIZE: Up to 1 m

HABITAT: Open woodland, hedgerows and orchards. Common in Southern England

IDENTIFICATION: Shrubby growth on deciduous trees. Evergreen with pairs of leathery leaves and sticky white berries from September to January

SIMILAR SPECIES: None

Despite the berries themselves being poisonous, mistletoe has been credited with preventing diseases, increasing fertility, warding off evil spirits and even extinguishing fire. The best known of many customs associated with it is kissing under a sprig of mistletoe at Christmas. This originates from Norse mythology after Balder, god of peace, was killed with an arrow tipped with mistletoe. The white berries are said to be the tears of joy his mother shed as she kissed everyone after restoring him to life. Traditionally, the mistletoe sprig is burnt on Twelfth Night otherwise the couples who kissed under it can never marry. Mistletoe is a semi-parasite forming a rounded mass where it grows on branches of host trees, its roots penetrating the bark to rob the tree of water and nutrients. Apple, poplar, hawthorn and lime are the most common hosts but the rare oak mistletoe was held in greatest reverence by the Druids.

WILD STRAWBERRY *(Fragaria vesca)*

SIZE:	10–25 cm high
HABITAT:	Woods, hedgerows, scrubland and grassland throughout the British Isles
IDENTIFICATION:	Creeping plant with long hairy runners, bright green leaves comprise three leaflets and are paler on the underside. White flowers in spring are followed by small red fruits from June to August.
SIMILAR SPECIES:	Barren strawberry

No commercial strawberry can compare with the sweet flavour of the tiny wild variety. Unfortunately, it takes a lot of careful searching to find the fruits before the birds have got there and a lot of time to gather enough to fill a bowl. The search can be further hampered by the barren strawberry growing among its more desirable cousin. Although the plants and leaves are similar, the fruits, or achenes, of the barren strawberry do not swell so remain dry and unpalatable.The wild strawberry is a perennial plant with a crown of long-stalked leaves. Runners bearing small leaf clusters radiate out, the clusters taking root to form new plantlets.Garden strawberries as we know them originated from America and were grown in France in the 18th century. The wild plant has been around much longer and remains have been found in Neolithic, Bronze Age, Iron Age and Roman sites in Europe.

SNOWDROP *(Galanthus nivalis)*

SIZE:	15–25 cm
HABITAT:	Woodland, hedgerows, meadows
IDENTIFICATION:	Clumps of bluish–green linear leaves. Solitary nodding white flowers with green markings. The three spreading, oval sepals are twice as long as the three petals.
SIMILAR SPECIES:	Summer snowflake

A delightful story tells why the snowdrop is the colour and shape it is. Apparently, the snowdrop was last in the queue for colours and God only had one drop of green left. At his suggestion, the snowdrop asked the other flowers to share some of their colour. When none would oblige, God felt so sorry for the sad snowdrop hanging its colourless head that he reached down and touched it with his last drop of green. Two Greek words meaning 'milk' and 'flower' gave the snowdrop its generic name of Galanthus, and its common name is from its likeness to a snowflake. 'Eve's tears' 'February fair maid' and 'snow piercer' are other local names. Village maidens used to wear bunches of these flowers as symbols of purity celebrating the Feast of Purification of St Mary on February 2nd.

WOOD PIGEON *(Columba palumbus)*

SIZE:	40 cm
HABITAT:	Widespread. Woodland, farmland, parks and gardens
IDENTIFICATION:	Greyish overall with faintly ruddy breast, white patches on neck and wings, black tail bar
SIMILAR SPECIES:	Stock dove

Here is one bird that has thrived with the mechanisation of farming and changes in land management. The wood pigeon used to be just that – a woodland bird. Winter fodder crops and machines that leave more waste corn on the land than did hand reaping and winnowing have expanded its range and boosted its numbers until it is now officially a pest. A large flock can strip a crop of beans or take the tops off a field of turnips before the farmer can get there with his gun. For all that, the wood pigeon's song is one of the sounds of summer, that soft, drowsy 'cu-*cooo*-coo-cu-cu' an accompaniment to many a village cricket match or berry-picking outing. The other sound associated with the wood pigeon is the wing clapping it does at the top of each climb in its display flight.

TREE PIPIT *(Anthus trivialis)*

SIZE:	15 cm
HABITAT:	Open woodland, scattered trees and bushes, open countryside, heaths, parks, pastures. Widespread summer visitor
IDENTIFICATION:	Similar to Meadow pipit but with yellower breast and shorter hind claws
SIMILAR SPECIES:	Meadow pipit, Rock pipit

Pipits are hard to tell apart, even for the experts. The *Bulletin of the British Museum* once published a light verse dealing with the taxonomy of birds which began: 'It's a pity pipits have/No diagnostic features/Specifically they are the least/Distinctive of God's creatures'. And with a name like *trivialis*, this is perhaps the most insignificant of all. Tree pipits winter in central Africa, and from April onwards they arrive here to breed and entertain us with their song flight, just as the other pipits do (see Meadow pipit p.133). The major difference with the tree pipits' performance is that it begins and ends on some roosting point high in a tree. To confuse the identification issue, there are also visits by the tawny pipit, the water pipit, the red-throated pipit, which is slightly easier to differentiate, and the rare Richard's pipit.

great spotted woodpecker

WOODPECKERS

The **Green woodpecker** (*Picus viridis*), 32 cm, is a real exotic which, when seen for the first time, takes the breath away. Its green back, yellow rump, creamy breast and neck, vivid red crown and cheek patches, and roguish black eyepatch make it look like an escapee from the tropical birdhouse. It is a big bird, and with its upright stance and raucous, laughing call, it demands attention. Of the three woodpeckers, it is the least likely to peck wood. It feeds mostly on the ground, taking beetles, larvae and insects and, particularly, ants and their grubs, which it licks up with its long tongue. Its range is wide, being absent only from the far north of Scotland.

The **Great spotted woodpecker** (*Dendrocopos major*), 23 cm, is gradually usurping the green woodpecker as the most numerous of the three. This is the one you are most likely to hear drumming away on a tree, not only to winkle out food, because it does the same to telegraph poles, but also to announce its presence. It is not nearly as colourful as the green woodpecker, but is still striking with its black and white upper parts and head, creamy underside and red flashes at the back of the head and undertail. It is more likely than the other two to be found in the woods, where the male performs elaborate courting flights, spiralling round branches in pursuit of its mate.

The smallest of the three British species is the **Lesser spotted woodpecker** (*Dendrocopos minor*), 14.5 cm. It has black and white plumage with a red crown and is very elusive. It is found in open woodland and parks, wooded gardens and old orchards, but its range is only from the Midlands down to the south coast. Its territorial 'drumming' is fainter but faster than that of the great spotted woodpecker and the male also has a distinctive display flight, fluttering like a moth from tree to tree.

Many cultures have legends that associate the woodpecker with water. It is known variously as the rain bird, weather cock or storm cock, and its call or its drumming are said to herald downpours. Common strands running through much woodpecker folklore are that the bird offended a god or that someone who did the offending was turned into a woodpecker.

green woodpecker

lesser spotted woodpecker

WOOD WARBLER *(Phylloscopus sibilatrix)*

SIZE:	12.5 cm
HABITAT:	Woodland, commonest in north and west. Summer visitor
IDENTIFICATION:	Green upper parts, yellow breast, dark stripe through eye and yellow stripe above, white undersides
SIMILAR SPECIES:	Willow warbler, Chiffchaff

The wood warbler is most easily marked out from the willow warbler and chiffchaff by its brighter colouring. It is also noticeably larger and, unlike the other two, confines itself to the habitat of its name, principally the mature oak woodlands of western Britain. It can also be found in beech, pine or birch woods, but whatever the habitat you will find it hard to spot. It spends its time flitting about in the upper foliage, hunting insects under the leaves (*phylloscopus* means 'leaf-explorer'). It will also take insects in flight. You are most likely to hear its song, a most distinctive and pretty melody in two parts: a series of accelerating single notes lasting 4–5 seconds ending in a trill interspersed by the second phase, a series of gradually diminishing notes with a mournful 'pew-pew-pew' sound. The nest, unlike that of the willow warbler, is all grass with no feathers.

MARSH TIT *(Parus palustris)*

SIZE:	12 cm
HABITAT:	Deciduous woodland and orchards. Widespread in England and Wales
IDENTIFICATION:	Olive brown upper parts with glossy black crown, pale under parts. Wings uniform colour
SIMILAR SPECIES:	Willow tit

The marsh tit is almost identical to the willow tit, but has a glossy rather than sooty black crown and no pale patch on its wing. It is also distinguishable by its call: the marsh tit has an angry 'pitchüü' and 'chicka*bee-bee-bee*', and the willow tit a loud 'tchay' and high 'zee-zee-zee'. The marsh tit's song also varies from a single, repeated note to something like 'pitch-a-*wee*ooo', whereas the willow tit has a more melodious song consisting of warbling 'chu-chu-chu' sounds. The marsh tit outnumbers the willow tit considerably in woodland but less so on farmland and, despite its name, is rarely found in marshland. It is the only tit that chips its nests out of tree trunks, sometimes enlarging existing holes, leaving a small pile of woodshavings underneath.

WILLOW WARBLER
(Phylloscopus trochilus)

SIZE: 12 cm

HABITAT: Widespread summer visitor in open woodlands and shrubbery

IDENTIFICATION: Dark olive upper parts, yellowish below with pale eye stripe and pale legs

SIMILAR SPECIES: Chiffchaff

As befits the most abundant warbler in Britain, this bird has a profusion of local names of diverse origin. The total breeding population has been estimated at 3 million pairs and willow warblers do not restrict themselves to willow trees. Local names include ground wren, fell peggy and nettle bird, and its tiny size gives tom thumb and golden wren. It has a most beautiful song: a liquid warble that mounts in volume, then skitters down the scale into a soft murmuring. Its nest is also distinctive – a dome with a side opening – and this lends it the names bank jug, ground oven, oven tit and oven bird. The chiffchaff *(P. collybita)* is paler all over and is distinguished by its dark legs and its song of just two notes, high (chiff) and low (chaff), repeated for a dozen or so seconds. It is infrequently seen in northern Scotland.

WILLOW TIT *(Parus montanus)*

SIZE: 12 cm

HABITAT: Widespread in England, favouring damp woodland

IDENTIFICATION: Olive brown upper parts with sooty, matt black crown, pale under parts. Pale wing patch

SIMILAR SPECIES: Marsh tit

The willow tit is unusual in having no local vernacular names. This is because it is a relatively recent discovery, and countrymen lumped it together with the marsh tit. The willow tit was thought to be absent from Britain until, in 1897, it was identified by Otto Kleinschmidt and Ernst Hartert, two European ornithologists, from skins they were studying in the British Museum. The skins had been marked as marsh tit, but the men noticed that two of them were definitely from a different species. It is not surprising that the species were not separated earlier as they are almost impossible to tell apart in the field, the black cap and pale wing patch giving the only guidance. Actually, the willow tit turned out to be almost as common as the marsh tit, favouring damp woodland, where it builds its nests in decaying willows, birches or alders.

PIED FLYCATCHER *(Ficedula hypoleuca)*

SIZE:	12.5 cm
HABITAT:	Coastal areas and deciduous woodland; S.W. and N. England, S. Scotland and Highlands
IDENTIFICATION:	Male black above and white below with white spot above bill and white wing patch. Female more grey–brown above and without bill spot
SIMILAR SPECIES:	Spotted flycatcher

The pied flycatcher is a passage migrant that has been extending its range in recent years. It used to be found only in Wales and upland England, but has benefited from the provision of nest boxes and is now a more common sight elsewhere. Unlike the spotted flycatcher, the pied does not return to its perch after catching prey but usually takes it to the ground. It relies on catching plenty of caterpillars and flies, often taking the former from the underside of leaves and the latter in flight. The male acts as the househunter, choosing a spot in a tree stump or dead branch for the nest when he arrives from Africa. The female arrives a little later and builds the nest which she lines with hair, wool and feathers.

TREECREEPER *(Certhia familiaris)*

SIZE:	13 cm
HABITAT:	Widespread in deciduous woodland and hedgerow trees
IDENTIFICATION:	Small with brown upper parts, paler below, white eye stripe and comparatively long, down-curved bill
SIMILAR SPECIES:	Short-toed treecreeper (rare)

Although a treecreeper might give away its presence by its high-pitched call of 'tsee-tree-tsee', you might not spot it until it moves. Its plumage is perfect camouflage against the rough bark of an oak and, even when you see it, you might at first glance think it is a mouse. One of its most fitting country names is tree mouse. It spirals up a trunk in a series of hops, clinging on with its huge claws and balancing on its stiff tail feathers. Unlike a nuthatch, it cannot climb down, so, once it reaches the top, it leaps off and flies to the foot of the next tree to begin another climb. It winkles out beetles, earwigs, weevils and woodlice from the bark with its long, curved bill, and also takes any spiders and moths from the surface. Sometimes it will hang upside down from a branch like a tit while feeding. It is often seen in gardens in winter.

REDPOLL *(Acanthis flammea disruptes)*

SIZE: 13–15 cm

HABITAT: Widespread all year among conifers, alders and birches; common near water. Often in gardens and hedgerows

IDENTIFICATION: Brownish upper parts, lighter below, with red forehead, black chin; male has pink breast and red rump

SIMILAR SPECIES: Linnet

Although not in any sense a water bird, the redpoll is likely to be seen near ponds or still pools in rivers, where it likes to bathe. As numbers increase and it spreads into more gardens, it is also a frequent visitor to bird baths. It also prefers damp woodlands of alder and birch, and has thrived as conifer plantations have crept across the countryside. Redpolls are naturally birds of the northern tundra and were once restricted to northern Britain, but have now spread throughout, and they are often joined by larger and paler European and Greenland redpolls in winter. It has the smallest bills of all finches and can pick out tiny grass seeds, but it feeds mostly on alder and birch seeds and willow flowers.

GOLDCREST *(Regulus regulus)*

SIZE: 9 cm

HABITAT: Widespread in conifer woods, occasional garden visitor

IDENTIFICATION: Tiny. Olive upper parts, creamy below. Male orange crest flanked by dark bars, female yellow crest

SIMILAR SPECIES: Firecrest

The boom in conifer plantations has led to the revival of the goldcrest, which has seen huge population fluctuations over the centuries. Once quite rare, it is now a fairly common sound, if not sight, in the upper branches of pines and firs. A delicate, and most apposite, call of 'cedar-cedar' floats down as it hops about seeking insects and their eggs. It is ironic that this tiny bird should be found on Douglas firs, sitka spruces and coast redwoods – our tallest trees.

The **firecrest** (*Regulus ignicapillus*) is a migrant, stopping off in Norway spruce forests and other woods on the way to its winter quarters. The first record of breeding was in 1962 in the New Forest and more are staying over winter, particularly in the south-west. Its breeding range has now expanded to northern and western England and into Wales and numbers are on the increase. It can be distinguished from the same-sized goldcrest by its black eye stripe.

WOODCOCK *(Scolopax rusticola)*

SIZE:	34 cm
HABITAT:	Widespread, but not abundant, in woods and forests. A few winter visitors near coasts
IDENTIFICATION:	Large and plump with long bill and short legs. Russet plumage above, lighter below with distinctive barred crown and under parts. Excellently camouflaged in woodland undergrowth
SIMILAR SPECIES:	Snipe

It was once believed, even among the learned, that the woodcock spent its summers on the moon. Although most woodcock are resident all year, some arrive near the coasts of south-west and eastern England, south Wales and northern Scotland in early November (traditionally around Hallowe'en). They seem to arrive out of nowhere, piloted, it is said, by goldcrests or short-eared owls, and they disappear as suddenly in the spring. One theory, before the more extraordinary one of migration was proved, was that it spent 2 months flying to the moon, 3 months there and 2 months flying back. The woodcock feeds on worms, which it 'feels out' with its flexible-tipped bill and people have long fed on the woodcock. It was laughably easy to net when such practice was common – so easy that it was believed it had no brain. The term 'woodcock' was applied to simpletons.

CAPERCAILLIE *(Tetrao urogallus)*

SIZE:	86 cm
HABITAT:	Ancient woodland and forests of Scotland
IDENTIFICATION:	Large. Male very dark with bushy throat feathers, iridescent green breast, white-flecked brownish wings and red patch over top of eye. Female mottled dark brown with chestnut breast
SIMILAR SPECIES:	Black grouse

Do not go near a male capercaillie in the breeding season – it will frighten you. This huge, aggressive, black creature will fan out its tail, throw back its head and utter a blood-curdling noise which builds from a few clicks into a frantic rattle, a loud 'clonck' and, finally, into a horrible rustling hiss. It is enough to send a full-grown stag on its way. The female is more reserved. The capercaillie was once widespread in Scotland but was wiped out by shooters, the last one being potted in 1785. It was reintroduced with some success in 1837 but numbers declined through loss of habitat, predation and shooting. It is now back on the increase, largely thanks to the work of the Royal Society for the Protection of Birds which is re-establishing areas of Caledonian pine forest in Scotland, principally at Corrimony, south-west of Inverness.

SPARROWHAWK *(Accipiter nisus)*

SIZE:	Wingspan 60–75 cm
HABITAT:	Woodlands, farmland. Widespread but not numerous
IDENTIFICATION:	Dark olive-grey upper parts, red–brown barred under parts, yellow legs. Female up to 10 cm larger than male and duller brown. Short, rounded wings, long tail
SIMILAR SPECIES:	Goshawk

A gentle woodland scene, morning sun filtering through the trees, finches twittering from branch to branch. From nowhere, a cutting, flashing streak of grey blasts through the clearing, a lightning flurry as needle-sharp talons grasp their prey and … gone. Nothing left but belated alarm calls and a few small feathers wavering down to the ground. A sparrowhawk has just got her breakfast. The fighter jet of the bird world, the sparrowhawk can take prey by surprise or outfly them in a thrilling display of power and skill: the only chance of escape is a dive into the undergrowth. It was once numerous but has been persecuted by gamekeepers and farmers who shot and poisoned it to near extinction until it was protected in 1963. Its larger cousin the goshawk *(A. gentilis)* was wiped out but is now re-establishing itself patchily through falconry escapes and introduced birds.

HOBBY *(Falco subbuteo)*

SIZE: Wingspan 70–85 cm

HABITAT: Small woods in southern England

IDENTIFICATION: Slate-coloured back, light, streaked under parts. Dark crown, black moustache. Short tail and long, angled-back, swift-like wings

SIMILAR SPECIES: Kestrel, Peregrine falcon

Here is the supreme flier. Like a giant swift, it scythes through the air with graceful beats of its long wings. It can swirl and cut before snatching a darting insect, or swoop with deadly speed on a frantic swallow. Pairs of hobbies put on dazzling displays of aerobatics, often passing food to each other in mid-air, and all this after having made a 2500 mile journey from south of the Sahara. The name hobby comes from the French *hobereau*, itself derived from Old French *hober*, meaning 'to stir', and this is what it seems to do to the air as it flies. It is a summer visitor, arriving and leaving with the swallows and martins, but only about 100 pairs breed in Britain, so it is a rare sight. The hobby's short tail distinguishes it from the kestrel in flight and it is appreciably smaller than the peregrine falcon.

GIANT WOOD WASP *(Urocerus gigas)*

SIZE:	30 mm
HABITAT:	Pine forests
IDENTIFICATION:	Large black and yellow wasp without a waist, sometimes mistaken for a hornet
SIMILAR SPECIES:	Hornet, Robber fly

What looks like a large sting on the female giant wood wasp is the long ovipositor which gives this wasp the common name of horntail. She uses this to lay eggs deep in rotten wood or sickly trees or sometimes in recently felled conifers. The larva takes up to 3 years to mature and runs the risk of having its nursery quarters sawn up for planks or packing cases and then being exported. This is thought to be how this species was accidentally introduced to Australia and New Zealand. If the larva is not lucky enough to unexpectedly emigrate, it might suffer a rather gruesome fate. The female of the ichneumon *Rhyssa persuasoria* has a 35 mm ovipositor (longer than her entire body length), which she uses to drill through the wood and lay her eggs directly into the wasp larva, which is then eaten alive by the emerging ichneumon larvae.

FOREST BUG *(Pentatoma rufipes)*

SIZE:	14 mm
HABITAT:	Woodlands and forests
IDENTIFICATION:	Reddish-brown bug with shield-shaped body and shiny legs. Orange coloured wing tips
SIMILAR SPECIES:	Sloe bug

The forest bug, like the shield bug and others of the *Hemiptera* order, has an incomplete metamorphosis: it goes from egg to nymph, then directly to adult, missing out the pupal stage of other insects. In August, the eggs are laid in cracks in the bark high up in trees. Some are eaten by birds, especially tits, but, if i survives, the nymph appears in April, and by July it is mature and ready to begin the cycle again. The forest bug is mainly found in oak forests but will also feed on other deciduous trees such as alder. It has also been known to develop a taste for cherries and can be a pest in orchards. The sloe bug usually inhabits hedgerows, particularly blackthorn, where it feeds on the sloes, hence its name. It can sometimes be found on damso trees, where both the nymphs and the adults feed on the flowers

WOOD ANT
(Formica rufa)

SIZE:	7–11 mm
HABITAT:	Dry woodlands, scrubland
IDENTIFICATION:	Black with brown thorax and legs
SIMILAR SPECIES:	Meadow ant (yellowish brown), Common red ant (red), Garden ant (black), Negro ant (black)

The wood ant is even more social than its relations. It not only builds nests, but forms groups of nests and thus a whole community. The ants within the community are friendly to each other, but have a defined territory for hunting, which is jealously guarded against hunters from other colonies. The reddish-brown workers form a trail when they go off hunting for food and can be seen hurrying to-and-fro along their designated route. Caterpillars and other insects form the main part of the diet. The wood ant builds a dome of twigs and leaves over its nest and guards it from intruders. If threatened, the ant squirts formic acid at its enemy and can also nip with its powerful jaws.

OAK APPLE GALL WASP *(Biorhiza pallida)*

SIZE:	4 mm
HABITAT:	Oak trees
IDENTIFICATION:	Small light brown wasp, females are without wings
SIMILAR SPECIES:	Many other species of gall wasp needing a microscope to differentiate. The type of gall is an easier method of identification

The galls of the grub of this wasp do, indeed, resemble apples, especially in early summer when they have a rosy pink appearance. Later they turn brownish-yellow. The fully grown adults emerge from several holes, winged males from one gall and wingless females from another. The female lays her eggs down in the roots of the oak tree and clusters of root galls are formed. This second generation is non-sexual and has no males. The young, wingless female climbs up the tree seeking oak buds to lay her eggs in. The cycle begins again with new oak apples forming. King Charles II escaped capture by hiding in an oak tree after defeat in the battle of Worcester in 1651 and May 29th was named Oak Apple Day to commemorate the restoration of his monarchy on that day in 1660.

WOLF SPIDER *(Pardosa lugubris)*

SIZE: 8–10 mm

HABITAT: Woodland and forest floors

IDENTIFICATION: Charcoal grey with a buff-coloured stripe down the middle of the thorax with a dotted pale band down each side

SIMILAR SPECIES: *Pardosa amenata* and other wolf spiders

With a name like wolf spider, you could be forgiven for being frightened of one. But it might have been more appropriate to name it 'grebe spider' after the female's endearing practice of carrying her young on her back, just as the waterfowl does. She does this for the first week or so after hatching, having already carried the eggs, wrapped in a silk cocoon, attached to the spinnerets at the tip of her abdomen. On sunny days in the spring you can sometimes see the male performing his courtship dance in front of the female. The way he dances has been likened to semaphore as he waves his hairy black legs or palps, sending his message of passion. The *Lycosa* family hunts by sight, chasing and leaping on some unfortunate insect. They move quite fast across the forest floor, and this method of hunting earned them the name of wolf spider.

SPECKLED WOOD BUTTERFLY

(Pararge aegeria tircis)

SIZE: Forewing 20–25 mm

HABITAT: Woodland rides and clearings, shady hedgerows. Likes damp places. Common in Wales and central and S. England and around the Great Glen in Scotland

IDENTIFICATION: Upper sides chocolate brown with creamy-yellow patches, 3 separate black eyes with white pupils along hindwings, 1 on forewing. Underside mosaic of grey and brown, resembling dead leaf when at rest

SIMILAR SPECIES: None

Changes in land management have favoured the speckled wood, unlike many other woodland butterflies. It became scarce during the 19th century but spread widely in the latter half of the 20th century, when the practice of coppicing died out, thereby creating shadier conditions. Both sexes feed on aphid honeydew, but the females spend more time in the tree-tops while the males patrol in search of a mate. The female is more evident when searching for suitable cocksfoot and couch grasses to deposit individual, pearly, thimble-shaped eggs. The mature caterpillar (25–30 mm) is yellowish-green with light and dark stripes. It is unique among British butterflies in that it overwinters as a caterpillar or a chrysalis. Late summer caterpillars either develop quickly and pupate or grow slowly through the winter, feeding in mild weather.

WOODLAND FUNGI

A walk in the woods will almost certainly include the chance to see some wonderful fungi. Springing white and erect from the leaf mould, poking in great brown slabs out of crevices in bark, creeping in rubbery yellow excrescences over rotting branches, fungi are everywhere and in great variety. Some are beautiful, some ugly and some will kill you horribly if you eat even the smallest bit.

Chief among the killers is the **destroying angel** (*Amanita virosa*), found in damp woods on acid soils, often under conifers or sometimes birch, particularly in highland areas, and responsible for 95% of mushroom-related deaths. The trouble is, it looks a lot like the common and very edible Agaricus mushrooms (*Agaricus arvensis*, the horse mushroom, is found almost everywhere and *A. bisporus*, although not found in the wild, accounts for 60% of world commercial production). Look at the gills under the white cap: if they are pinky–brown, you can probably eat it, if they are white, don't even touch it.

Unlike most poisonous fungi, which make you sick almost immediately and leave you feeling a bit below par, destroying angel kills you slowly and extremely unpleasantly: by the time you realise something is wrong, it is too late. The first symptoms of phalloidin syndrome appear 6–12 hours after ingestion. They begin with dizziness, difficulty breathing and vague discomfort followed by vomiting, severe, evil smelling, cholera-like, diarrhoea and intense dehydration. This lasts 3 or 4 days – if you don't die sooner of heart failure. Then comes apparent remission for a couple of days. But all the while your liver is failing and, after a minimum of 6 days from ingestion, it gives up the struggle and you die. The only cure shown to work consistently is one developed by a French doctor, M. Bastien. This must be administered very early on and involves injecting vitamin C intravenously followed by the antiseptic Ercefuril and the antibiotic Neomycin.

The **sickener** (*Russula emetica*), on the other hand, doesn't waste time making you ill and merely teaches you not to tamper with this quite pretty, red-capped, white stemmed little fungus found

the sickner

stinkhorn fungus

destroying angel

in moist coniferous woodland. The beechwood sickener *(R. mairei)* is smaller with firmer flesh and grows under beech trees.

It is extremely unlikely you would even consider eating a **stinkhorn** *(Phallus impudicus)*. This distinctive fungus is found poking up its thick white stem and dark slimy head in deciduous woodland and sometimes in gardens. It really does smell horrible yet, in its egg form, before the stem and head, or fruit body, has emerged, it is edible.

Just as you enter the wood you might wonder why someone has been so careless as to leave little piles of orange peel scattered about. Take a closer look and you will see it is orange peel fungus *(Aleuria aurantia* or *Peziza aurantia)*. This brittle-fleshed fungus is common either on its own or in groups on bare soil or in the low growth at the edge of woods. It is supposed to be edible if well cooked though it doesn't offer much of a meal.

In picking up old fallen branches for the fire you might find your hand slithering over a disgusting rubbery yellow mess of jelly. You will have discovered *Tremella mesenterica*, known as yellow brain fungus or witch's butter. This, too, is said to be edible though why anyone should want to eat it is a mystery.

MANY-ZONED POLYPORE

(Trametes versicolor or *Coriolus versicolor)*

SIZE:	Up to 10 cm across
HABITAT:	Deciduous woods
IDENTIFICATION:	Semi-circular brackets with concentric rings of different colours
SIMILAR SPECIES:	*Trametes hirsuta, Trametes gibbosa*

Bracket fungi are usually found on fallen branches or dead trees, although many of them do attack living trees and can eventually destroy them. The fungi either feed on the sap of the wood, or on the wood itself. Some trees such as the Californian redwood and the yew are immune. The many-zoned polypore favours hardwoods such as beech or oak and is usually seen flush with the surface of fallen branches. This species can be seen all year round, although it is at its best during the early winter. The brackets often grow in tiers and sometimes turn upwards showing the pale tubes on the underside. The upper surface is velvety and variable in colour from yellow through greenish-brown to grey, sometimes tinged with red or blue.

COMMON PUFFBALL

(Lycoperdon perlatum)

SIZE:	Up to 7 cm tall
HABITAT:	Mixed woodlands, heaths and pastures
IDENTIFICATION:	Whitish-grey, almost spherical cap with a thick stalk
SIMILAR SPECIES:	*Lycoperdon molle* or *umbrinum, Lycoperdon pyriforme*

The edible puffball is best picked young if it is intended for the kitchen. Although the warts do not develop on the skin until the plant is older, the puffball is best peeled and sliced before frying in bacon fat until golden brown. Widespread and common, it is usually found on woodland floors in clusters pushing its way up through decaying matter in summer and autumn. Creamy-white when young, the plant becomes yellowish-brown and wrinkled with age. When mature, the body is covered with long spines which fall off to leave pale spots and the characteristic stubby warts. Puffballs growing directly on decaying wood are likely to be the pear-shaped *L. pyriforme*. In conifer woods, a shorter puffball can be found; this is *L. molle* or *L. umbrinum*.

The death cap *(amanita phalloides)* is one of the deadliest fungi

HAZEL DORMOUSE
(Muscardinus avellenarius)

SIZE:	8–9 cm excluding tail
HABITAT:	Deciduous woodland and hedgerows in S. England and Wales
IDENTIFICATION:	Golden-brown fur, large black eyes and a long furry tail
SIMILAR SPECIES:	Edible dormouse (rare)

The dozy dormouse in *Alice in Wonderland* was a perfect portrayal of this little creature, which seems to spend a good deal of its time asleep. Not only does it hibernate in winter and sleep during the day in summer, but if food is scarce in spring it will curl up into a ball and sleep to conserve energy. While awake, this nocturnal animal spends most of its time climbing among branches foraging for hazel nuts, acorns and blackberries. The summer breeding nest, often high above ground, is loosely woven, often with bark stripped from honeysuckle. When the young leave, they build their own, smaller shelter nests. Hibernation nests are built at ground level under leaves or in among tree roots. Numbers have declined over the past 100 years and in 1999, conservationists were providing more nesting sites.

GREY SQUIRREL *(Sciurus carolinensis)*

SIZE: 30 cm excluding tail

HABITAT: Deciduous woods, parks, orchards and gardens, occasionally coniferous woods

IDENTIFICATION: Grey fur tinged with orange–red on back. Large bushy tail

SIMILAR SPECIES: Red squirrel

The grey squirrel was introduced from North America at the end of the 19th century and has now replaced our native red squirrel over most of England and Wales. It is less common in Scotland and Ireland. Numbers are such that it is now considered a serious pest, damaging trees in gardens and orchards as it strips the bark to eat the softer tissue below. It is hated by bird lovers because it raids nests for eggs and nestlings and even steals food put out on the bird table. Hazel nuts and acorns are also a favourite food and some are stored for winter use. The squirrel builds its nest, or drey, in the branches of trees or, in suburban areas, under roofs. The female has two litters a year each with up to seven young.

BADGER *(Meles meles)*

SIZE: 80–90 cm

HABITAT: Deciduous woods, near cultivated land. Widespread over mainland Britain, commonest in the south-west

IDENTIFICATION: Dark grey body with distinctive black and white striped face

SIMILAR SPECIES: None

The badger has been hunted, baited and persecuted for hundreds of years, but this relatively harmless creature and its home are now protected by the *Badgers Act 1992*. It can have bovine TB, but the debate as to whether or not it passes it on to cattle continues into the 21st century. An unobtrusive, nocturnal animal, the badger is seldom seen except perhaps as a road casualty – now its major threat. Worms are its main food, but it also eats insects and small mammals and will break open a bees' nest for honey. A large spoil (heap of soil), old bedding and hairs near one of the entrance holes indicates a badger's sett in use. This underground home might have been used for hundreds of years. It has several interconnecting passages with resting chambers and separate nests. A social group of 4–12 adults occupy a sett, but only one female breeds at a time.

DEER

Deer can be beautiful and serene or sprightly and charming so they are always popular – with everyone except the farmer and landowner. They eat crops and damage trees and, as good swimmers and jumpers, are extremely difficult to keep enclosed. For the most part, however, they are tolerated as they are wonderful to watch.

The **Reeves muntjac** *(Muntiacus reevesi)*, height 43–46 cm at shoulder, weight 11–16 kg, doe smaller than buck, a native of south-east Asia, has adapted superbly to life in Britain, having been released from Whipsnade Zoo in 1921. Although a relative newcomer here, it is part of the oldest of all known deer families and its hardiness has seen it spread throughout England and into parts of Wales and southern Scotland. It is even being reported in urban areas. The muntjac, or barking deer, was introduced to Woburn Park in the 19th century and some were released, but the Whipsnade deer are thought to have led to the current feral population.

The native **roe deer** *(Capreolus capreolus)*, height 60–75 cm at shoulder, weight 24–30 kg, doe smaller than buck, was in Britain at least 400,000 years ago, and was numerous until 1338 when it was declared unworthy of being hunted by noblemen and became fair game for the starving peasants. Numbers plummeted. By the late 1500s it was extinct in Wales and gone from large parts of England and Scotland. The forestry boom in the 18th and 19th centuries, and the increase in game shooting and associated conservancy, brought it back into areas it had been missing from for hundreds of years, and it can now be found all over England, most of Scotland and into Wales.

The first Japanese **sika deer** *(Cervus nippon nippon)*, height 70–95 cm at shoulder, weight 30–70 kg, hind smaller than stag, in Britain were probably a pair presented to the Zoological Society of London in 1860. It became a popular park and zoo animal, and many escaped or were released. It is now widespread but patchy throughout Britain, with the largest populations around Poole

in Dorset, the New Forest, the Lake District and Lancashire. Numbers are increasing, but the sika is hybridising with red deer to the extent that some experts predict there will soon be few, if any, pure-bred red deer or sika left in mainland Britain.

If you order venison in a restaurant, you will probably eat either **fallow deer** *(Dama dama dama)*, height 80–95 cm at shoulder, weight 45–70 kg, doe smaller than buck, or red deer. The fallow is our most widespread deer, even found on the Inner Hebridean islands, and it is a docile, herding species that likes parklands, making it ideal for farming. It was in Britain before the last Ice Age, became extinct and was then re-introduced, so it does not count as truly native, yet it is deeply embedded in our tradition. It was hunted by knights, kings and queens in the royal forests and appears on coats of arms and pub signs. The buck's rutting call, accurately described as a 'groaning belch', is a common sound in the autumn woods.

sika deer

oe deer

RED SQUIRREL *(Sciurus vulgari)*

SIZE: 18–24 mm excluding tail

HABITAT: Mixed woodland and coniferous forests

IDENTIFICATION: Reddish-brown fur, with tufts of hair on ears, long bushy plume-like tail

SIMILAR SPECIES: Grey squirrel

The red squirrel is now more likely to be seen on a wildlife programme than on a walk in the woods, especially if you live in the south. This is our native squirrel, once widespread, but now confined to four or five isolated populations in Wales and centra England. In the coniferous woods further north and in Scotland it fares better, although its range is contracting. The introduction of the grey squirrel is to blame for the decline. They do not seem to fight or spread disease, so competition for food and space is the probable cause. Nuts, seeds and pine cones make up most of the red squirrel's diet and it spends most of its time in trees. During the mating season, several males chase one female, leaping spectacularly through the branches and up and down the tree-trunks. The female has one or two litters a year, each with two or three young.

PINE MARTEN *(Martes martes)*

SIZE:	45–55 cm excluding tail. Tail length 18–27 cm
HABITAT:	Coniferous forests and mixed woodland
IDENTIFICATION:	Reddish-brown fur, yellowish-white throat, long body and long fluffy tail
SIMILAR SPECIES:	Resembles a weasel but is more than twice as big

The pine marten was common throughout mainland Britain until the 19th century, but it was hunted for its fur and persecuted by gamekeepers until, by 1926, it was only found in north-west Scotland. Now fully protected by the *Wildlife and Countryside Act (1981)*, it is increasing its range. Living in well-wooded areas, the pine marten makes its den among the roots of Scots pine or in a hollow tree. It climbs with great agility, but hunts by night on the ground, mainly for voles. Berries and fungi are eaten in season, with beetles and carrion adding variety. Sometimes taking over a disused squirrel's nest, the female spends 6 weeks bringing up her single litter of up to five young, which are born blind and helpless. She is very susceptible to disturbance, and human interference could cause her to move, or even eat, her young.

WILD BOAR *(Sus scrofa scrofa)*

SIZE:	Length 1.1–1.8 m; height 1 m; weight 50–200 kg (male), 35–150 kg (female)
HABITAT:	Marshland, reed-beds, woods and thickets or on farmland with areas of dense woodland. Avoids exposed sites. Mainly Kent and E. Sussex but other scattered sightings
IDENTIFICATION:	Strong neck, conical elongated head, small eyes, erect triangular ears. Compact flanks. Coat of long, coarse bristles and thick down. Male has sharp tusks. Mostly active at night, dusk and dawn
SIMILAR SPECIES:	Domestic pig (but easily distinguished)

We are in the early stages of an unofficial, and mostly accidental, re-introduction of a once common but officially extinct species. As recently as 1997, the Government told concerned country dwellers that, although there were some farm escapees living free, the boar was not breeding in the wild; by 1998, hunting enthusiasts in Devon were holding boar shoots. In mid-1999, the Government acknowledged there were 100 living wild in Kent and Sussex and up to 20 in Dorset, but there are now very many more. Sightings, some of family groups, have been made in Tyneside, Norfolk and Derbyshire. The sow can be aggressive if her piglets are threatened, and any boar is dangerous if cornered. It eats roots, bulbs, berries and nuts, mice, birds' eggs, insects, reptiles and carrion. Farm crops might also be raided. Boar meat is highly regarded and costly.

Heaths, Downs, Moors and Mountains

*Buttoned from the blowing
      mist*

*Walk the ridges of the
      ruined stone.*

*What humbles these hills
      has raised*

*The arrogance of blood
      and bone*

CROW HILL
TED HUGHES

RHODODENDRON *(Rhododendron ponticum)*

SIZE: Up to 12 m tall but usually much less

HABITAT: Widespread in heaths, moors, scrubland, gardens and parks

IDENTIFICATION: Alternate, long, waxy leaves broadening to a short tip, paler beneath. Purplish flowers in dense clusters producing green seed capsules. Cultivated species vary in flower colour

SIMILAR SPECIES: Azaleas are of the Rhododendron genus. Cherry laurels look similar at first glance

The first rhododendrons, natives of Asia Minor, were brought to Britain in 1763. Liking the climate and soil, they soon escaped from gardens into the wild and have since flourished. This tough, woody shrub is very hard to eradicate and has become a real pest in some areas. The real passion for rhododendrons took off in the mid-19th century, when new varieties were discovered in the Himalayas, Burma, Assam and China. They flooded into gardens and parks and were eagerly cross-bred by nurserymen and amateur enthusiasts. There are now more than 600 recognised species, varying from squat ground creepers to tall trees. Flower colours vary from scarlet and pink to purple and almost blue. The name comes from the Greek: *rhodon* (a rose) and *dendron* (a tree).

WAYFARING TREE *(Viburnum lantana)*

SIZE: Up to 6 m but usually shorter

HABITAT: Heaths, scrubland, wood margins, hedgerows. Chalk and limestone soils

IDENTIFICATION: Opposite, oval leaves, undersides covered in whitish hairs. Dense clusters of white flowers producing shiny oval, red to black berries

SIMILAR SPECIES: Guelder rose

This tree was christened the wayfarer's tree by the botanist, John Gerard, in the 16th century and its current name is merely a corruption of this. Gerard was struck by the number of these trees lining the lanes of southern England, where they give the traveller some shelter, but also provide colour in their white flowers and red berries and a pretty fluttering of their downy, two-toned leaves. One old name for the tree is the hoarwithy: 'hoar' meaning frosty white, the colour of the silk on the undersides of the leaves, and 'withy' meaning the flexible twigs which were once used as cord. The wood is very hard and used to be made into pipe stems, while the black berries, which birds love, were crushed to make ink.

ROWAN *(Sorbus aucuparia)*

SIZE: Up to 20 m tall but usually shorter

HABITAT: Mountains and moors, often by streams

IDENTIFICATION: Alternate leaves made up of several sharp, paired, stalkless leaflets. Abundant flowers in clusters forming bright red berries. Smooth, grey bark

SIMILAR SPECIES: Bastard service tree, Hupeh rowan

Rich in folklore, the rowan, or mountain ash, clings to its spot in the wilderness with a tenacity and vitality which make it worthy of such reverence. Greek myth tells how the leaves, which turn golden in the autumn, and the berries, were formed from the feathers and blood of an eagle sent by the gods to fight demons. In Norse myth, the first woman was made from a rowan and the tree saved the god Thor by bending over to rescue him from a torrent. In Britain the rowan was thought to stave off witchcraft, the tiny five-pointed star on each berry echoing the ancient protective pentagram symbol. The berries were historically used to lure birds into traps: *aucuparia* comes from words meaning 'to catch a bird'. Rowans thrive in poor soils and are also common around ancient settlements. The berries make excellent jelly and wine.

BIRD CHERRY *(Prunus padus)*

SIZE:	Up to 9 m tall, usually shorter
HABITAT:	Northern uplands and moors. Limestone soils
IDENTIFICATION:	Dark green, leathery leaves with red stalks. Drooping spikes of white flowers ripening to round, black berries. Smooth, dark bark with orange flecks
SIMILAR SPECIES:	Wild cherry

This is the most beautiful of all wild *prunus* and replaces the wild cherry in upland Britain, where it favours limestone country. In May this small, neat tree has long, pendulous bunches of almond-scented blossom, which shine out against the often dour surroundings of the northern moors. The black fruit is even more bitter than wild cherry, but is a treat for birds and can be steeped in spirits like rum and vodka to give them a delicious cherry flavour. The bird cherry seldom grows large enough to provide any timber but, in any case, the cut wood smells unpleasant – which is probably why the bark was once hung outside front doors to keep away infections. The infused bark was also used as an antacid and laxative.

COMMON GORSE *(Ulex europaeus)*

SIZE:	Up to 2 m tall
HABITAT:	Heathland, throughout the British Isles
IDENTIFICATION:	Spiny evergreen shrub, covered with bright yellow flowers
SIMILAR SPECIES:	Western gorse, Dwarf gorse

In May and June, whole hillsides can glow with the golden flowers of gorse, or furze as it is sometimes known. The coconut-scented flowers are at their best in early summer but can appear throughout the year, leading to such country sayings as 'When the gorse is out of bloom, kissing is out of fashion'. They are followed by black seed pods which dry and burst to disperse their seeds. In the north and west of Britain, gorse is widespread on acid soils, not restricted solely to heaths. Although the sharp spines make them difficult to pick, the flowers can be used to make a fragrant country wine. Gardeners make use of these spines by laying branches over seed beds to discourage mice.

BROOM *(Cytisus scoparius)*

SIZE:	Up to 2 m tall
HABITAT:	Heaths and hedgerows
IDENTIFICATION:	Trefoil leaves, yellow pea-like flowers April to June
SIMILAR SPECIES:	Dyer's greenweed, Petty whin

Like the common gorse, the hairy, black seed pods of broom explode with an audible crack in hot dry weather. It is a deciduous shrub with graceful, arching twigs with angled ridges. The trefoil leaves (*trefoil* means having three leaflets) distinguish it from dyer's greenweed (*Genista tinctoria)* and petty whin (*G. angelica)*. Dyer's greenweed was, as its name suggests, used to make a yellow dye. A good green dye was made when mixed with woad. This shrub grows in grassland and heaths in England, Wales and southern Scotland. Further north, into the Scottish Highlands, the small shrub with its yellow pea-like flower is likely to be the earlier-flowering petty whin.

BELL HEATHER *(Erica cinerea)*

SIZE:	Up to 60 cm tall
HABITAT:	Dry heaths and moors throughout Britain
IDENTIFICATION:	Evergreen shrub with whorls of leaves up the stem, bell-shaped purple flowers from June to September
SIMILAR SPECIES:	Cross-leaved heath, Heather (Ling)

Emily Dickinson wrote, in *From Time and Eternity*: 'I never saw a moor,/I never saw the sea;/Yet know I how the heather looks,/And what a wave must be'. Almost everyone knows what heather looks like. It is one of our best known wild flowers and bell heather has larger, brighter flowers than the others. They are carried in clusters at the top of the stems. Widespread on dry acid soils, it is most common in the north and west of Britain, sometimes appearing as clumps on the driest part of an otherwise boggy area. Bell heather has been brought into cultivation, where its ability to flourish on the poorest soils is much appreciated by gardeners.

HEATHER (LING) *(Calluna vulgaris)*

SIZE: Up to 60 cm tall

HABITAT: Heaths and moors

IDENTIFICATION: Straggly evergreen shrub with tiny linear leaves, spikes of purple flowers during August and September

SIMILAR SPECIES: Bell heather, Cross-leaved heath

Every August, hillsides and heaths are turned purple by the prolific flowers of this, our most common heather. Only occasionally can the white, 'lucky' flowers be found. It is a tough and aggressive plant surviving grazing by sheep in upland areas, and new shoots spring up after it has been burned. The shoots provide the main food for red grouse, whereas the flowers are sought by bee-keepers to make a superior honey. The flower heads are used to make herb tea and country wines. In the Scottish Highlands and Islands, heather was used as bedding material for cattle and the stems woven into baskets. The blackhouses of the Outer Hebrides were traditionally thatched with heather as it grows in abundance all over the islands.

CROSS-LEAVED HEATH

(Erica tetralix)

SIZE: Up to 50 cm tall

HABITAT: Wet heaths and moorland

IDENTIFICATION: Evergreen shrub with whorls of grey–green leaves, clusters of pink flowers from June to September

SIMILAR SPECIES: Bell heather, Ling

Cross-leaved heath is often found growing alongside ling, but its pink, bell-shaped flowers appear earlier and are larger than thos of its neighbour. The flowers are similar to bell heather, but are clustered at the top of the stems rather than spaced out in spikes As the fruits ripen, the drooping flowers become upright and fade to a pale brown. The leaves are also different from bell heather, being grouped in whorls of four resembling a cross when looked at from above. It is a neat, bushy plant when youn but sprawls with age, the branches rooting where they droop on to the wet ground.

Broad Buckler Fern
(Dryopteris dilatata)

SIZE:	Up to 1 m tall
HABITAT:	Heaths, woodland and mountain slopes
IDENTIFICATION:	Dark-green divided fronds, stalks with dark-centred scales
SIMILAR SPECIES:	Bracken, Hay-scented fern, Lady fern

he density of trees in woodlands greatly affects the condition of
e soil. Dead leaves and twigs accumulate and increase the
umus, and the canopy of leaves affects the water distribution
nd mineral content of the soil. This rich, moist woodland soil
nds to be acid and is the perfect growing medium for most
rns. The broad buckler fern is no exception and is common
nd widespread throughout Britain and Ireland, from April to
November. The fronds emerge as curled tufts and grow on to
eir typical feathery shape. The main lobes are divided into
0–20 smaller lobes which in turn are divided. Kidney-shaped
cales protect the spore cases on the under side of the fronds.

Lousewort *(Pedicularis sylvatica)*

SIZE:	7–25 cm tall
HABITAT:	Moors, damp heaths and bogs, throughout Britain
IDENTIFICATION:	Creeping plant with feathery leaves and pink flowers from April to July
SIMILAR SPECIES:	Marsh lousewort

In upland areas where the soil is poor and vegetation grazed by
hill sheep, lousewort and tormentil are often the only wild
flowers to flourish. The 20–25 mm long flower has a cylindrical
sepal tube and two-lipped, pink petals. The louseworts are 'semi-
parasites', which fix their roots to those of an adjoining plant
such as grass, extracting minerals and water without seeming to
harm the host. The lousewort was named because it was believed
to infest sheep with lice, a theory which is unproven today. The
marsh lousewort *(P. palustris)* is common in northern Britain,
flourishing in bogs and marshes. When the seed pods ripen, the
seeds shrink away from the walls of the pod and rattle when
blown in the wind, hence its alternative name of red rattle.

COMMON MILKWORT
(Polygala vulgaris)

SIZE:	5–10cm tall
HABITAT:	Heaths, dunes and grassland
IDENTIFICATION:	Trailing or upright, branched stems with narrow alternate leaves and clusters of bell-like flowers from May to September
SIMILAR SPECIES:	Heath milkwort, Chalk milkwort

According to Scottish legend, milkwort was one of four flowers made into a magical hoop and placed under the milk vessel to protect the cows and the milk from witchcraft. The name was more likely to have come from the belief that an infusion of the plant increased the flow of a mother's milk. Although usually blue, the flowers of this creeping plant can be pink, mauve or white. Despite being so small, the flowers are very pretty when looked at closely. The two inner sepals are brightly coloured and almost obscure the petals which might be white, giving the appearance of a bi-coloured flower. Heath milkwort is a smaller plant with opposite leaves instead of alternate. As its name suggests, it grows on heaths, moors and acid grassland.

COMMON EYEBRIGHT
(Euphrasia nemorosa)

SIZE:	Up to 30 cm tall
HABITAT:	Heaths, moors, downs and grasslands
IDENTIFICATION:	Branched stem with sharply toothed leaves and white flowers from June to September
SIMILAR SPECIES:	Eyebright (*E. officinalis*)

This pretty little plant with its painted flowers is a common sight all over the British Isles. It favours chalky soils but also grows in acid conditions on lowland moors and high up in the mountains. The lower lip of the white flower is longer than the upper and has a yellow patch and purple lines, not unlike a pansy. It has long been thought to improve bad eyesight, perhaps stemming from the 17th century story that it was used by a linnet to improve its sight. Some eye lotions today contain an extract from the plant. There are 25 species of eyebright, all are 'semi-parasites', fixing their roots to those of an adjoining plant such as grass or clover, extracting minerals and water without seeming to harm the host.

WILD THYME *(Thymus praecox* ssp *arcticus)*

SIZE: Up to 8 cm tall

HABITAT: Heaths and downs

IDENTIFICATION: Prostrate, creeping plant with small oval leaves and dense
                     pinkish-purple flower heads from June to August

SIMILAR SPECIES: Large thyme

In upland areas and downs the hill sheep graze on this aromatic herb and it is said that the lamb comes ready seasoned. They would need to consume quite a lot of it, as the wild thyme is considerably milder than the garden variety. Nevertheless, the honey-scented flowers and fragrant leaves have long been loved by insects, cooks, poets and herbalists as well as by the sheep.
It is common and widespread on both limy and acid soils, often forming dense mats on short turf. The aromatic oil in the leaves contains thymol, used as a preservative and an antiseptic.
It was therefore one of the main herbs used in the Sovereign's Maundy Thursday posy to protect against the infectious diseases of the poor.

TORMENTIL *(Potentilla erecta)*

SIZE:	5–50 cm tall
HABITAT:	Heaths, moors, mountains
IDENTIFICATION:	Upright stems with trifoliate leaves and small bright yellow flowers from May to October
SIMILAR SPECIES:	Creeping tormentil, Silverweed, Creeping cinquefoil

On grazed moorland throughout the British Isles, the ground is studded with these bright yellow flowers throughout the whole summer. On poor soils, it is often the only splash of colour apart from the lousewort. Tormentil has similar flowers to silverweed but they are smaller and have only four petals. At first sight, the leaves appear to be five-lobed, but actually comprise three leaflets and two leafy stipules. The roots were valued as a red dye and were used when tanning hides. Herbalists powdered the roots and used them to treat toothache. The similar creeping tormentil is found in hedgerows and on waste ground, the stems creeping and rooting as suggested by the name.

PYRAMIDAL ORCHID
(Anacamptis pyramidalis)

SIZE:	20–45 cm tall
HABITAT:	Downs, grassland and sand dunes
IDENTIFICATION:	Narrow, unspotted leaves, pyramid-shaped spike of rose pink flowers from June to August
SIMILAR SPECIES:	Green-winged orchid, Early purple orchid, Fragrant orchid

This distinctive orchid, with its densely packed flower spike, is widespread on downland in southern and eastern England but rarely seen in Scotland. It favours dry chalk and grassland, where it is often seen surrounded by butterflies and moths seeking nectar from its long spurs. The insects carry the orchid's stamens away with them on their tongues as they fly off. These will then come into direct contact with the stigma of the next flower visited, thus ensuring a high rate of pollination. The flowers are at their best in mid-July, later than other downland orchids, and have a marked 'foxy' smell. This is different from the sweet scent of the fragrant orchid, which also has a more elongated spike of flowers.

Autumn Gentian ▶
(Gentianella amarella)

SIZE:	5–30 cm tall
HABITAT:	Downs, dunes and grassland
IDENTIFICATION:	Upright branched plant with lance-shaped stem leaves. Dull purple flowers with a fringed tube from August to September
SIMILAR SPECIES:	Field gentian, Alpine gentian

The autumn gentian is the commonest of our gentians, although different species of the plant favour different areas of Britain. It prefers grassy plains and grows well on chalk or limestone mostly in the south, scarcer in the north. It was valued by 17th century herbalists and credited with curing snakebites and even treating people bitten by mad dogs. In the north you are more likely to see the field gentian, which has slightly brighter, bluish-purple flowers. These usually form a four-pointed star where the petal tube opens, compared to the five-pointed star of the autumn gentian. One of the rarest mountain flowers in Britain is the alpine gentian, its beautiful deep blue flowers seldom seen except on postcards.

Mossy Saxifrage
(Saxifraga hypnoides)

SIZE:	5–20 cm tall
HABITAT:	Mountains, hillside, rocky ground
IDENTIFICATION:	Small, 3-lobed leaves, clusters of white flowers from May to July
SIMILAR SPECIES:	Starry saxifrage, Meadow saxifrage

In upland areas, the vegetation and character of the habitat is markedly different from the lowlands, and mossy saxifrage is one of the plants seldom seen at lower levels. It can be found in chalky parts of the Lake District, Snowdonia and the Scottish Highlands up to 1220 m above sea level. In dry conditions, it forms tight cushions similar to clumps of moss with the branched flowering stalks held high above the foliage. In wetter areas, it becomes more straggly, trailing rather than creeping and looking, at first sight, like a completely different plant. The white flowers have five petals which are sometimes tipped with pink. Starry saxifrage and meadow saxifrage have similar flowers but their leaves are very different, the former having kidney-shaped, stalked leaves and the latter a basal rosette.

HAREBELL *(Campanula rotundifolia)*

SIZE:	15–40 cm tall
HABITAT:	Heaths and downs
IDENTIFICATION:	Heart-shaped basal leaves, bell-shaped pale blue flowers from July to October
SIMILAR SPECIES:	Ivy-leaved bellflower, clustered bellflower

On the west coast of the Outer Hebridean islands of Lewis, Harris and the Uists the wind-blown shell sand has formed a unique fertile soil known in Gaelic as machair. The machair sustains over a thousand species of wild flower, and many breeding birds, the rare corncrake in particular, make their home on this type of foreshore. Large, flat areas are cultivated by crofters but the smaller, less accessible places support their own incomparable blend of plants. The harebell, or bluebell as it is known in Scotland, is one of the key flowers that make up this remarkable sea of colour. The bell-shaped flowers, related to the garden Canterbury bells, are carried singly or in clusters and hang their heads, nodding in the breeze. The plants can survive on poor soil, and can be found in dry grassy places all over the British Isles. Although the flowers are not scented, they attract many butterflies and bees. The Harebell Fairy is one of the best known of Cicely Barker's famous flower fairies. The flower is known in the south west as the fairy plant and in the Isle of Man as the fairies' thimble. It is also known as the flower of witches who, according to legend, used its juice to make up their flying ointment. One tale of how the harebell got its name relates to witches using extracts of the plant to transform themselves into hares. The clustered bellflower grows on dry chalky soils and its flowers are, as the name suggests, grouped together rather than single. A rarer plant is the ivy-leafed bellflower which, with its violet blue flowers, is common only on damp moors and heaths in south-west England and Wales.

WHITETHROAT *(Sylvia communis)*

SIZE: 14 cm

HABITAT: Scrubland, heaths, overgrown hedgerows, coastal cliffs, occasionally gardens

IDENTIFICATION: Grey–brown upper parts, rusty-coloured wings, white throat. Male has grey head, crown feathers sometimes raised; female brown-headed. White outer tail feathers noticeable in flight

SIMILAR SPECIES: Lesser Whitethroat

The whitethroat, once common over almost the whole of Britain, is now recovering after droughts wiped out huge numbers in its wintering grounds of Central Africa in the late 1960s and early 1970s. Over 5 years the number of visitors fell to a sixth of normal, and its short, rather scratchy, but quite musical song – one of the features of the British summer – was seldom heard. The whitethroat favours sunny gorse and bramble covered coastal cliffs, and the male sometimes accompanies his song with a short, dancing display flight. The song obviously does not please everyone: in parts of Scotland it is known as blethering tam. The lesser whitethroat (only 0.5 cm smaller) prefers mature hedgerows and woodland with dense undergrowth. It is more shy and retiring with a tune-less rattle of a song, sung on one note. Its wings have no red tinge.

LINNET *(Acanthis cannabina)*

SIZE: 13.5 cm

HABITAT: Widespread on heaths, moors, scrubland

IDENTIFICATION: Male with chestnut back, greyish head with red forehead, greyish under parts with red breast. Female without red, more streaked. Both sexes white-edged wings and tail feathers in flight

SIMILAR SPECIES: Redpoll

Linnets used to be kept in cages to entertain with their delicate, twittering song. So many were trapped for this purpose that, in the early 1900s, laws had to be brought in to protect this charming little bird. Now it is threatened again, this time by loss of food supply due to greater use of weedkillers. The linnet relies on weed and wild flower seeds, although the young get a supplement of insects and grubs for the fortnight they are in the nest. Its name comes from *linece*, the Old English word for flax, although flax no longer plays an important role in its diet. It has a short, wide bill which cannot deal with larger seeds or ones that are hard to get at, so it feeds mainly on plants with seeds on the stem, like dock and chickweed. Linnets nest in small communities that gather at dusk, flying around and singing before settling down.

RAVEN *(Corvus corax)*

SIZE:	64 cm
HABITAT:	Mountains and moors
IDENTIFICATION:	Large black bird. Stout bill, shaggy throat feathers, splayed primary feathers in flight
SIMILAR SPECIES:	Rook, Carrion crow (both much smaller)

This huge dark bird, the largest of the *Corvidae*, and the largest perching bird in the world, is sometimes mistaken for an eagle by enthusiastic but inexpert Scottish tourists (see Buzzard p.241). It is, of course, much smaller with different plumage and tail shape but it does not lack gravitas. Its brooding presence and carrion-eating habits (particularly that of feeding on hanged corpses) have always made this a bird of ill omen with numerous legends and superstitions attached to it. Shelley wrote of 'The obscene ravens, clamorous o'er the dead' and one ditty runs: 'To see one raven is lucky, 'tis true/But it's certain misfortune to light upon two/And meeting with three is the devil'. Ravens often perform aerobatics, folding their wings and dropping like stones before looping the loop or even flying upside down for short stretches.

STONECHAT *(Saxicola torquata)*

SIZE:	12.5 cm
HABITAT:	Heaths, moors, mountains, downland, forestry plantations
IDENTIFICATION:	Male with dark upper parts, black head, white neck patch, white rump, chestnut red breast, white under parts. Female less contrasting, streaky upper parts and no rump patch
SIMILAR SPECIES:	Whinchat

Take two round, golf ball-sized pebbles, hold them lightly between forefinger and thumb of each hand and knock them together two or three times: you have produced the call of the stonechat. The stonechat makes its distinctive sound perched on a telegraph wire, bush or rock as it looks out for insects or spiders on the ground. It will also eat worms and grubs and has been known to tackle lizards. The stonechat stays in Britain all year, unlike its cousin the whinchat, and is severely affected by bad winters, with many birds dying off. Consequently, it raises three broods each year to cover the losses. In flight, the stonechat can be distinguished from the whinchat by its lack of tail markings. The whinchat *(Saxicola rubetra)* winters in central Africa and favours areas of gorse, which is called 'whin' in some parts.

WHEATEAR *(Oenanthe oenanthe)*

SIZE:	15 cm
HABITAT:	Uplands, moors and heaths, also farmland. Widespread but less common in central England
IDENTIFICATION:	Male grey above, buff beneath, white rump, black cheeks and wings. Black 'T' on white tail. Female brown above without cheek markings, otherwise similar
SIMILAR SPECIES:	Black-eared wheatear (very rare)

The name wheatear has nothing to do with wheat or ears. It comes from the Anglo-Saxon *hwit oers*, meaning 'white arse', which is the most noticeable thing about the bird as it flies low to the ground from one vantage point to another. The wheatear spends most of its life at low level, hunting out insects, larvae and worms in ploughed land or between rocks. It even makes its nest at ground level, usually under a large rock or in a crevice. It will sometimes use an old rabbit burrow for nesting, giving rise to its Norfolk name of coney chuck: 'coney' being another word for rabbit and 'chuck' echoing the bird's call, similar to that of the stonechat. It migrates from Africa very early in the year, sometimes arriving in southern England in the second week of March. The black-eared wheatear is a rare visitor on its travels to and from southern Europe.

STONE CURLEW *(Burhinus oedicnemus)*

SIZE:	41 cm
HABITAT:	Chalky downs and sandy heaths, S. and E. England. Rare, summer visitor
IDENTIFICATION:	Sandy brown plumage, long yellow legs, yellow bill with black tip, large yellow eyes. Long, thin body
SIMILAR SPECIES:	None

There is a haunted look in the wide yellow eye of the stone curlew. This, and its ducking, almost apologetic, stance and wailing cry, make it seem a persecuted bird, whereas it is really only very shy. It can sometimes be seen during the day, but is most active at dusk and through the night, when its curlew-like keening floats out across the eerie landscape. It prefers open, hedgeless tracts where it can see danger approaching and scuttle away to the safety of the undergrowth. When caught in the open, however, it will crouch and 'freeze', its colouring hiding it against the earth. It makes an insignificant scrape of a nest in which it lays well-camouflaged eggs. Everything about the stone curlew speaks of keeping a low profile. Even its courting display has both birds lowering their heads and making a slow march – away from each other.

NIGHTINGALE *(Luscinia megarhynchos)*

SIZE: 16.5 cm

HABITAT: Open deciduous woodland, thorn thickets. Midlands and S.E. England. Summer visitor

IDENTIFICATION: Brown upper parts, pale below with buff tinge to breast. Longish chestnut tail. Like a large robin in shape and stance

SIMILAR SPECIES: Nightingale thrush

The nightingale figures so large in poetry that it might be thought to be the only songbird on earth. Almost all references, from Tennyson's 'hundred-throated nightingale' to the 'matchless songs' described by Marvell, are to the sounds the bird makes. This is proper as its song is exquisite. But it also highlights the fact that it is seldom seen. Swinburne and Arnold are among the few who refer to its appearance, calling it, respectively, 'brown, bright' and 'tawny throated'. It certainly is elusive, skulking about in the bushes and undergrowth of its favourite woodland. It also does most of its singing at night – hence its name. The singing phase lasts just over a month and it is all done by the male not, as in poetry, by the female. By August most nightingales are on their way back to Africa, where they are just another brownish bird.

DARTFORD WARBLER
(Sylvia undata)

SIZE:	12.5 cm
HABITAT:	Heathland in S. England – Surrey, Hampshire and Dorset
IDENTIFICATION:	Male blue–grey above, reddish below, white belly; female similar but duller
SIMILAR SPECIES:	Whitethroat

The Dartford warbler is unusual in being the only British warbler that does not migrate, southern Britain being at the extreme N.W. range of this essentially Mediterranean bird. Already rare, this can make it rarer still as harsh winters cut a swathe through the population, reducing it to fewer than 12 pairs in 1962/3. However, a succession of mild winters in the late 1990s allowed it to spread its breeding range as far as East Anglia and Suffolk, and its more southern strongholds were estimated to be holding as many as 1000 pairs. It is usually seen as a blob in the distance, sitting in the top of a gorse bush twittering out its scratchy little song, its long tail cocked up at an angle. It was once widespread in southern Britain, but the dry heaths it favours disappeared under tree plantations, were dug up for minerals, or ravaged by fire.

NIGHTJAR *(Caprimulgus europaeus)*

SIZE:	25–28 cm
HABITAT:	Summer breeding visitor to moorland, heaths, dunes and young conifer plantations in S. and E. England. Small numbers and lower densities in Wales, Midlands, N.E. England and S.W. Scotland
IDENTIFICATION:	Long, back-curving wings in flight. Long tail. Mottled grey–brown, plumage like tree bark. Male has faint white spots near wing tips and corners of tail
SIMILAR SPECIES:	In flight similar to cuckoo, falcon or large swift but differs in holding wings above horizontal

Known locally in Lancashire as the flying toad, the nightjar at rest has a creepy, reptilian demeanour. This spooky bird, rarely seen by day, favours dead branches to crouch along in its cat-like way and at twilight the roosting male makes a weird 'churring' sound (shown to contain 1,900 notes per minute). Its Latin name means 'goat milker' and, in times past, this visitor from the sub-Sahara was thought to suckle from the udders of goats and cows, infecting them with an illness called puckeridge (another of its names is puck – linking it with that elfin troublemaker). An insect eater, it used to spend its evenings in byres and barns, hunting moths and bugs and was often in the vicinity of lactating beasts, hence the myth. Now its range is decreasing due to loss of heathland though numbers in the UK went up from 2100 males in 1981 to 3400 in 1992.

GOLDEN PLOVER (*Pluvialis apricaria*)

SIZE:	28 cm
HABITAT:	High moors in summer, spreading to lowlands in winter
IDENTIFICATION:	Speckled gold above with pale under parts becoming black in summer
SIMILAR SPECIES:	Grey plover

The piping 'klew-*eee*' of the golden plover is a familiar sound to hillwalkers and upland farmers. At breeding time the bird delivers its call from a prominent rock and, if approached, it flits to another not too far away, stands erect and calls again, and so on, probably leading you away from its nest. At the height of summer the plumage is a brilliant flecked gold offset by black under parts – a striking sight on a barren hillside. The display flight and song is also impressive, both birds circling high above the moor repeating a hooting 'kooo-roo' interspersed with a plaintive 'per-*eee*-oo' call which carries several hundred metres. In winter, Icelandic and Scandinavian golden plovers visit Britain, along with Arctic grey plovers (*P. squatarola*) from their breeding grounds in Canada and Russia. Grey plovers stay around the coasts.

BLACK GROUSE (*Tetrao tetrix*)

SIZE:	40–55 cm
HABITAT:	Uplands in Scotland, N. and S.W. England and Wales. Moorland near woodland. Local and declining
IDENTIFICATION:	Male all black with red eye wattles, white wing blotches and white-centred, lyre-shaped tail when displaying. Female orange–brown, no wattles
SIMILAR SPECIES:	Capercaillie

The male black grouse is pretty full of himself when performing his courtship display with his bright red wattles, hooked out wings and spreading, lyre-shaped tail with a flare of white feathers at its centre. Other males are treated to a posturing dance with bubbling, cooing sounds separated by loud scratchy noises. If no attention is paid to this ritual, then it comes to fisticuffs with feet, wings and bills slashing. The winner struts about in front of the submissive female. Where many grouse gather for such courtship displays, usually in the early morning, it is known as a 'lek' and the same site might be used for years. There were fewer than 7000 adult males left in Britain in 1996, but a project in the northern Pennines involving local people and conservation groups led to a population increase of a third in 3 years, promising hope for other regions.

RED GROUSE *(Lagopus lagopus scoticus)*

SIZE: 38 cm

HABITAT: Scotland, upland England and Wales

IDENTIFICATION: Dark, red–brown plumage with white legs
                   and red eye wattles. Female paler,
                   smaller wattles

SIMILAR SPECIES: Ptarmigan

The blaring 'quar*aaa*-kra-kra-kra' of a startled grouse is very often followed, fairly promptly, by the light click of a safety catch and the thunder of a charge of gunpowder. If the shooter is skilled, the bird will tumble into the heather in a froth of feathers, if not, then, like the rest of us, he will see the grouse coast low to the ground and settle in the undergrowth 50 m or so away. The species was once thought to be uniquely British but has been reclassified as a subspecies of the willow ptarmigan. Shooting stocks are maintained by landlords, and this involves major and costly land management, including systematic heather burning. It is not unknown for keepers to kill protected birds of prey which, they think, predate stocks. The ptarmigan *(L. mutus)*, found only in Scotland above 760 m, is similar to the red grouse but has pure white winter plumage.

BUZZARD *(Buteo buteo)*

SIZE:	Wingspan 115–125 cm
HABITAT:	Moorland, heath and mountains, occasionally near urban areas
IDENTIFICATION:	Colours vary from dark or pale grey to brown. Paler undersides. Short neck, barred tail
SIMILAR SPECIES:	Golden eagle, Honey buzzard, Rough-legged buzzard (rare visitor)

The buzzard has always been a common sight in upland and moorland Britain, but its range seems to be spreading and it is now often seen on a gatepost or telegraph pole quite close to human habitation and large urban areas, probably living off road kills. It lives in the shadow of the golden eagle as far as public regard is concerned but, apart from its smaller size, it is still imposing. When hunting, it locks into rising columns of air and soars, wings forward and raised, primary feathers splayed and tail raised, keeping an eye out for small mammals. When the prey is spotted, it half-folds its wings into a 'W' and rushes down to snatch the victim in its powerful talons. In parts of Scotland it is known as 'the tourist's eagle', circling over the glens and fooling many a hopeful, but starry-eyed, eagle seeker.

RED KITE *(Milvus milvus)* ▼

SIZE:	Wingspan 145–165 cm
HABITAT:	Moors and heathland, over woodland and plantations
IDENTIFICATION:	Brownish-red upper parts, pale head and underwing patches. Distinctive long, forked tail
SIMILAR SPECIES:	Black kite (rare)

Red kites used to be both widespread and common, but human persecution led to their extinction in England in 1870 and in Scotland in 1890. A few pairs survived in central Wales in the early 1900s, and protection allowed this population to increase to about 160 pairs by 2000. A red kite reintroduction project began in 1989 and, over five years, 93 young European birds were released at sites in southern England and northern Scotland. Other schemes in the Midlands and central Scotland established breeding populations, and by 1998 at least 71 pairs raised 143 young in southern England and four pairs were found in the Midlands. In Scotland, 25 pairs successfully raised 44 young. It is a beautiful bird and we are fortunate to see it soaring again over our countryside; however, only a tiny fraction of the red kite's former range is occupied today.

HEN HARRIER *(Circus cyaneus)*

SIZE:	Wingspan 100–120 cm
HABITAT:	Moorland and uplands of Scotland, N. England and N. Wales, spreading along E. and S. coasts in winter
IDENTIFICATION:	Male very pale, white and grey, with black wing tips. Females and young birds (known as ringtails), brownish but share male's white rump. Typical V-shaped wings in flight
SIMILAR SPECIES:	Montagu's harrier (rare), Marsh harrier

Probably Scotland's and Britain's most persecuted bird, the hen harrier is a beautiful ground nester, usually found on remote moorland. It is reviled by some gamekeepers because it includes young grouse in its extremely varied diet, which takes in small mammals, frogs, beetles, eggs and even chicks of other birds of prey. Hundreds of hen harriers have been killed systematically over the years, adults shot or poisoned, young trampled to death in the nest. By 2001, there were only 520 pairs in the UK, fewer than a dozen in England where they risked extinction. The hen harrier is protected under UK and European law, and the first successful conviction for shooting one came in 2001. Hen harriers began nesting on the Isle of Man in 1977, and more than 40 pairs now breed there, with more than 80 making up the largest communal winter roost in Western Europe.

PEREGRINE FALCON *(Falco peregrinus)*

SIZE:	Wingspan 95–115 cm
HABITAT:	Coastal cliffs, mountains and moorland. Occasionally cities. Patchy distribution, breeding mainly in the N. and W., more widespread in winter
IDENTIFICATION:	Blackish hood, slate upperparts, barred below. Juveniles brown above with streaked under parts. Distinctive anchor shape in flight. Female larger than male
SIMILAR SPECIES:	Hobby, Merlin (both smaller)

A stunningly powerful flier, the peregrine was protected as the falcon of noblemen in the Middle Ages. Law now protects it again, but in the early 2000s a campaign of destruction was apparently being waged against it by pigeon fanciers who mistakenly believed it responsible for high mortality among racing pigeons. It declined sharply in the 1950s and 1960s through pesticide poisoning, but made a good recovery, and Britain now has the most significant population in Europe with an estimated 1300 pairs. It hunts a wide range of birds: well over 100 species have been recorded in Britain, from goldcrest to grey

heron and even geese. Near coasts it takes puffins, rock doves, fulmars and guillemots. It is a sure and skilful hunter, circling high overhead and then descending in a breathtaking swoop to shatter its victim with a blow of its talons.

MERLIN *(Falco columbarius)*

SIZE: Wingspan 60–65 cm

HABITAT: Widespread but scarce in uplands of N. and W., rare in English Midlands. Breeds on moorland, heaths and forest edge. In winter on coastal farmland, marshes and other open habitats

IDENTIFICATION: Upper parts bluish-grey on male, brownish on female. Black tail band. Size of large mistle thrush, male smaller than female. Quick dashing flight

SIMILAR SPECIES: None of same size

The merlin's size sets it apart from other raptors. Hardly larger than a mistle thrush, it was the 'ladies falcon' in medieval times, trained to hunt skylarks. In the wild it is usually a solitary hunter, but two have been seen hunting together making repeated, alternate stoops on a meadow pipit. In the breeding season it will fearlessly assault any large bird approaching the nest, even golden eagles and ravens. In splendid aerial displays it climbs hundreds of metres before stooping at tremendous speed and peeling off almost at ground level. At long range in poor light, immature birds can be confused with hen kestrels, but are more compact with a shorter tail and deep brown, not reddish-brown, above. Also, the flight is very different, swifter and dashing with rapid wing beats and intervals of gliding, often inches from ground.

GOLDEN EAGLE *(Aquila chrysaetos)*

SIZE: Wingspan 190–250 cm

HABITAT: Scottish highlands, Hebrides

IDENTIFICATION: Large and powerful. Dark brown plumage, golden brown head, yellow feet. Gliding flight with few flaps, long primary feathers. All dark below in flight, immatures showing pale underwing patches

SIMILAR SPECIES: Sea eagle

If you 'think' you see a golden eagle, it probably is not one. You will know for certain when you see the real thing: it is huge. On the wing it looks like a small aeroplane; perched on a rock more like an oversized statue. It is majestic. Throughout history it has been the bird of rulers and nations. Numbers in Britain fell to dangerously low levels about 150 years ago through persecution, and some hill farmers still think it kills lambs, although this has never been proved. Shooting and poisoning is not unknown. Nevertheless, about 422 pairs breed and just over 1000 winter in Britain. It nests on rocky outcrops in the mountains, on sea cliffs

or in large trees, each pair usually producing one eaglet. There is one pair in the Lake District, around Haweswater. The population scattered because each pair needs 1200 hectares (3000 acres) of hunting ground where they take grouse, ptarmigan, hares and occasionally foxes. It also eats carrion, mostly dead sheep and deer.

The larger **sea eagle** *(Haliaeetus albicilla,* wingspan up to 250 cm) was once widespread in Scotland and the Lake District but persecution wiped it out by 1916. Reintroduction programmes began in 1975 on the Inner Hebridean island of Rhum, with the first successful breeding in 1985. It is now more scattered along the west coast of Scotland where, by 2000, 12 out of about 20 breeding pairs had successfully produced 100 chicks. It is bulkier and more vulture-like than the golden eagle and adults are unmistakable with their short gleaming white tails. The Anglo-Saxons thought sea eagle bone marrow had healing properties (although, like all birds, it has hollow bones with no marrow), while the Faroese were convinced that the talons could cure jaundice. Shetland fishermen used to anoint their bait with sea eagle fat to improve the catch.

EMPEROR MOTH *(Saturnia pavonia)*

SIZE: Forewing 40 mm (female), 21 mm (male)

HABITAT: Heaths, moors, marshes and similar open country. Widespread and locally common, particularly in Scotland and the Northern Isles

IDENTIFICATION: Distinctive large eye-spots on all 4 wings in both sexes. Male with grey–green or grey–brown forewings and tawny hindwings. Female larger, lighter coloured without tawny hindwings

SIMILAR SPECIES: None in Britain

This is the British representative of the silk-moth family. The caterpillar spins a large, commercially worthless, rough silken cocoon in the undergrowth to overwinter the pupa. The brown, pear-shaped cocoon has a ring of spines at the sharp end. These open when the emerging moth presses from the inside, but cannot be forced apart from the outside by a predator. The most colourful specimens are found in Scotland and the Northern Isles and the large caterpillar (up to 60 mm) is bright green with black bristles and bands of black circles. This seems garish, but provides surprisingly good camouflage in heather, its principal foodplant. It also eats bramble, hawthorn, blackthorn, sallow and meadowsweet. The day-flying male's antennae can pick up the scent of an unmated female from as far as 2 km away. The female flies at night.

COMMON LIZARD *(Lacerta vivipara)*

SIZE:	10–15 cm long, including the tail
HABITAT:	Heaths, downs, moors, coastal cliffs and dunes
IDENTIFICATION:	Brown or grey–brown with darker blotched markings along its length
SIMILAR SPECIES:	Sand lizard (rare)

On a still summer day you might come across a common lizard basking in the sunlight on a warm rock or log. Like other reptiles, it relies on external heat sources to maintain its body temperature. It does this either by soaking up the sun or by lying on rocks that have already been warmed. In the right conditions, on dry light soils, the common lizard can be found throughout Britain. It is the only reptile in Ireland. The young are born alive, not hatched from eggs, and feed on the same insects and spiders as the parent. The rare sand lizard is found only in parts of Southern England and Lancashire. It is slightly larger than the common lizard and the male has green flanks which are brightest during the breeding season. Unlike the common lizard, the sand lizard lays eggs in holes and the young appear from June to August.

SMOOTH SNAKE *(Coronella austriaca)*

SIZE:	55–75 cm
HABITAT:	Sandy heaths
IDENTIFICATION:	Grey–brown slender body with indistinct darker markings down its back
SIMILAR SPECIES:	Adder, Grass snake, Slow worm

This is Britain's equivalent of a boa constrictor, killing or subduing its prey by squeezing. Gruesome as it might sound, this fate is only suffered by lizards and the non-venomous smooth snake is harmless to humans. It is Britain's rarest reptile, found only in Hampshire and Dorset and infrequently in Surrey and West Sussex. It is strictly protected by law and it is an offence to kill, capture, injure or disturb one. Like other snakes, it basks in the sun, sometimes superbly camouflaged, entwined around heather stems. The young are born live in summer, the eggs hatching within the female. If you get close enough to see its eyes, you will notice that the smooth snake has round pupils whereas the adder has vertical slits, like a cat. The adder is also distinguishable from the smooth snake by its dark zigzag stripe.

ADDER *(Vipera berus)*

SIZE: 50–60 cm

HABITAT: Heaths, moors, downs and sand dunes

IDENTIFICATION: Distinctive dark zig-zag pattern runs down the length of its back and a dark V-shaped mark on the head

SIMILAR SPECIES: Grass snake, Smooth snake, Slow worm

The adder is Britain's only poisonous snake, but it poses little threat to a healthy adult. About 40% of the bites release no venom into the victim, but if venom is released it can cause painful swelling, sickness and fever and anti-venom treatment should be sought from a hospital. Sometimes called the viper, it is a shy creature and will slink away if approached. Whatever you do, do not hit one with a stick: all indigenous snakes in the UK are protected by law and it is an offence to kill or injure one. The adder hibernates underground and emerges in spring often sunbathing in groups. It can cover quite a large territory and sometimes hibernates some distance away from its summer haunts. As with the smooth snake, the eggs hatch within the mother and the young are born live.

FLY AGARIC *(Amanita muscaria)*

SIZE: Up to 20 cm tall

HABITAT: Heaths, birch and mixed woodland

IDENTIFICATION: Red cap with white flecks and white gills

SIMILAR SPECIES: Blusher, Panther cap

This is our most familiar toadstool, often pictured in children's story books or reproduced as garden ornaments. In Germany, marzipan *Glückspilz* are imitation fly agaric mushrooms, offered for good luck on New Year's Eve. The fly agaric has been known for centuries and was first illustrated in a fresco in France dating back to 1291. It is poisonous and there is considerable folklore associated with deeds carried out while under the influence of its hallucinogens. Also known as magic mushroom or liberty cap, fly agaric was reputed to induce erotic energy, prophetic sight and outstanding muscular strength. In the 13th century it was discovered that when broken up and soaked in milk, this fungus attracted and killed flies, so earning its common name.

CLADONIA IMPEXA

SIZE:	Low, spreading
HABITAT:	Heaths, moors and mountains
IDENTIFICATION:	Cushions of branched stems, greyish-green
SIMILAR SPECIES:	Reindeer moss (*Cladonia rangiferina*)

On heaths and moors, the genus *Cladonia* is usually dominant with 10–25 different species of lichens flourishing. *Cladonia impexa* is the most common, often seen in dense cushions growing in among heather or ling. The hollow stems often branch in groups of three, facing in different directions with small brown spores sometimes developing at the tips. Not confined to heaths and moors, it can be found high up in the mountains such as in the Cairngorms. The rarer, bluish-grey reindeer moss (*C. rangiferina*) is only found at these higher altitudes in Scotland and Wales. It grows abundantly in Arctic regions, where it forms the staple diet of reindeer and is imported for use in potpourri as it absorbs the perfumed oils and slowly releases the aroma.

STAGHORN CLUBMOSS (*Lycopodium clavatum*)

SIZE:	Up to 10 cm tall
HABITAT:	Moors and mountains
IDENTIFICATION:	Creeping, branched stems, dense leaves
SIMILAR SPECIES:	Fir clubmoss

More commonly found in northern England, Wales and Scotland, staghorn clubmoss has evergreen antler-like upright stems branching off the creeping main stems. It produces sporecases in long-stalked cones, usually in pairs. A bright-yellow powder called 'Lycopodium powder' was once collected from the spores and used in fireworks as an ingredient of 'flash powder'. The same powder was used by chemists for coating pills. Fir clubmoss is rarely seen in the lowlands, but is widespread in Scotland and Ireland where it can be found growing on rocky ledges or clefts between boulders. The upright plants resemble miniature fir trees and they are less branched than the staghorn clubmoss.

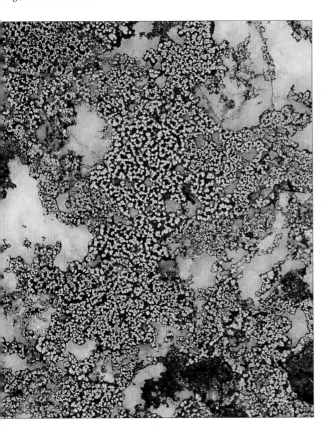

MAP LICHEN *(Rhizocarpon geographicum)*

SIZE:	Flat, spreading
HABITAT:	Uplands and mountains
IDENTIFICATION:	Yellowish green blotches with black dividing lines, usually on rocks and boulders
SIMILAR SPECIES:	None

At first glance it is easy to see how this lichen got its name, with black lines forming boundaries between coloured blotches, like borders between counties. Closer examination reveals the black lines as the lower layer of the lichen, showing through where the upper layer has cracked or where two colonies meet. These lines are also emphasised where map lichen grows alongside other, different coloured species. Lichens are thought to be among the slowest growing organisms and map lichen was measured in one analysis to have grown only 0.09 mm per year. However, environmental conditions do affect the growth, and a study of map lichen on tombstones across Scotland found a considerable increase in growth rate in the rainy west coast compared with the drier east. Air pollution also slows development.

CROTTLE *(Parmelia saxatilis)*

SIZE:	Flattish, spreading
HABITAT:	Moors, woods, throughout the British Isles
IDENTIFICATION:	Flat grey rosettes growing on rocks, walls or trees
SIMILAR SPECIES:	*Parmelia sulcata*

Travelling through the Scottish islands during the 1920s and 1930s, the visitor was likely to see a large black, three-legged iron pot outside nearly every crofthouse. This was used to dye wool with crottle collected by the crofters and weavers. It was scraped off the rocks, sometimes using a seashell, and layered with the wool before boiling. The colour of the dye varied from gold through reddish brown to a deep chocolate colour, lending the resultant tweeds their familiar hues. During the Napoleonic Wars, a famous victory was brought about because of the rich red crottle dye used by Welsh women. The French army mistook the red cloaks of the women for uniforms of advancing soldiers and surrendered without a shot being fired.

Fox *(Vulpes vulpes)*

Size: Body up to 90 cm, tail 60 cm

Habitat: Widespread in countryside and urban areas but absent from Scottish islands

Identification: Reddish colour with long bushy tail, white undersides and tail tip. Paws and backs of ears usually dark

Similar species: None in Britain

The fox is the mammal equivalent of the herring gull – an accomplished scavenger, found everywhere from the wild countryside to busy city centres. It will eat everything from earthworms to restaurant left-overs, and it is partial to poultry and game birds, which is why it is persecuted. It is also blamed for killing lambs but, like the golden eagle, it probably eats those that have already died rather than going to the trouble of killing them. It hunts for food mostly at night and spends the daytime underground in its 'earth'. This is where the young are born – usually a litter of four to six cubs – in the springtime. You know when you have come across a fox's den by the musty smell. The call of a female fox, or vixen, during the mating season is a bloodcurdling scream which some farmers learn to emulate to draw males, or dog foxes, towards their guns.

RED DEER *(Cervus elaphus scoticus)*

SIZE: Male 101–112 cm at shoulder, 90–190 kg; female 42–54 cm, 57–115 kg

HABITAT: Mountain and moorland, forests and woods. Mostly Scotland but also New Forest, Exmoor, Quantocks, Suffolk, and the Lake District

IDENTIFICATION: In summer, dark red or brown with lighter cream underbelly, inner thighs and rump. Possibly some spots along spine. In winter, darker brown or grey, lighter patches on rump and undersides. Tail patch reaches higher up than other deer. Stags can grow large, multi-tined antlers

SIMILAR SPECIES: Sika deer

The arrogant stag silhouetted on the skyline, antlered head thrown back, roaring an autumnal challenge to his rivals; the delicate gangle-legged calf nosing into the cream fur of its mother's belly for a feed; the startled herd flowing with supple ease over rough mountain terrain like russet smoke: the red deer, our biggest land mammal, is wonderful to watch. This tough native species survived the Ice Age to populate post-glacial woodland. As people removed the wolf, bear and lynx, it prospered, but the human proved a more rapacious predator. Only royal protection in the 17th–18th centuries prevented it being hunted to extinction by commoners. Woodland clearance forced it to adapt, which it did too successfully in parts of Scotland, where numbers are beyond grazing capacity, and many animals die of starvation. There are fears that it is being hybridised out of existence as a pure breed by the sika.

STOAT *(Mustela ermina)*

SIZE: 30 cm excluding tail

HABITAT: Moors, heaths, downs, woods and farmland

IDENTIFICATION: Long body, short legs, reddish-brown fur with white underside, long tail with black tip

SIMILAR SPECIES: Weasel

The ceremonial ermine cloak worn by medieval kings and queens was made from the winter coat of the stoat. In Scotland, Wales and some parts of western England, the stoat moults in winter to become completely white (apart from the tip of its tail), giving excellent camouflage in the snow. The black tip to its tail is the easiest way to tell it apart from the smaller weasel. The stoat is a curious, playful creature and will explore holes or buildings, usually at night. A bold hunter, it preys on small mammals, particularly rabbits, killing with a swift bite to the back of the neck. It sometimes occupies the burrow of the unfortunate rabbit and might use its victim's fur to line the nest. Apart from on some islands, the stoat can be found throughout Britain wherever there is suitable undergrowth for cover.

MOUNTAIN HARE *(Lepus timidus)*

ZE: 50–65 cm

ABITAT: Heather moorland, upland areas and mountains

ENTIFICATION: Blue–grey fur in summer, white in winter, long, black-tipped ears

MILAR SPECIES: Brown hare

In winter, the mountain hare's coat becomes completely white except for the tips of its ears, giving superb camouflage in the snow. It is our only indigenous hare and is better adapted to living at high altitudes than the brown hare. In England there is a small population in the Peak District, but in Scotland it is common on grouse moors, mountains and on several Scottish islands where it is an important food for golden eagles. In the Cairngorms it has been known to breed as high as 1200 m. The mountain hare, or blue hare as it is also called, shelters during the day in a form or scrape and is most active at dawn and dusk, grazing on grass or heather. In bad weather it will gnaw bark above the level of the snow. Usually a solitary animal, it sometimes gathers in groups on the leeward side of the hill, scraping away shallow snow in order to feed.

POLECAT *(Mustela putorius)*

SIZE: 45–55 cm

HABITAT: Woodland, heaths and downland. Wales and N. England

IDENTIFICATION: Dark golden brown with darker paws and tail, dark eye band and whitish chin and ears

SIMILAR SPECIES: Mink (smaller), domestic ferret (dark form)

The polecat, once widespread but persecuted almost to extinction by gamekeepers and hunters, is now protected and spreading from its Welsh stronghold, re-establishing itself in northern England. In the 10 years up to 1999 there were occasional reports of polecats in Cheshire, particularly in the Delamare Forest and other local woodland sites and a UK-wide survey throughout the 1990s recorded more than 1000 specimens (mostly road kill, unfortunately). Worcestershire was reported as completely re-populated by 2000. Numbers of the true form are hard to verify as polecat hybridise with feral domestic ferrets but a 1999 survey by the Vincent Wildlife Trust suggested a dramatic 93% increase since 1991 in the area occupied by polecats in Britain. The widespread use of rodenticide is still a threat as polecats eat small mammals as well as birds and invertebrates.

WILD CAT *(Felis sylvestris)*

SIZE: 75–95 cm (specimen of 122 cm recorded)

HABITAT: Remote forests, hills and grouse moors in Scottish Highlands. Some in Scottish borders and Northumberland.

IDENTIFICATION: Tabby grey to rufous with distinct striping and bushy, blunt-ended tail marked with black rings. Golden amber eyes, black paw pads. Broad head with distinctive 'M' on forehead

SIMILAR SPECIES: Domestic and feral cats

The Scottish wild cat (F. silvestris grampia) is the only true wild cat you are likely to see in the UK. Other cats living in the wild will almost certainly be feral domestics. Its cousin the lynx was hunted to extinction in Scotland centuries ago and the wild cat almost went the same way. Some estates killed hundreds a year before it was awarded some legal protection in 1981. However, in a court case in 1990 a gamekeeper was acquitted of killing three wild cats because an expert witness could not positively identify the remains as pure specimens. The estimated population of 5000 is barely enough to overcome the effects of interbreeding with ferals and domestics but only the true wild cat, with its thicker, warmer coat and stockier, more muscular build, can survive really harsh conditions. Rabbits, voles and other rodents form the largest part of its diet but frogs, fish and small birds are also taken.

Rivers,
Lakes, Ponds and
Marshes

And out again I curve and flow
To join the brimming river,
For men may come and men
  may go,
But I go on for ever.

THE BROOK
ALFRED TENNYSON

CRACK WILLOW *(Salix fragilis)*

SIZE: Up to 25 m tall but often pollarded

HABITAT: Widespread beside water

IDENTIFICATION: Long, narrow, bright green leaves. Twigs snap off easily. Hanging yellow male catkins, short green female catkins maturing into woolly seeds. Deeply ridged grey–green bark

SIMILAR SPECIES: White willow, Weeping willow, Almond willow

Willow regrows quickly when coppiced or pollarded (sometimes several feet a year) and a twig stuck in the ground will usually root and grow, so the tree has become a widespread symbol of renewal, vitality and immortality. Crack willow twigs snap off easily, float away and root in the bank downstream. However, willows generally, particularly larger trees, are dwindling as they are grubbed out to make waterway management easier. Willow wood is pinkish, soft, light, brittle and splits easily. It has been used for house building, coracle frames, toys, clogs, artificial limbs, charcoal and the sound boxes of harps. Its ability to absorb shock makes it perfect for cricket bats and stumps. The bark was used to make a reddish-brown dye, for tanning leather and as animal feed. A folk remedy for numerous ills, willow's active ingredient is salicylic acid, synthesised into acetylasylic acid in aspirin.

OSIER *(Salix viminalis)*

SIZE:	Up 10 m tall but usually coppiced low
HABITAT:	Widespread by water, particularly in Somerset
IDENTIFICATION:	Very long (up to 25 mm), alternate, narrow leaves, dense silver hair on undersides. Catkins short, male yellow, female green. Long, whippy branches when coppiced
SIMILAR SPECIES:	Sallow, Bay willow, Grey willow, Eared willow

Supermarkets and plastic bags have virtually killed off shopping baskets but there is something very satisfying about these sturdy, functional and ecologically sound load carriers. They also provide a direct link to history, as basketwork has been with us almost unchanged for thousands of years. A 6th century basket unearthed on Shetland used the same weaving techniques as are still practised in Scotland. The coppiced stems, or withies, have been used to make chairs and fish traps, beehives and lobster pots and a great deal more. Willow weaving is reappearing in new applications like landscape sculptures, outdoor seating, children's play huts and urban screening, all made from live cuttings, grown *in situ*, woven and sculpted into living structures. Withies, harvested at 1 year old, can be used unprocessed (coloured green), steamed and dried (brown), boiled and stripped of bark (buff) or stored over winter in water then stripped (white).

ALDER *(Alnus glutinosa)*

SIZE:	Up to 22 m tall but sometimes coppiced
HABITAT:	Widespread by water
IDENTIFICATION:	Alternate, rounded leaves, sometimes indented at tip. Male catkins with purple scales, yellow flowers, female catkins small and purple–brown ripening into small cones
SIMILAR SPECIES:	Grey alder, Italian alder

If you like Venice you should thank this tree as most of the piles driven into the lagoon to support the city are alder trunks. Alder grows like a weed in wet places but out of water its timber is not very useful as it rots easily. It was used for clogs, perhaps because it is a poor heat conductor, and although poor firewood, it makes first-class charcoal. This was used for gunpowder, and small plantations of coppiced alder were often established near powder factories. Live alder wood is pale but turns deep orange when cut, giving the impression of bleeding. This led to many superstitions about the tree. Seasoned alder is a richer brown and was sought after by furniture makers. However, it is prone to woodworm and an old custom was to put an alder branch in cupboards to attract the beetle, which prefers alder to any other wood as the place to lay eggs.

Bog Myrtle *(Myrica gale)*

SIZE:	Up to 1.5 m tall
HABITAT:	Common in wet, peaty areas of north, scattered in south
IDENTIFICATION:	Alternate, narrow, grey–green leaves, widening near tip, on upright, red–brown stems. Short, orange–brown male catkins, slightly longer reddish female
SIMILAR SPECIES:	In US: Bayberry, Wax myrtle

Myrtle is a very useful little shrub. If caught in a cloud of Highland midges without a protective spray, find a myrtle bush, crush some leaves in your hands and rub your palms over your face and neck. The peppery sweet scent is supposed to repel biting flies. Perhaps it was this quality which led Clan MacDonald to adopt it as their badge. The dried leaves were used to perfume linen, and the branches replaced hops as flavouring in Yorkshire's extremely thirst-quenching 'gale beer'. The catkins, boiled in water, release scummy wax, once used to make candles. The bark, used to tan calfskins, will, if gathered in autumn, dye wool yellow. The Swedes boil up a strong myrtle liquor to kill insects, vermin and to cure itching. The dried berries can be put into broth and used as spice and, in China myrtle leaf tea is used as a gastric stimulant and cordial.

Bulrush *(Typha latifolia)*

SIZE:	135–230 cm tall
HABITAT:	Fresh water margins, swamps
IDENTIFICATION:	Long stems, flat, narrow leaves and brown sausage-like flowers during June and July
SIMILAR SPECIES:	Lesser bulrush

This plant used to be called greater reedmace until it was depicted in the celebrated painting *Moses in the Bulrushes*. Sir Lawrence Alma-Tadema, the Victorian painter, was illustrating the Biblical story and painted these striking plants instead of *Schoenoplectus lacustris* which was then known as bulrush. As his painting was so well known, the greater reedmace became known as the bulrush and the original bulrush renamed common clubrush. Whatever its name, the plant is unmistakable with its brown, sausage-shaped female flower head, made up of thousands of tiny flowers. The male flowers appear as a thinner spike growing from the tip. The greyish-green leaves are up to 20 mm wide and have a cellular interior. They were once used for weaving baskets and reed boats.

WHITE WATER LILY *(Nymphaea alba)*

IZE: Flowerheads up to 20 cm across

ABITAT: Lakes, ponds, slow-moving water

DENTIFICATION: Large, almost circular leaves, and large white flowers floating on fresh water from June to August

IMILAR SPECIES: Yellow water lily

The white water lily is one of the largest of Britain's wild flowers and one of the most beautiful. Floating on still or slow-moving water, its beauty is fleeting. The flower lasts for just 3 days and only opens in the middle of the day, sinking partly below the surface as it closes. The flower is a symbol of purity and the roots and leaves have medicinal properties that have been used for centuries. They were popular as an infusion for soft skin, to combat wrinkles and as an antiseptic. The roots can be as much as 2 m below the surface of the water yet, on the island of Jura off north-west Scotland, they were once sought to make a dark, chestnut brown dye.

MARSH MARIGOLD *(Caltha palustris)*

SIZE: 30–60 cm tall

HABITAT: Marshes, damp woodland and other wet areas

IDENTIFICATION: Dark green mottled, kidney-shaped leaves; yellow, cup-shaped flowers from March to July

SIMILAR SPECIES: Greater spearwort and other buttercups

These semi-aquatic perennial plants with their golden flowers are members of the buttercup family. The glossy, kidney- or heart-shaped leaves make it a handsome plant even before the flowers appear. The flowers, up to 50 mm across, have five yellow sepals and no petals. They are cup shaped and an alternative name for the plant is kingcup: the botanical name *Caltha* is from the Greek for goblet or cup. Although once used as a treatment for rheumatic pain, the plant should be treated with care as the raw leaves and buds are poisonous. The juice is caustic and was used in folk medicine to make warts fall off, a remedy that was probably effective, although perhaps not altogether pleasant.

BOGBEAN *(Menyanthes trifoliata)* ▲

SIZE: Up to 15 cm above water

HABITAT: Shallow fresh water bogs, fens and marshes

IDENTIFICATION: Leaves with three leaflets, spikes of pink and white flowers during May and June

SIMILAR SPECIES: None

It is a pity that the bogbean chooses such inhospitable places to grow as it means the average walker does not stumble across them. Perhaps he would not want to as they grow in shallow lochs and lagoons with the flowers and foliage held above the water. Nevertheless, they are startlingly beautiful and well worth a wet walk to find. The trifoliate leaves emerge from the surface of the water and are followed by clusters of pink buds opening into star-shaped, pink and white flowers, fringed with white hairs. Early herbalists used the plant as a general tonic, a cure for scurvy and to get rid of boils. The leaves are bitter but have been used in the past to flavour beer.

COMPACT RUSH *(Juncus conglomeratus)*

SIZE: Up to 1 m tall

HABITAT: Bogs, marshes, wet grassland and woods

IDENTIFICATION: Ridged stems with round clusters of brown flowers from May to July

SIMILAR SPECIES: Hard rush, Soft rush

When the compact rush, or clustered rush as it is sometimes called, is in flower, it looks as if the flower is appearing part way up the stem but, in fact, the flower cluster emerges from the top of the stem and is topped by a long bract. The soft rush is very similar but the flower heads have stalks and branches, causing them to hang more loosely. Rushes have been put to many uses in the home in rural areas. The pith from inside the stems used to be made into wicks for candles. Common throughout Britain, especially on acid soils, rushes were plaited for baskets and strewn on stone floors to add warmth.

RAGGED ROBIN *(Lychnis flos-cuculi)*

SIZE: 30–70 cm

HABITAT: Marshes, fens, damp meadows and woodlands, throughout Britain

IDENTIFICATION: Upright plant with narrow leaves, pink flowers May to August

SIMILAR SPECIES: Red campion

At first glance you might think that this flower has had a battering from the wind, leaving its flowers in tatters. Looking more closely, the four-lobed petals are symmetrical and the flower itself has a delicate beauty. The sepals form a tube behind the flower in a similar way to those of the red campion. Both are members of the pink family but the flowers of the ragged robin are quite unmistakable because of their deeply divided petals. Cuckoo-flower and bachelor's buttons are alternative common names, but these are given to other wild flowers as well. Country girls used the flower buds to foretell whom they were to marry. A girl would pick buds and give each one the name of a local bachelor. She would then hide the buds in her clothes, and the first one to open would determine which boy she would marry.

Yellow Iris *(Iris pseudacorus)*

SIZE:	40–150 cm
HABITAT:	Pond margins, river banks and marshes
IDENTIFICATION:	Sword-shaped leaves, three-petalled yellow flowers from May to August
SIMILAR SPECIES:	Stinking Iris

his robust perennial with its clusters of two or three large ellow flowers is a familiar sight surrounding ponds and on the anks of streams. It can survive in water up to 25 cm deep and as spread to salt marshes in Scotland. The roots or rhizomes of e plant have been put to a variety of uses over the ages, some ather bizarre. Crushed roots mixed with daisies and strained, roduced a liquid which was poured into the patient's nose to eat toothache. A more practical use in some of the Scottish lands was to make a black dye or, boiled with copperas (proto-lphate of iron) to make ink. In the language of flowers, iris eans ardour, and has inspired writers and poets to ng its praises.

Common Cotton-Grass
(Eriophorum angustifolium)

SIZE:	Up to 75 cm tall
HABITAT:	Bogs and wet peaty places
IDENTIFICATION:	Three-sided stem with drooping, insignificant flowers followed by white, fluffy flower heads during May and June
SIMILAR SPECIES:	Hare's-tail cotton-grass

On very boggy ground, with acid, peaty soil, scattered white tufts appear during May and June as if a flock of sheep had walked by leaving clumps of their wool behind on thorns or spikes. You might need to put your boots on to get close enough to investigate, but then you'll find that there is nothing prickly or harsh about these tufts. They are the fruiting heads of common cotton-grass and softer than the best cotton wool. Once used to stuff pillows, probably equivalent to the best goose down, the plant is most common in the north and west of Britain but is declining as drainage reduces our bog land. Hare's-tail cotton-grass is similar but the flowers are borne singly rather than in clusters.

ROSEBAY WILLOWHERB
(Epilobium angustifolium)

SIZE: Up to 1.5 m tall

HABITAT: River banks, damp meadows and waste ground

IDENTIFICATION: Long stems with wavy narrow leaves, spikes of pinkish-purple flowers from July to September

SIMILAR SPECIES: Great willowherb, Marsh willowherb, Broad-leaved willowherb

This is the most beautiful of all our willowherbs and the most common since it sprang up in city bomb sites during the Second World War. It is still seen flourishing on waste ground, as well as on river banks, with its densely clustered flowers on tall, straight spikes. This is the only willowherb to have unequal petals – the upper two are broader than the lower two. The taller great willowherb can be found in ditches or beside streams, particularly in the south. Both willowherbs have been used medicinally, for their astringent qualities, and the powdered root was said to stop internal bleeding. Today, an infusion of rosebay willowherb is sometimes used to treat asthma.

COMMON BUTTERWORT
(Pinguicula vulgaris)

SIZE: 5–10 cm

HABITAT: Bogs, fens, wet moors and heaths, mainly in the north and west of Britain

IDENTIFICATION: Star-shaped basal rosette of leaves with a single violet-like flower

SIMILAR SPECIES: Pale butterwort

The pale green basal leaves are the first things you notice about this plant, as they look like starfish washed up from the seashore. During May and June a single flower stem emerges from the centre bearing two-lipped, violet-like flowers. Innocent though it looks, this plant is one of our few insectivorous plants; it traps and digests insects unfortunate enough to land on its leaves. The insect sticks to the surface while the leaf curls round to hold it fast. The butterwort extracts mineral salts from its victim and, when it is of no further use, the leaf opens and the remains are washed or blown away. The pale butterwort is only found in the west and, as its name suggests, has paler, pinkish-lilac flowers.

WATER FORGET-ME-NOT
(Mysotis scorpioides)

SIZE: Up to 12 cm tall

HABITAT: River banks, stream edges

IDENTIFICATION: Branching stems with narrow leaves and bright blue flowers from June to September

SIMILAR SPECIES: Field forget-me-not, Tufted forget-me-not, Wood forget-me-not

The romantic tragedy that gave this flower its well-known name originated in Germany. It is said that a knight was picking a bunch of these beautiful blue flowers for his companion when he lost his balance and fell into the river. As he was swept away, he threw the bunch to his lady, crying out for her not to forget him. The water forget-me-not is common on neutral soils throughout the British Isles and has the largest flower of the forget-me-nots found in wet places. Usually the curved flower clusters are sky blue, but occasionally the five petals can be white or pale pink. Many of the forget-me-nots were used by herbalists to make a syrup to treat coughs or lung complaints.

COMMON COMFREY
(Symphytum officinale)

SIZE:	30–120 cm tall
HABITAT:	Marshes, ditches and by rivers and streams
IDENTIFICATION:	Bushy plant with spear shaped leaves, clusters of dull purple flowers from May to July
SIMILAR SPECIES:	Russian comfrey

This hairy perennial plant has clusters of nodding, rather luscious flowers, which are usually a dull purple colour, but can also be cream, white, mauve or pink. The plant is widespread throughout Britain but is commonest in central and southern England. The dark green, spear-shaped leaves are edible, sometimes cooked like spinach. A more interesting way to eat them is to leave the stalks on, dip them into a thin batter and fry them for 2 minutes. The grated roots of comfrey were used as a plaster to set broken bones by medieval herbalists, thus earning the plant the alternative names of 'Boneset' and 'Knitbone'. Russian comfrey prefers drier conditions and is widely established on verges and hedgerows. It has distinctive blue–purple flowers from June to August.

EARLY MARSH ORCHID

(Dactylorhiza incarnata)

SIZE:	Up to 60 cm tall
HABITAT:	Marshes, damp meadows and fens
IDENTIFICATION:	Narrow, unmarked leaves, spikes of flowers usually pink with the sides of the lower lip folded back
SIMILAR SPECIES:	Southern marsh orchid, Northern marsh orchid

The early marsh orchid with its narrow, yellowish-green leaves is widespread but usually prefers calcareous soils. The flower colour varies; although usually salmon pink it may be white, yellow, purple or dark red. The folded lower lip is the best way to tell it from the other marsh orchids. The southern marsh orchid is slightly taller and is locally common in southern and central England and in south Wales. The darker lanceolate leaves are also unmarked. The rosy purple flowers can be distinguished from the early marsh orchid, as the petals have unfolded sides. North of a line from the Humber to South Wales, the marshes are home to the northern marsh orchid. Its flowers are deep purple and have a tapering spur.

FLOWERING RUSH *(Butomus umbellatus)*

SIZE:	Up to 150 cm tall
HABITAT:	At the edge of fresh water, still or slow moving
IDENTIFICATION:	Three-angled, long leaves, clusters of pink flowers in July and August
SIMILAR SPECIES:	None

No chapter on aquatic or semi-aquatic plants would be complete without the inclusion of this handsome plant. It is not a true rush and has no close relations, but the long, slender leaves are rush-like and it favours similar growing conditions. Close examination shows that the grey–green leaves are an unusual shape, triangular in cross-section. However, it is the magnificent clusters of bright pink flowers that are so impressive. Each stem carries a single cluster of flowers, but several stems of different lengths are likely to emerge from each plant. The pink flowers with their dark veins are followed by egg-shaped fruits, which eventually turn a purplish-brown as they ripen. The flowering rush is common is central and southern England, but scarce in Wales and not found in Scotland.

MEADOWSWEET *(Filipendula ulmaria)*

SIZE:	Up to 1.25 m tall
HABITAT:	Fens, marshes and damp woods and stream margins
IDENTIFICATION:	Reddish stems, toothed leaves, silver on the underside. Sprays of creamy flowers from June to September
SIMILAR SPECIES:	Dropwort

A tall, distinctive plant, widespread and frequently abundant in the damp conditions it favours. The frothy flowers are fragrant, but the crushed leaves have a sharper smell. This led to one of its many common names, courtship-and-matrimony, referring to the difference before and after crushing, i.e. before and after the wedding. Another local name, sweet hay, was given because, when the plant is cut and dried, both parts smell of newly cut hay. For this reason, it was commonly used as a strewing herb to cover floors in Elizabethan times. The dried leaves were also used to flavour beverages such as mead, port and claret. Dropwort is a similar but less showy plant, growing on dry grassland on chalk or limestone.

BOG ASPHODEL *(Narthecium ossifragum)*

SIZE:	5–40 cm
HABITAT:	Bogs, wet heaths and mountain areas
IDENTIFICATION:	Sword-shaped leaves, spikes of yellow flowers from July to September
SIMILAR SPECIES:	Yellow star of Bethlehem

This distinctive plant likes peaty bogs and heaths or mountainous areas with acid soil. In areas where most wild flowers are low growing, the upright, orange–yellow flower spikes demand attention during the summer months. Look very closely at one of the flowers and you will see what looks like a tiny daffodil, a plant to which this is distantly related. After flowering, the stems and capsules turn a deeper reddish-orange. In Lancashire, the plant is known as maiden hair because country women used a dye made from the yellow flowers to colour their hair. Bog asphodel has been found at altitudes up to 900 m as well as being common on lowland wet heaths. It is absent from central and eastern England. In these areas you are more likely to come across the flowering yellow star of Bethlehem as it prefers chalky soils.

COMMON DUCKWEED (Lemna minor)

SIZE:	Up to 5 mm across
HABITAT:	Ponds and lakes
IDENTIFICATION:	Floating green leaf-like fronds covering large patches of water
SIMILAR SPECIES:	Ivy-leafed duckweed

Ponds, lakes and other areas of still water can be seen covered with a green blanket of tiny floating plants, especially in summer. This is common duckweed, so named because it forms a valuable part of the diet for wild ducks, swans and other water birds. Thanks to its high protein content, it could also prove viable to harvest for domestic animal fodder. It is already being cultivated as a water treatment medium, as duckweed acts as a bio-filter by feeding on organic waste. In order to keep children away from the dangers of ponds, parents used to tell them fairy stories about 'Jenny-green-teeth', an underwater goblin waiting for them beneath the duckweed. Flowers rarely appear; the duckweeds usually reproduce by forming buds and dividing.

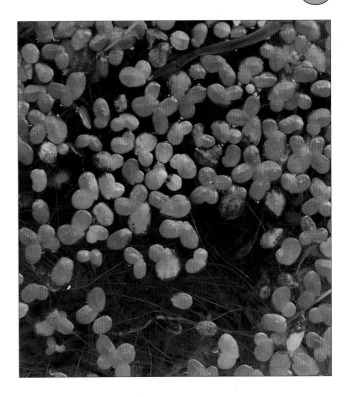

WATERCRESS (Nasturtium officinale)

SIZE:	10–40 cm high
HABITAT:	Streams, shallow ponds and wet mud
IDENTIFICATION:	Dark green pinnate leaves turning bronze in cold weather. Loose clusters of small white flowers from June to October
SIMILAR SPECIES:	Fool's watercress

The bunch of dark green watercress in the supermarket might have been commercially grown but it is probably no different from the wild variety. Unchanged by cultivation only the original and one hybrid are produced. The Latin name, from nasitortium meaning nose twisting, and the Yorkshire name of 'tang tongue' reflect its peppery taste. Unusually, it's not the young leaves that provide the best flavour but the sturdier, older shoots with dark, slightly burnished leaves. Rich in vitamins and minerals especially iron, this leafy member of the cabbage family makes wonderful tangy soups and salads alone or mixed with oranges and nuts. For culinary use, watercress should not be picked from streams flowing through pasture land or from stagnant water as the hollow stems could contain the eggs of liver fluke. This parasite destroys the liver of sheep and is quite at home in humans.

HEMLOCK *(Conium maculata)*

SIZE: Up to 2 m high

HABITAT: By streams, ditches and on waste ground

IDENTIFICATION: Purple-spotted stems with finely divided leaves. Umbrella shaped clusters of white flowers in June and July

SIMILAR SPECIES: Hogweed, sweet cicely, cow parsley

Many of the white umbellifers are loosely called hemlock but this true variety is best avoided as it one of Britain's most poisonous plants. The Greek philosopher Socrates was found guilty of 'neglect of the gods' and 'corruption of the young' and sentenced to death by drinking a cup of hemlock juice. All parts of the plant are poisonous and the witches' brew in Shakespeare's Macbeth contained a root of hemlock. In modern times children have been known to die after using the stout, smooth stems to make whistles or pea shooters. If any part of the plant is bruised, it gives off an offensive mousy smell which is helpful in distinguishing it from hogweed or other similar species. The hogweeds, particularly giant hogweed, contain substances which can irritate or blister the skin but are unlikely to prove fatal.

ROUND-LEAVED SUNDEW

(Drosera rotundifolia)

SIZE: 5-25 cm tall

HABITAT: Bogs, wet heaths and moors

IDENTIFICATION: Round, hairy leaves, curving flower spike of white flowers from June to August

SIMILAR SPECIES: Great sundew, Oblong-leaved sundew

Anyone who has spent any time outdoors in Scotland during August will tell you that there are not enough sundews. These fascinating plants feed on insects and are reputed to consume up to 2000 midges each during the summer. The round-leaved sundew is the most widespread of the three, flourishing on nutrient-poor, acid soils, making up the deficiency from the insects it devours. The round-bladed leaves are covered with red hairs, each with a drop of sticky fluid looking like dew. The midges land, thinking these drops are water, and are then trapped. Great sundew and oblong-leaved sundew have elongated leaves, and are found mainly in the north. The distinguishing feature for oblong-leaved sundew is the flowering stem coming from beneath the basal rosette rather than up from the centre.

MOORHEN *(Gallinula chloropus)*

SIZE:	33 cm
HABITAT:	Widespread except in far N.W. Scotland. All freshwater environments
IDENTIFICATION:	Mostly dark brown and black with red bill base and forehead, white undertail
SIMILAR SPECIES:	Coot

The moorhen is a creature of surprisingly volatile temperament. Most of the time it skulks about in the reeds and waterside vegetation, eager to keep out of sight and rarely venturing into the open. When threatened, it will sometimes submerge itself until only its bill is above water. At breeding time, however, it becomes extremely aggressive towards intruders near the nest, slashing with toes and pecking violently, and pairs can even be pretty rough with each other during their otherwise quite elegantly expressive mating displays. Birds often return each year to a favourite nesting place where they build up a platform or raft of dried plants. For a water bird, the moorhen is a particularly bad swimmer, having no webbing between its toes, and its rocking, rolling technique gives it a comic appearance.

COOT *(Fulica atra)*

SIZE:	38 cm
HABITAT:	Widespread except in N.W. Scotland. All freshwater
IDENTIFICATION:	All black plumage with white bill and frontal shield. Stubby body with large feet and lobed toes
SIMILAR SPECIES:	Moorhen

The coot is easily differentiated from the moorhen by the colour of its bill and forehead. In all other respects it is very similar, even down to its aggressiveness at mating and nesting times. The two birds are often seen together on the same stretch of water but the coots, with lobed toes allowing more efficient paddling, will venture further out in large groups, leaving the moorhens to lurk at the edges. The coot is an energetic but clumsy diver, submersing itself with a jump and splash and then bobbing back up all tumblewise, often tail first. This could be the origin of the phrase 'as crazy as a coot', although it could also have sprung from the bird's often unprovoked flurrying attacks on fellow coots. In Horsey, Norfolk there is a traditional Coot Custard Fair at which sweets made of coots' and gulls' eggs are sold.

DIPPER *(Cinclus cinclus)*

SIZE: 18 cm

HABITAT: Widespread but infrequent in Scotland, Wales, N. and W. England. Near fast-flowing rivers and streams

IDENTIFICATION: Dark upper parts, white throat and chest, faint reddish 'waistband'. Dumpy with short tail, relatively long legs and large feet

SIMILAR SPECIES: None

It is alarming to watch a dipper at work: one moment this perky little bird, like a huge wren, is bobbing about on a rock beside a powerful river and the next it has launched itself into, and under, the water. You might think it doomed, but it is actually walking on the riverbed, hunting aquatic insects. It sometimes performs this trick from the air, diving from one of its low, darting flights. It nests in rocky banks, behind waterfalls or on bridges and walls. In winter it moves to lower altitudes and is seen at weirs, slower-moving parts of streams and lakeshores. The British race *gularis* has a strongly chestnut 'waistband' but, in the darker brown *hibernicus* from Ireland, Outer Hebrides and western Scotland, the waistband is duller and less extensive. The Scandinavian Black-bellied race *C.c.cinclus* overwinters on the east coast.

KINGFISHER *(Alcedo atthis)* ▶

SIZE: 16.5 cm

HABITAT: Widespread as far as S. Scotland. Rivers and lakes

IDENTIFICATION: Distinctive. Iridescent blue–green above, orange–chestnut below. Large head, white throat and cheeks, dark eyestripe. Long bill

SIMILAR SPECIES: None

Fishermen are just as likely to brag about having seen a kingfisher as about the size of their catch. It is a very elusive little bird, the usual sighting being just a flash of iridescent colour as it dashes past along the bank. It fishes by perching above the water and diving to snatch fish, tadpoles, insects and molluscs on, or beneath, the surface. Where there are no perches it will hover before diving. It stays in Britain all year, so when the rivers and lakes freeze over it is at risk and might move to coastal rock pools for sustenance. It also dives to clean itself when digging the burrow in which it builds its nest. The burrow entrance is usually in the bank of a slow stream. Dead kingfishers, hung outside houses, were thought to ward off lightning and, put among stored clothes, they actually did keep away moths.

SWANS

The swan has been a royal bird since ancient times and many myths and legends surround it, particularly those involving beautiful 'swan maidens' who took on human form and married or fell in love but tragically reverted and flew away when accidentally touched by iron.

Britain's royal, and fairy-tale, swan is the **mute swan** (*Cygnus olor*), (*pictured overleaf*) present all year and widespread except in the very far north-west of Scotland. It is mute in that it doesn't hoot but it does hiss and grunt when angry – quite common during the breeding season. It is large (152 cm) and an irate adult should be avoided: if one puffs itself up, pushes out its chest and paddles rapidly towards you, it is time to go. The mute is distinguished from the other two British swans by its long curved neck and orange bill with a pronounced black knob at its base.

The swan was once a prized table bird and many were semi-domesticated. It was given Royal status in the 12th century, and any escaped bird became crown property. Later Henry VI made it an offence punishable by imprisonment for a year and a day (plus a

ine) to steal a swan's egg. To this day all the mute swans on the River Thames between London Bridge and Henley belong to the Crown or to one of two London livery companies. Each year, in the Swan Upping ceremony, the cygnets along this entire stretch of water are gathered and those belonging to the companies are marked with bill notches.

Discarded lead fishing weights, which mute swans ingested as they grazed riverbottom and bankside plants, led to widespread poisoning which severely depleted the population until lead weights were banned in 1987.

A mute swan in flight is a beautiful spectacle with its outstretched neck and powerful wing beats, each beat producing a twanging, thrumming sound as the flight feathers vibrate.

The **whooper swan** (*C. cygnus*) is, like the Bewick's, a Siberian-breeding winter visitor to northern Britain but a few nest in Scotland, particularly in the Outer Hebrides. It is the same size as the mute but has a shorter neck. It has a broad black bill with

a large yellow patch covering the back half. The rising, double-noted, musical call, which gives the whooper its name, made it the subject of many folk tales about people falling under the spell of the mournful sound and might be the basis of the legend that swans sing before they die. Unlike the mute swan, it makes no wing noise when flying.

The **Bewick's swan** (*C. bewickii* is the smallest and most truly wild, steering clear of human beings far more than the other two. It grows to 120 cm and has a much shorter, goose-like neck. Its black bill has a smaller, less jagged yellow patch than the whooper's. Although it comes further south than the whooper, it is found only at a few coastal sites, principally around the Wash and the Severn Estuary where individual birds (identifiable by their distinctive bill patterns) have been studied over many years at Slimbridge Wildfowl Trust. One alarming outcome of this close study is that, despite being protected, more than a third of the Slimbridge Bewick's have been found to be carrying shotgun pellets.

GREY HERON *(Ardea cinerea)*

SIZE: 90 cm

HABITAT: Very widespread and numerous on all waters

IDENTIFICATION: Distinctive, large, long-necked. Grey with long yellow–orange bill, long legs and big wingspan. Harsh, crawking call. In flight neck drawn back, wings arched

SIMILAR SPECIES: Little egret (rare summer visitor),
White stork (rare stray)

The grey heron is a wildlife photographer's dream, standing still for minutes at a time while it patiently waits for a fish or eel to venture into the water at its feet. Sometimes it wades incredibly slowly, hardly stirring the surface, but when it strikes it does so with lightning speed and grasps the prey in its long bill. Captured eels will writhe themselves around its head before it manages to gobble them down in one piece. The heron was once quarry itself. It was deemed great sport to hunt it with hawks, although it earned a reputation as a coward for flying high and avoiding the fight. Those killed were often served at the table. Like the kingfisher, the heron suffers in harsh winters when the waters freeze over. It makes a huge nest which it returns to year after year, adding material until it grows 2 m or more across.

TUFTED DUCK *(Aythya fuligula)*

SIZE: 43 cm

HABITAT: Widespread on freshwater throughout Britain. Present all year but some winter migrants visit western areas

IDENTIFICATION: Male with dark upper parts, glossy purple head and pure white flanks; female brownish all over with lighter belly. Both with 'pigtail' tufts on head and golden eyes

SIMILAR SPECIES: Scaup (female), Pochard (female)

In just over 150 years the tufted duck has gone from the first record of breeding in Britain to its present status as our most common diving duck, with up to 8000 nesting pairs. It is an impressive ecological success story and one brought about largely because of human reshaping of the landscape. Abandoned gravel pits, reservoirs and ornamental lakes have helped this pretty little duck to thrive. Another boost for it was the introduction from Russia, and rapid spread of, the zebra mussel, a favourite food, along with fish, amphibians and insects. It has some colourful local names including magpie diver, black topping duck and blue-billed curre, this last probably echoing the purring noise it makes in flight or when alarmed. It can be distinguished from the pochard in flight by its longer, more pointed wings.

MALLARD *(Anas platyrhynchos)*

SIZE: 58 cm

HABITAT: Extremely widespread on all waters

IDENTIFICATION: Male has green head, maroon breast, yellow bill, greyish body and black tail. Female dullish buff and brown, greenish-yellow bill and violet–blue wing patch

SIMILAR SPECIES: Shoveler, Pintail

The mallard is the archetypal duck. This, the largest surface-feeding duck in Britain, is everywhere: dabbling about on brook and pond, river and lake. The town mallard is tame and will take bread from your fingers; the wild one will be away before you get within 100 m – it has been shot at more often. It was once known simply as the wild duck, and it was only the male that was called a mallard (derived via Old French from the Latin *masculus*, meaning 'male', and the Old High German *hart*, meaning 'hardy' or 'bold'). The bold male has a reputation for uninhibited courtship, with several males hotly pursuing the same female before engaging in spirited mating. Where there are too many drakes chasing too few ducks, this mating frenzy can end in the duck's death. It is the female that makes the typical 'quacking' noise.

POCHARD *(Aythya ferina)*

SIZE:	45 cm
HABITAT:	Widespread on lakes, ponds, reservoirs, gravel pits; joined in winter by migrants
IDENTIFICATION:	Male with red head, red eye, black breast, grey back and dark tail; female dull brown with pale face, back and flank markings
SIMILAR SPECIES:	Tufted duck (female), Scaup (female)

The pochard breeds in Britain in relatively small numbers, and the huge flocks we see on inland waters in the winter are composed mostly of migrants. Those that do nest choose their site very carefully so that they have food nearby and not too deep – they only dive to a maximum of 2.5 m. They eat worms, insects, leaves, molluscs, crustaceans, seeds and leaves which they glean from the bottom of stretches of open water where there are no floating plants. The male has a courtship ritual in which he throws his head back and makes a wheezing noise, and his already vivid red eye becomes even redder when he is sexually aroused. The name, which can be pronounced 'potchard', 'poachard' or 'pockard', possibly came from the Old French *pocher*, meaning to poke about, referring to the bird's feeding manner.

TEAL *(Anas crecca)*

SIZE:	36 cm
HABITAT:	Widespread but thinly distributed on freshwater all year with many winter migrants and passage birds
IDENTIFICATION:	Male with chestnut head, green eye mask edged in white, dappled breast and white belly; grey wings with green patch; white tail with yellow patch edged in black. Female dappled brown with black-and-green wing patch
SIMILAR SPECIES:	Wigeon, Gadwall, Garganey

This is our smallest duck and a very attractive one too, particularly the male, which shows off its brilliant head and tail colours in a dashing courtship display. However, even when its numbers are at their highest during the winter, it is difficult to see the teal close up because, as a quarry for hunters, it is extremely wary. Shooters probably like it because it is small, agile and fast, making it a challenging target. It shows this agility when alarmed, springing vertically into the air and beating its wings rapidly to get up quick speed. The collective name is a spring of teal – a perfect description. The male has a distinctive and melodious, bell-like call, which echoes out over the wintry marshes. Unfortunately, numbers are on the decline.

WIGEON *(Anas penelope)*

SIZE:	46 cm
HABITAT:	Widespread on shallow, still freshwater and coastal marshes all year, boosted by winter migrants
IDENTIFICATION:	Male grey above, white belly, chestnut-brown head with cream crown, white and green wing patches in flight. Female light brown with grey wings in flight
SIMILAR SPECIES:	Teal, Gadwall, Garganey

The wigeon is an oddity in having changed its habitat and feeding patterns over the past 70–80 years. It used to be almost exclusively a coastal duck, seen roosting in large rafts just offshore and coming ashore to feed on *Zostera* grass (sometimes called wigeon grass). *Zostera* was hit by disease in the 1930s and 1970s and the wigeon had to adapt, coming inland to graze, just like geese, on other plants and then moving on to freshwater lakes and reservoirs. They are still found in the coastal marshes where they are a favourite target for wildfowlers. The male wigeon makes a musical high whistling call, while the female has only a purring growl. Breeding occurs only in Scotland and northern England.

GREBE FAMILY

The **little grebe** *(Tachybaptus ruficolis)*, 25–30 cm, is ubiquitous and numerous on still or slow-moving fresh water, all year round. *Tachybaptus* comes from the Greek meaning 'rapid dipper' and that describes the little grebe, or dabchick, perfectly. It is forever submerging, and some of its colloquial names echo the 'plip-plop' of its plunge: divedapper, divedop, dobchick and doucker, and so on. It is a shy bird and keeps a very low profile – sometimes literally, by sinking itself in the water until only its head and upper neck show. It is mostly grey–brown and in summer has a distinctive red neck and a little upturned pale patch at the corner of its bill, which gives it an enigmatic smile.

The largest and only other year-round resident in the family is the **great crested grebe** *(Podiceps cristatus)*, 48 cm. Found everywhere except north-west Scotland on shallow lakes and ponds, it was almost wiped out in the mid-1800s through the demand for its feathers, which had become fashionable. Just a few dozen pairs remained when the *Birds Protection Act* took it under its wing and recolonisation was able to start. It has an elaborate courting display in which both birds rise breast-to-breast in the water, shaking their heads and presenting bits of vegetation to each other. The breeding plumage shows a prominent dark double crest, a neck ruff and a white face with ruddy ear coverts. The chicks have bold zebra markings and are often carried by the parents.

The **red-necked grebe** *(P. grisegena)*, 43 cm, is a winter visitor to eastern coasts and inland waters, not easily distinguished from the great crested. However, it prefers smaller, shallower waters with more surface vegetation.

The breeding plumage of the **Slavonian grebe** *(P. auritus)*, 33 cm, is the brightest of them all: a black head with horn-like golden tufts, grey–brown upper parts and chestnut neck and flanks. Only about 650 individuals are scattered around British coasts in winter and about 70 pairs breed in the Highland and Grampian regions of Scotland.

The **black-necked grebe** *(P. nigricollis)*, 30 cm, is unusual in preferring enclosed pools with plenty of vegetation in and around the water. These are not common in Britain, so it winters in a few sites around the south coast and the Midlands and manages to breed in just a handful of Scottish lochans. It has a black head, neck and back, rufous flanks and a dramatic golden ear tuft.

great crested grebe

little grebe

OTHER WILDFOWL

There are not many **ruddy ducks** (*Oxyura jamaicensis*), 40 cm, in Britain but they are causing a huge uproar. This American bird was introduced at the Wildfowl and Wetlands Trust, Slimbridge, in the 1940s. Some escaped in 1952 and the attractive freshwater diving duck, with its distinctive upright tail, colourful plumage and bright blue bill, spread across Europe. However, it mated with the endangered white-headed duck in Spain, resulting in a hybrid which some conservation groups did not like. The suggested remedy was a cull of all ruddy ducks, and trial shootings took place in Britain in 1993 and 1994. Sadly, some birds died in protracted agony, so the Government cancelled plans for a cull. In 1997, the Bern Convention ordered the Government to cull all 4000 British ruddy ducks 'to protect European wildlife and habitats'. In 1999, trial shootings began in Anglesey, the Midlands and Scotland. By the end of 2001, half had been killed and it was estimated that complete eradication would take 10 years. See them while you can.

The **goldeneye** (*Bucephala clangula*), 45 cm, is a widespread and numerous winter visitor, which bred for the first time in Britain in 1970 on a Scottish loch. There are now several hundred nesting pairs. The male is a striking black-and-white with a distinctive green-sheened head, high forehead and white cheek spots. The female's head is the same shape but brown and lacking the spot, and her plumage is brown-and-white.

Huge flocks of overwintering **pintails** (*Anas acuta*), below, 55 cm, gather over stretches of inland water, but this elegant bird is Britain's rarest breeding dabbling duck with perhaps only 50 or so nesting pairs. The male has a chocolate-and-white patterned head, black-and-yellow undertail and long, dark tail feathers. The female is mottled pale brown.

The huge, wide bill of the **shoveler** (*Anas clypeata*) 50 cm, distinguishes it from all other wildfowl. The shoveler is present all year, widespread but patchy, and numbers are boosted by winter migrants. The spade-like bill has hundreds of little 'teeth', which filter food out of the water. The male has a green head, white breast and chestnut belly while the female is mottled brown with a light blue wing patch.

The **red-breasted merganser** (*Mergus serrator*) and the **goosander** (*M. merganser*), 55–65 cm, both have a reputation as fish stock predators. The merganser, with its distinctive crest, is present all year in Scotland and north-west England, where it is reviled for taking young salmon and trout in rivers. It is present inland but spends most of the winter near estuaries, where it steals from salmon farms if it can. The goosander, more of an inland bird, is persecuted for attacking trout farms. It first nested in 1871 in Scotland and has since spread across the whole of Britain. The males of both species have dark green heads; the females brownish heads. All have a narrow orange–red bill. The male goosander is mostly white; the merganser red–brown breasted and greyish white.

ruddy duck

pintail

BLACK-THROATED DIVER
(Gavia arctica)

SIZE:	58–68 cm
HABITAT:	Freshwater lochs in Scotland in summer; coasts around Britain in winter
IDENTIFICATION:	Breeding plumage: grey head, black-and-white upper parts, pale belly. Winter plumage: grey upper parts sharply distinct from pale neck and belly. Red–orange eye
SIMILAR SPECIES:	Red-throated diver, Great northern diver

The black-throated diver has a reptilian look about it, especially in its summer plumage of black, grey and white checks and stripes. It sits on its mossy nest beside the dark, lapping waters of a Scottish loch looking like a prehistoric cross between a snake and a bird, coddling its olive-coloured eggs. When it throws out its haunting call to echo round the ancient hillsides, it sends shivers down the spine of many a hillwalker. In flight it makes a rapid 'quark-quark' which seems to come from nearby, even when the bird is almost too high to see. No wonder it and its fellow divers have generated so much folklore – they are spooky birds (see great northern diver, p.360). The red-throated diver *(Gavia stallata)* has almost the same range but breeds in greater numbers. It is distinguished by its lighter plumage, red throat and uptilted head carriage.

SNIPE *(Gallinago gallinago)*

SIZE:	27 cm
HABITAT:	Widespread all year in Britain near inland water. Some winter migrants
IDENTIFICATION:	Brownish with light and dark stripes along length of head, long legs and very long, straight bill
SIMILAR SPECIES:	Jack snipe

The Gaelic name for the snipe is *gabhar athair* – the 'goat of the air'. With its enormous bill it does not look like a goat but, in the early summer, it sounds like one. The courtship flight involves swooping dives in which the tail feathers are extended sideways to vibrate, making a swelling, bleating noise. When heard at night, which is not uncommon, there is no obvious source for this eerie sound which seems to surround the listener. The snipe's stripy camouflage is so good that, crouched in a ditch or puddle, it is almost trodden on by the walker before it erupts into its swerving escape flight, scraping out a raucous call. It uses its hugely long beak – a third of its total length – to probe for worms in the soft ground. The jack snipe *(Lymnocryptes minimus)* is a winter visitor and, as its name suggests, is smaller.

CURLEW (*Numenius arquata*)

SIZE:	55 cm
HABITAT:	Widespread on marshes, moors and mudflats all year. Some winter migrants
IDENTIFICATION:	Lightish, speckled brown plumage with distinctive, long down-curved bill
SIMILAR SPECIES:	Whimbrel

Although the curlew's name is an imitation of its call, no official notation can accurately mimic the plaintive wail. One local name, courlie, from Sussex, comes closest if the first syllable is dwelt on and rolled low and the second snapped off high. It is a melancholy sound that makes cold, dank marshes seem even more desolate. The male's courting song, delivered on the wing, is a richer, friendlier noise. This is Europe's largest wader, but it does not spend all its time on the shoreline; it also feeds inland, tweaking out worms and snails with its long bill. It also eats small frogs, crabs, shrimps and, on the mudflats, cockles. The rarer whimbrel (*N. phaeopus*) is darker with a shorter bill and a striped crown. It visits between May and September and a few breed.

BLACK-TAILED GODWIT
(*Limosa lapponica*)

SIZE:	38 cm
HABITAT:	All round the British coastline in winter. A few summer visitors
IDENTIFICATION:	Winter plumage greyish with streaks, paler beneath. Typical wader's legs and long bill. Summer plumage with russet under parts
SIMILAR SPECIES:	Bar-tailed godwit

Both godwits are apparently wonderful to eat, although it is unlikely that they end up on tables nowadays – particularly the black-tailed, which has only recently recovered after being down to just four breeding pairs in the 1950s. Sir Thomas Browne, in his *Notes and Letters on the Natural History of Norfolk* (1662–8) said 'godwyts…were accounted the daintiest dish in England and…for the bignesse, of the biggest price'. The bar-tailed godwit does not breed in Britain, but some non-breeding birds stay all summer and many all winter. Big flocks march about the mudflats digging out crabs, sandhoppers and worms with their long bills. Black-tailed godwits have a prominent white wing bar as well as a solid black, rather than barred, tail. They are both very noisy, and several local names refer to this: shrieker, barker, whelp, and so on.

WATER RAIL *(Rallus aquaticus)*

SIZE: 28 cm

HABITAT: Widespread near fresh water all year except in far N.W. Scotland. Some winter visitors. Migrants sometimes near built-up areas

IDENTIFICATION: Very marked brown upper parts, grey beneath with striped flanks and long red bill. Long legs, very large feet. 'Cowering' gait

SIMILAR SPECIES: Spotted crake (rare visitor), Corncrake

All crakes and rails are elusive and prefer to creep away rather than fly when disturbed, but the water rail is the champion skulker. It has huge feet for its size and they pad quickly and softly through mud and rushes carrying the crouching bird to safety. Many of the local names allude to this scuttling getaway: brook runner, skitty, skitty coot and grey skit, among several. Its long bill leads a way through the close-packed reeds, which scarcely part for its narrow body, and it leaves no track to guide predators to its nest. The spotted crake *(Porzana porzana)* was probably common in Britain 250 years ago before large areas were drained for agriculture. Now its rare April–December presence is confirmed by its distinctive, loud, whipcrack call among the marshland reeds. It looks like the water rail but has a very short bill.

BITTERN *(Botaurus stellaris)*

SIZE:	76 cm
HABITAT:	A few present all year in East Anglia fens and on Lancashire coast. Some winter visitors in S.E. England
IDENTIFICATION:	Like a heron but slightly smaller with shorter neck, dark-streaked brown plumage, long green legs and medium-length sharp bill
SIMILAR SPECIES:	Little bittern (rare summer visitor)

There are local names for the bittern in almost all parts of Britain, indicating how widespread it must once have been. Two things led to its eventual disappearance as a breeding bird: loss of its habitat and the flavour of its meat. It favours the sort of reedy fens that have been drained in their hundreds of square miles to make arable land over the past couple of centuries. On top of this came the shooting: in the early 1800s this shy and fascinating bird was thought to be a delicacy and was stalked in special bittern-shooting parties. By the late 1800s it was extinct as a breeding bird. Continental birds recolonised early in the last century but found it a struggle, and now just a handful breed in East Anglia and Lancashire. The resonant 'boom' of the male's mating call, carrying up to a mile, is now a rare sound.

ROCK PIPIT *(Anthus spinoletta)*

SIZE:	16–17 cm
HABITAT:	All round British coastline and just inland by water meadows, reservoirs, sewage farms. Present all year
IDENTIFICATION:	Larger than tree and meadow pipits. Very streaked breast, dark olive brown upper parts. Soles of feet orange. Grey lines along edges of tail
SIMILAR SPECIES:	Water pipit, Tree pipit, Meadow pipit

The rock pipit is essentially a bird of the seashore, darting about among the boulders and seaweed, but it can also be found near stretches of still water inland, especially in winter. The water pipit is the mountain race of rock pipit as it lives beside streams and lakes. In Orkney the rock pipit is known as the tangle sparrow: it spends a great deal of time picking about among the rotting tangle, or oarweed, looking for insects and vegetable matter to eat. Kelp flies are a favourite food, along with ants, beetles and larvae. Like the other pipits it has an impressive song flight (see Meadow pipit p.133). The water pipit breeds in Europe and is mostly seen in Britain as a winter migrant, frequenting watercress beds. The name pipit is echoic of the bird's call note, coming from the Latin *pipio*, meaning chirper.

GREY WAGTAIL *(Motacilla cinerea)*

SIZE: 18 cm

HABITAT: Widespread throughout Britain all year, mostly in uplands by fast-moving water

IDENTIFICATION: Male grey above, yellow below with black throat, white eye stripe, yellow rump and long dark tail; female duller without black throat. Constant bobbing motion

SIMILAR SPECIES: Yellow wagtail, Pied wagtail

Like the other wagtails, this dapper little bird is almost tiring to watch with its constant, frenetic bobbing and ducking, dashing about and flitting into the air – always on the move. It is as if it cannot decide what to do next and just turns towards whatever catches its eye at the time. It often feeds over water, taking insects like mayflies or small dragonflies in flight with quick little hovering darts. It is very susceptible to severe cold weather and many birds move into towns or further south or even across to the Continent for the winter, returning in the spring. All the wagtails have rural names including the words 'wash' or washer'. These refer back to the days when country women used to go down to the water's edge to wash clothes or dishes, scrubbing with an up-and-down motion mirrored by the bobbing of the wagtails.

SAND MARTIN (*Riparia riparia*)

SIZE: 12 cm

HABITAT: Widespread summer visitor, nesting in sandbanks, quarry faces, riverbanks, soft cliffs, railway cuttings, etc. Uncommon in N. Scotland

IDENTIFICATION: Smaller than house martin, all brown above, white below with distinctive brown band across white breast

SIMILAR SPECIES: House martin

If you come across a high riverbank peppered with holes, as if blasted by a giant shotgun, you are most probably looking at a sand martin colony. These busy little birds share their tunnelling skills with kingfishers, digging in horizontally for up to 90 cm before widening out a gallery at the end for a nesting chamber. They will nest in just about any vertical or semi-vertical face of soft enough material. Artificial features such as road and rail cuttings, quarries and other excavations give them more choice as the years go by. Traditionally, any quarrymen who find martins' nests will leave them alone until the young have flown, even if this means delays as, in the same way as it is lucky to have house martins nesting under the eaves of your house, it is deemed good luck to have them at your place of work.

MARSH HARRIER (*Circus aeruginosus*)

SIZE: Wingspan 110–125 cm

HABITAT: Wetlands, particularly reedbeds, in East Anglia. Seen migrating elsewhere

IDENTIFICATION: Male reddish-brown with blue–grey head and long grey, unbarred tail; female dark brown with pale shoulders, pale head with dark eye stripe. Long wings and long tail

SIMILAR SPECIES: Hen harrier, Montagu's harrier (both much lighter colour)

Like most birds of prey, the large, powerful marsh harrier was itself harried by human beings, almost to extinction as a British breeding bird. Between 1960 and 1973 just a handful of chicks were raised in Suffolk and Norfolk. However, with protection and the withdrawal of organochlorine pesticides, there was a remarkable recovery, and it now breeds in much larger numbers in the reserves at Minsmere, Titchwell and Cley on the E. Anglian coast. About 250 young are raised each year, mostly in reedbeds but also in arable crops. During incubation and while the female tends the young, her partner provides food in spectacular aerial food passes, as 'rehearsed' in the display ritual. As the cock approaches the nest, the hen rises and flies at him from below, turns upside down and catches the prey – a small mammal or duck – as he drops it. In high wind the pass is made claw-to-claw.

OSPREY *(Pandion haliaetus)*

SIZE: Wingspan 145–160 cm

HABITAT: Summer visitor to sites in Scotland and the Lake District where forests are near large lakes and rivers

IDENTIFICATION: Dark brown above with white under parts, slightly speckled breast, crested head with dark eye streak. In flight rather like huge gull

SIMILAR SPECIES: No other bird of prey very similar

The osprey is so popular that enthusiasts can monitor a nest in Loch Garten, Inverness-shire, on 24-hour webcam during the breeding season. Millions of people have visited the two Scottish nest sites in person and, in 2001, the first wild pair to breed in England for 150 years were seen by more than 25,000 people from a viewpoint above Bassenthwaite Lake near Keswick in the Lake District. The osprey, which winters in Africa, was made extinct as a British breeding bird by the guns and poison of gamekeepers and river bailiffs, who objected to its taking trout and salmon. After an absence of 50 years a few osprey returned to Scotland and, in 1959, the first chicks were raised. Conservation groups now erect partially built nests in the tops of trees and on electricity poles, and the birds add twigs and branches to these each year to create huge structures. A constant guard has to be kept against egg thieves. The osprey's fishing technique is breathtaking: it climbs high over the water where it can spot the fish, preferably near the surface, then makes a spectacular dive, plunging feet first, sometimes right under, to grasp the prey in its talons. It then carries the fish, anything up to 2 kg, back to its nest.

Pond Skater *(Gerris lacustris)*

Size:	8–10 mm
Habitat:	Ponds and lakes
Identification:	Slender brown body with short front legs and long mid and hind legs
Similar species:	Water measurer

There are no prizes for guessing how this bug got its name. It skims over the surface of the water, supporting its body on the tips of its legs, looking as if it is skating on ice. The middle legs are used as oars and the hind legs as rudders. It preys on insects that have fallen into the water, seeing them or detecting their distress movements as they start to drown, and it uses its shorter front legs to grab hold of them. The adults winter in sheltered places away from the water, returning in the spring ready to lay eggs in May. The water measurer *(Hydrometra stagnorum)* is a longer and thinner bug, which also walks on the surface of the water and is commonly found wandering among the vegetation on the edge of the pond. It is on the stems of plants at water level that the female lays her long narrow eggs.

WATER BOATMAN *(Notonecta glauca)*

SIZE:	14 mm
HABITAT:	Ponds and lakes throughout the British Isles
IDENTIFICATION:	Brown with darker markings, large eyes and long, fringed hind legs
SIMILAR SPECIES:	Lesser water boatman

If you have ever seen what looks like a bug rowing itself across a pond, it is almost certainly a water boatman. It swims upside down, suspended just under the water by the surface tension and using its powerful, fringed hind legs as paddles. It is an energetic swimmer and an aggressive hunter, diving after tadpoles and beetle larvae and has even been reported to attack fish. Its large eyes help it to see prey and it also detects vibrations in the water. In trout hatcheries it has been known to reduce the number of fry considerably. The smaller, lesser water boatman swims the right way up, so is easy to differentiate. It does not hunt, but uses its flat hairy forelegs as a sieve to catch passing food, whether of plant or animal origin. Males stridulate or 'sing' in a similar way to crickets.

WHIRLIGIG BEETLE *(Gyrinus marinus)*

SIZE:	3–6 mm
HABITAT:	Lakes, canals and other slow moving water
IDENTIFICATION:	Small black oval body with short stubby legs
SIMILAR SPECIES:	Hairy whirligig beetle

The whirligig beetle has eyes in the back of its head – or eyes in the front of its head, depending on whether you are a human observing it from above or potential prey trying to sneak away underwater. In any event, it has two pairs of eyes, one adapted to see above water and one below. It also uses antennae to detect ripples, which could mean an insect or an obstacle in its path. The long slender front legs are used to gather prey and the rear paddle-like legs act as oars. The whirligig beetle usually congregates in groups, gyrating around each other and making a wake of ripples as they whirl. Active from spring to autumn, it swims along the surface of the water, half-submerged and will rapidly dive if disturbed. Eggs are laid underwater on submerged plants and the larvae do not come to the surface until almost fully grown.

EMPEROR DRAGONFLY
(Anax imperator)

SIZE:	78 mm body length
HABITAT:	Around ponds, lakes and canals
IDENTIFICATION:	Large dragonfly, male's abdomen is sky blue and the females a greenish-blue, both have a black stripe running down the length of their back.
SIMILAR SPECIES:	Common aeshna

It seems strange that a creature as beautiful and ethereal as the dragonfly should be surrounded by so much folklore associating it with the devil. It has about 70 common names in Britain, 'devil's darning needle' being one of them. The conception varies from country to country: in Japan it is a symbol of courage, success, strength and happiness. The emperor is Britain's largest dragonfly having a wingspan of nearly 100 mm. It is confined to south-east England, and is seen from June to September hunting over water and swooping down on its prey. The male is a perfect gentleman, supporting the female as she lays her eggs in the water then helping her up into the air again. The acid waters of heaths and moors in the north and west are the home of the common aeshna, a colourful but slightly smaller species than the emperor dragonfly.

GREAT RED SEDGE (CADDIS FLY) *(Phryganea grandis)*

SIZE:	25 mm
HABITAT:	Lakes and slow moving rivers
IDENTIFICATION:	Marbled brown and buff coloured wings
SIMILAR SPECIES:	Several other sedge flies and caddis flies

Trout are said to be driven wild when the sedges are hatching, which is why the sedge or caddis fly is used for bait both in its adult and larval form. Many of the artificial flies used by fly fishermen have designs based on different species of caddis fly. With its 65 mm wingspan, the great red sedge is one of the largest caddis flies in Britain and can be seen on the wing from May to July. When at rest, it holds its velvety wings in a tented peak or roof-like shape over its back. The adult cannot feed, although it might sip nectar, whereas the larva is omnivorous and has been known to attack small fish. Eggs are laid in, or beside, the water, and the larva builds itself an extraordinary spiral-shaped protective case of leaves and other plant debris.

WATER SPIDER *(Argyroneta aquatica)*

SIZE: Up to 14 mm

HABITAT: Ponds, lakes, bogs and ditches

IDENTIFICATION: Dull velvety black when out of water

SIMILAR SPECIES: None

This is the only spider in the world to spend its life under water, despite breathing air and needing a supply of oxygen. It solves this problem by building itself a 'diving bell'. It spins a dome of silk large enough to live in, and attaches it to submerged plants. Periodically, it renews its air supply by surfacing, trapping air bubbles in its body hairs and taking them down to its lair. As it makes the trip back, the bubbles give it a silvery appearance. The eggs are laid inside the dome during the summer and, when the spiderling leaves home, it takes up temporary accommodation in an empty snail shell or something similar. This home must have an air supply which the young spider collects from the surface in the same way. This unique way of living makes it an impressive aquarium pet which seems to adapt well to captivity.

Jenkins' Spire Shell *(Potamopyrgus jenkinsi)*

SIZE: 4–6 mm high

HABITAT: Brackish water and freshwater rivers and streams throughout the British isles

IDENTIFICATION: Dark brown slender spiral shell

SIMILAR SPECIES: Mud snail

This remarkable little snail is a relative newcomer to Britain, and is thought to have been introduced via drinking water barrels in ships coming over from Australia in the middle of the 19th century. As it can survive brackish water, it would have been quite happy being released into the estuary of the River Thames. Since then, it has spread rapidly through rivers and canals and then through streams and ditches to become common throughout Britain from Shetland to the Isles of Scilly. In mainland Scotland it is rarely found inland, being usually confined to the coasts. In the early 1900s, it was reported to be choking up London's fresh water supply, but engineers overcame the problem by using filters. The mud snail is more likely to be found in ponds, although it is amphibious and also inhabits wet meadows and temporary ponds.

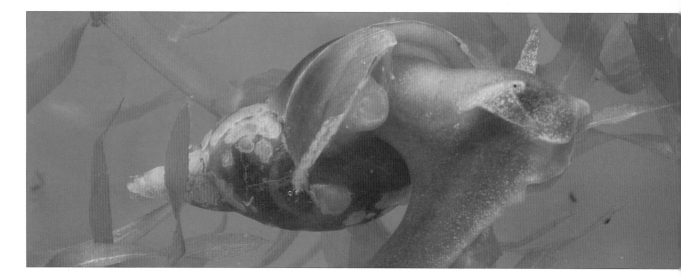

Great Pond Snail *(Limnaea stagnalis)*

SIZE: Up to 50 mm high

HABITAT: Ponds, lakes and canals throughout England and Wales, less common in Scotland

IDENTIFICATION: Brown conical shell

SIMILAR SPECIES: Wandering snail

The great pond snail is thought by some small boys to make an interesting pet, so is captured, taken home and watched for a while and then released or forgotten. If it has laid some eggs, these sausage-shaped gelatinous masses can be seen on the underside of waterweed leaves. After about a month, the young snails hatch and immediately rise to the surface for a supply of air. They grow quite rapidly at first but do not reach full size for about 2 years. In the wild, this snail prefers stagnant water and can sometimes be seen gliding along beneath the surface film, coming up for air from time to time. It feeds on algae and other vegetable or animal matter and has been known to attack live fish or newts.

RAMSHORN SNAIL *(Planorbis planorbis)*

SIZE: Shell size 18 mm diameter

HABITAT: Ponds, lakes and ditches

IDENTIFICATION: Pale brown flattened shell resembling a miniature ram's horn

SIMILAR SPECIES: Great ramshorn

The ramshorn snail is easily identified by the flattened shape of its shell which has a ridge or keel running round the widest part.

It also has the curious habit of carrying its shell to one side, almost upside down, when crawling on vegetation. This species prefers shallow water with plenty of weed and is common throughout lowland Britain. It is entirely herbivorous and grazes on algae or any tiny plant on the surface of rocks or larger water plants. It can tolerate almost stagnant water as its blood contains haemoglobin, so is more efficient at carrying oxygen than that of other pond snails. Sometimes known as trumpet snail, it is frequently kept in aquaria to rid the tanks of algae. The great ramshorn snail is larger – up to 25 mm across – and is a more local species, absent from some western areas and Scotland.

SMOOTH NEWT *(Triturus vulgaris)*

SIZE: 7–10 cm

HABITAT: Ponds and streams

IDENTIFICATION: Dull, yellowish-brown spotted body, cream and orange
                underbelly

SIMILAR SPECIES: Palmate newt

It is a pity that, according to Shakespeare at least, witches were so fond of putting newts into their evil brews, as they are now not so common as they used to be. Another reason, and the one favoured by scientists, is that their habitat is diminishing. The village pond is becoming a thing of the past and it is the garden pond that is now attracting the smooth newt. This is the commonest of our three newts and is widespread on the British mainland. During the breeding season, the male becomes brightly coloured with an undulating crest along the back. The eggs are laid singly and wrapped in a leaf of pondweed to conceal them before they hatch out into tadpoles called efts. The rarer palmate newt looks similar to the female smooth newt, but can be distinguished by the lack of spots on its throat and by its distinctive webbed feet.

RIVER LIMPET *(Ancylastrum fluviatilis)*

SIZE:	6–9 mm across
HABITAT:	Rivers, streams and small lakes
IDENTIFICATION:	Flattened, cone-shaped shell
SIMILAR SPECIES:	Lake limpet

Imagine the shape of a home-made meringue as it emerges from the oven, a flattish, oval cone with a little peak of egg white drooping slightly to the side: that is the shape of the river limpet's shell. Another similarity with a meringue is that the margin of the shell is soft, allowing the limpet to pull it down snugly over any irregularities on the surface it is moving over. This is to protect the limpet from sediment, which it cannot tolerate. The river limpet attaches itself to weeds as well as to stones or rocks, and the streamlined, flattened shape of the shell allows it to cling on in fast-moving water. It can be seen under fresh water throughout most of Britain. Its lung-sacs always contain water and it cannot breathe or survive out of water. The less common lake limpet has a flatter shell and prefers still water.

GREAT CRESTED NEWT
(Triturus cristatus)

SIZE:	14 cm
HABITAT:	Ponds and small lakes, widespread but extremely local on mainland Britain
IDENTIFICATION:	Warty skin with slate grey spotted body, orange spotted belly. Male has striking crest down the centre of its back
SIMILAR SPECIES:	Smooth newt, Palmate newt

Development, farming, waste disposal, neglect and a lowering of the water table have all been blamed for the loss of breeding ponds leading to the decline of this species. In the last 20 years of the 20th century, 42% of the great crested newt population in the London area was lost. It has now been afforded legal protection, and conservation groups plan to restore populations in 100 unoccupied sites between 2000 and 2005. Unaware of the efforts being made on its behalf, the great crested newt carries on with its own efforts to ensure survival, spawning in the spring and continuing the egg to eft (tadpole) to adult, cycle. Unlike other newts, it does not always hibernate, sometimes staying in the water where it will spawn.

COMMON TOAD *(Bufo bufo)*

SIZE:	8–13 cm
HABITAT:	Ponds and lakes in breeding season. Woodland, marshes and moors at other times
IDENTIFICATION:	Warty olive brown skin, more colourful than frogs and with a rounder snout
SIMILAR SPECIES:	Natterjack toad

Is the squat, ugly thing in the grass a frog or a toad? To find out, give it a gentle prod with your finger: frogs hop, toads walk. In fact, a toad will walk a long way and with great determination, when it moves from its hibernation quarters to its breeding pond. It is fastidious about where it breeds and will pass by other bodies of water *en route*, rejecting them as unsuitable. Obstacles such as roads or walls will not deter it, but unfortunately there are hundreds of traffic victims each year. Animal lovers have gone to great lengths to ensure its survival, including putting up road signs to warn motorists of toad crossing points. The female toad produces strings of double-stranded spawn, 2–3 m long, at the end of April. The tadpoles are jet black compared with the dark brown frog tadpoles. The natterjack toad is endangered and is only found in a few sites in Britain.

COMMON FROG *(Rana Temporaria)* ▶

SIZE:	6–9 cm long
HABITAT:	Ponds and slow moving water
IDENTIFICATION:	A variety of colours, mainly olive green, speckled with brown. Always a dark triangular patch behind the eye
SIMILAR SPECIES:	Marsh frog

In the days when every village had a pond, the frog and its life cycle were part of every small boy's Saturday afternoon. Wellies donned, a jam jar with string handle in one hand, a fine mesh net on a long cane in the other, and he was ready to go off tadpoling. The contents of the jar were watched carefully as the tadpoles developed legs (hind legs first) and absorbed their tails into their bodies. The time soon came when tiny frogs were escaping and becoming unwelcome visitors in the kitchen. Left to its own devices, the frog will hide in damp places during the day and search for food during the cooler night or on rainy days. Insects, spiders, snails and worms make up its diet. It hibernates in mud or at the bottom of the pond. Reaching sexual maturity after three years, it returns to its home pond to spawn, the male attracting its mate by croaking.

BOG MOSS *(Sphagnum recurvum)*

SIZE:	Up to 5 cm tall
HABITAT:	Bogs and marshes
IDENTIFICATION:	Clumps of feathery moss, usually dark green
SIMILAR SPECIES:	Many other sphagnum mosses

Sphagnum mosses dominate stagnant water in acid bogs, usually in northern and western Britain, where rainfall is high. Slightly different species are found according to the acidity of the bogs and they are often difficult to tell apart, so are generally just called sphagnum moss. The species *Sphagnum recurvum*, or bog moss, is typical of the wetter heathlands. When dry, the leaf tips curve back. Sphagnum moss has natural antiseptic properties as well as being a great absorber of fluids, and was used as a surgical dressing for many years. During the Second World War, it was used to apply raw garlic juice, which is one of the best antiseptics. War workers in areas where it grew were kept busy harvesting the moss to be sent to the front. Lapland mothers were said to use this moss as a mattress for babies, its absorbency keeping the child warm and dry.

WATER HORSETAIL *(Equisetum fluviatile)*

SIZE:	Up to 1 m tall
HABITAT:	Marshes and shallow water
IDENTIFICATION:	Thick, green stems with whorls of short branches, some stems carry brown spore cones at the tip
SIMILAR SPECIES:	Marsh horsetails, Field horsetail, Giant horsetail

Water horsetail can be seen throughout the British Isles growing at the margins of lakes and rivers as well as in marshes. The stems are buried in the mud and the hollow stems grow up through the water as much as a metre tall. The short, oval cones at the tips are black and green when young, turning to brown when the spores ripen. The similar field horsetail is a persistent weed in gardens, but has been put to good use over the ages. The hard green stems were used as scourers by housewives and as fine sandpaper by cabinet makers. The branching shoots, which have been described as 'moth-eaten asparagus', are rich in silica and are used by gardeners to make an effective fungicide.

FRESHWATER SHRIMP

(Gammarus pulex)

SIZE:	Up to 3 cm, usually smaller
HABITAT:	Clean ponds, rivers and streams
IDENTIFICATION:	Light brown semi-translucent segmented body
SIMILAR SPECIES:	Fairy shrimp

The freshwater shrimp is more closely related to the seashore sandhopper than to the marine shrimp. It is quite fussy about where it chooses to live and will not tolerate polluted water or insufficient oxygen. Synthetic pyrethroid sheep dips are thought to have been responsible for the disappearance of freshwater shrimps from 30 km of the river Caldew, near Carlisle in 1996. In areas of chalk and limestone, the freshwater shrimp is abundant and is one of the main sources of food for water shrews. It spends a lot of time beneath stones and leaves, feeding on decaying matter. It swims on its side, quite fast, with jerky movements. The fairy shrimp is one of Britain's rarest crustaceans and lives in unlikely places like puddles in tyre ruts. These beautiful creatures are completely transparent and swim upside down.

THREE-SPINED STICKLEBACK

(Gasterosteus aculeatus)

SIZE: 4–10 cm

HABITAT: Widespread in ponds, lakes, ditches and rivers. Also estuaries and coastal waters

IDENTIFICATION: Spindle-shaped body with three heavy spines on greenish or bluish-silver back. Pale underside.
No scales but bony plates on sides: either along whole length, or at front and tail, or at front only

SIMILAR SPECIES: Nine-spined stickleback

In the far north, the stickleback is more likely to be a migrant, spending winter in the sea and returning to fresh water to spawn in spring. Elsewhere, certainly in the south of England, it remains in fresh water all year. The northern form has the heavier 'armour' of bony plates, extending the length of the body, whereas full-time river fish have plates only at the front. The male is normally silvery, but changes colour at spawning time with a bright red belly and blue eyes. He builds a nest of twigs and entices passing females to lay eggs in it by putting on a courtship dance. He then spends up to 25 days fanning the eggs with water until they hatch. The stickleback is important in the food chain, eating fish fry and eggs and small animals, and in its turn being eaten by cod, salmon, eels, pike, birds and mammals. It was once used to make fish oil.

FRESHWATER CRAYFISH
(Astacus pallipes)

SIZE:	Up to 10 cm long
HABITAT:	Rivers and streams
IDENTIFICATION:	Olive green or brown crustacean resembling a miniature lobster
SIMILAR SPECIES:	Signal crayfish

This native species is under threat from a foreign invader – the American signal crayfish. Numbers are declining drastically following the escape of signal crayfish from farms. Apart from competing for habitat, the signal carries a fungus disease against which the indigenous crayfish has no resistance. The white-clawed crayfish, as it is sometimes known, is Britain's largest and only native freshwater crustacean. It requires well-oxygenated, fast-flowing water, and prefers calcareous water that has run across chalk or limestone. It crawls under stones or digs burrows in river banks to hide in during the day, emerging at night to feed on the river bed. Insect larvae, tadpoles and snails make up most of its diet. The female carries fertilised eggs, sticking to her abdomen, and the young cling to their mother with their pincers.

BULLHEAD *(Cottus gobio)*

SIZE:	10–15 cm
HABITAT:	Cool, clear, well-oxygenated waters with stony bottoms and strong to moderate currents. Can occur in brackish water. Widespread, but absent in Scotland
IDENTIFICATION:	Huge head compared to body. Broad and squat with wide mouth. Small eyes set high on head
SIMILAR SPECIES:	None in Britain

The ugly-looking little bullhead, also known as the miller's thumb, uses jet propulsion to make quick getaways. It sucks in water and ejects it explosively through its gills when it needs a boost to escape its two main predators: the eel and the trout. The bullhead gets its own back on the trout by eating large quantities of its eggs and fry, along with worms and the larvae of mayfly, blackfly and caddisfly. It is a real pest in trout rivers. When it is not feeding, it lurks about under stones and never moves very far unless forced to. The male digs a hollow in the river bottom or under a stone into which the female lays 100–500 large (2.5 mm) sticky eggs, which the male guards until they hatch 3–4 weeks later. The larvae live on yolk sacs for 10–12 days and then eat small animals. The bullhead matures in its second year and probably lives for 3–5 years.

STONE LOACH *(Nemacheilus barbatulus)*

SIZE:	8–12 cm
HABITAT:	Cool, clear, well-oxygenated waters and brooks and shore region of clear lakes. Tolerates weak brackish water. Widespread except in Scotland
IDENTIFICATION:	Body long and rounded, blotched greenish-brown above, paler below. Six barbels around the downturned mouth
SIMILAR SPECIES:	Spined loach

The stone loach usually prowls about at night on the river bed, feeling with its barbels for shrimps, worms, leeches, larvae and occasionally snails. It spends the day under cover, unless it is overcast and gloomy. Spawning is in April and May with up to 800,000 eggs laid in separate places, some in hollows and some stuck to plants and stones. It is a good bait fish and was once cultivated in ponds for food, although it would make a pretty poor meal. The spined loach *(Cobitis teania)* is smaller at 5–10 cm and more localised, not being recorded in Scotland or Wales. It has a pair of spines on its head that serve as weapons, which it uses readily when handled. It often lies still on the bottom with just its head protruding from the sand or stones. It tolerates less well-oxygenated water than the stone loach and feeds on crustaceans and rotifers.

MINNOW *(Phoxinus phoxinus)*

SIZE:	8–10 cm
HABITAT:	Common in fast-flowing fresh water and vegetated zones. Not present in Scotland
IDENTIFICATION:	Small, slender, dark-coloured with blunt snout and small scales. Belly cream to pearly, changing in male to red in spawning season
SIMILAR SPECIES:	Gudgeon (but lighter in colour, with small barbels, and up to 15 cm)

The minnow is a companionable little fish, sometimes seen in compact schools feeding on small crustaceans, molluscs and larvae. It frequents the 'trout zone' – the fast-flowing streams of the uplands – and fly-fishermen would rather it was not there. It competes with young trout for food, often rising to the surface to take a midge, and eats trout eggs. On the other hand, it is a tasty meal for a larger trout and is often taken by perch, pike and chub. The gudgeon *(Gobio gobio)* is another small member of the Cyprinidae family, a bottom feeder sometimes living in slower, waters. Parents in Britain would probably balk at being asked by an eager young angler to prepare one of these limp little creatures for tea, but in France the child would be praised and then served with their catch, rolled in flour and quickly fried, for a delicious treat.

ATLANTIC SALMON *(Salmo salar)*

SIZE: Up to 1.3 m

HABITAT: Life cycle includes time in sea, lower and upper reaches of suitable rivers. Spawns in well-oxygenated streams with gravel beds

IDENTIFICATION: Streamlined, silvery body, dotted above, with thinner 'wrist' at tail than trout. Sharpish head, eye in line with rearmost part of mouth (see Trout p.331). Back margin of tailfin curved inward. Spawning colours yellow and golden red with purple spots and markings

SIMILAR SPECIES: Trout

The salmon is a majestic fish with glorious looks, immense power and a life cycle to rival any other creature. Seeing one of these beautiful fish, either holding a lazy drift in the shadow of a bridge or making spectacular leaps up a crashing torrent, sends a tingle up the spine. Even a farmed salmon, with its tattered fins and subdued colour, is magnificent. There was good news towards the latter half of the 20th century when waterways in England began to get clean enough to attract the odd salmon back to rivers they had been missing from for years. Sadly, this was more than offset by the huge decline in wild salmon numbers in the traditional fishing rivers of Ireland and Scotland. The two main reasons suggested for the decline were overfishing by trawlers in the feeding grounds and installation of fish farms near the mouths of salmon rivers. Other factors could include the rise in the number of seals, the redistribution of prey species, warming of the seas and pollution. The salmon hatches from an egg laid in the gravel of the upper reaches of a river and lives there, eating insects, small fish and shrimps, until it becomes a smolt at about 2 years. It then descends to the sea and makes the trip across the North Atlantic to the feeding grounds off Greenland, where it spends anything between 14 months and 5 years eating herring, sprat and shrimps. Then it returns to its birth river, to almost the exact same spot, in order to spawn. This involves a trip of thousands of miles across the ocean, the pinpointing of the correct river outlet and a journey upstream through rapids and waterfalls. Once in the river, usually in the early summer, it stops feeding, so by the time it has completed its energetic spawning it is extremely emaciated and weak. The survival rate after spawning is 2–5%. A survivor begins to feed and makes its way back to sea, perhaps to return again in 2–3 years. Very few fish manage three journeys. The salmon is a formidable navigator. In the open sea it uses water temperature and salinity and possibly magnetic fields to steer a course to within a few miles, perhaps as many as 10 or even 20, of its home river. Once within sensory range it follows the chemical trail of bile salts it deposited in the river as a departing smolt. This final tracking can be greatly affected by pollution, and the salmon might fail to spawn because it cannot find its river.

ROACH *(Rutilus rutilus)*

SIZE:	10–25 cm
HABITAT:	Common in lakes and slow-flowing rivers of England, less so in W. Wales and Scotland
IDENTIFICATION:	Silvery, spindle-shaped body with reddish fins
SIMILAR SPECIES:	Rudd

The roach is a great favourite with anglers and, in the right conditions without overcrowding, can grow to 40 cm and weigh 1 kg. Usually, however, it is less than half that size.

It is easily mistaken for a rudd (confusingly called a roach in Ireland), which looks identical at first glance but which is slightly deeper in the body and with a dorsal fin set back from the line of its anal fin. The rudd *(Scardinius erythrophthalmus)* hybridises with roach, bleak and bream to further confuse matters. The roach is abundant and important in the river food chain, eating water thyme, duckweed, stonewort, worms, insect larvae and crustaceans and being eaten by pike, zander, perch and eels. It is also caught by heron. In eastern Europe it is sold locally as a cheap food – fresh, smoked or salted – but in Britain it is only of interest to anglers.

TENCH *(Tinca tinca)*

SIZE:	15–30 cm (up to 50 cm)
HABITAT:	Widespread in sluggish waters of muddy lakes and ponds as far north as Loch Lomond, Scotland
IDENTIFICATION:	Deep body, back and sides dark green or blackish-brown with bronze lustre, pinkish below. Thin barbel at each corner of mouth. Thick at the tail
SIMILAR SPECIES:	None

If its pond dries up it does not bother the tench much. This handsome fish just digs itself into the mud and waits for the water to rise. It can survive like this for some time and it will even stay alive out of water in a damp sack for 2–3 hours. It is a very hardy fish, able to live in poorly oxygenated, polluted waters. The tench feeds by rooting around in the mud for bloodworms, insect larvae, snails, mussels and even small fish. More very large tench are being caught in Britain and one suggested reason is that farm fertilisers, leaching through to the water, have nourished the weeds and invertebrate life on which the tench feeds. It used to be called the 'doctor fish', as its slime was thought to have magical medical properties. It was used in the Middle Ages as a supposed cure for headaches, toothache, jaundice and other illnesses.

COMMON CARP *(Cyprinus carpio)*

SIZE: 25–60 cm (up to 100 cm)

HABITAT: Widespread in still, warmer waters with thick vegetation and muddy bottom. Commonest in Thames basin and E. Anglia

IDENTIFICATION: Original form olive-gold with even-sized scales. Deep, heavy-set body. Two barbels each side of mouth. Many various forms

SIMILAR SPECIES: Crucian carp

The carp, probably introduced to Europe from Asia by the Romans, has been bred, fished for and used as a pond decoration for thousands of years. Wild varieties are more slender with uniform scales; cultivated forms have a higher back and a huge variety of scale patterns, from complete absence in the leather carp to the bulky 'armour plating' of the mirror carp. Its natural food includes worms, water bugs, larvae, spiders and snails, but anglers have conditioned it to take most baits including sweetcorn, luncheon meat, bread, potatoes, fruit, tinned pet food and spicy dumplings called 'boilies'. It can grow large on this diet: the British record is 25.23 kg. When temperatures fall in winter, it digs itself deep into the silt and stops feeding. The crucian carp *(Carissius carissius)* is browner with a very humped back and no barbels.

COMMON BREAM *(Abramis brama)*

SIZE: 30–40 cm (up to 75 cm)

HABITAT: Lakes, slow-flowing streams and lower reaches of large rivers. Common on Norfolk Broads, not found north of Loch Lomond

IDENTIFICATION: Greyish above, lighter below with humped back. Laterally compressed with large anal fin

SIMILAR SPECIES: Silver (or White) bream

If you happen to catch a bream, do not bother taking it home to eat – it is soft, particularly tasteless and full of bones. But the bream does serve a purpose other than providing a quarry for anglers: it is the specific 'marker' species which identifies the fourth level of a watercourse – the lower reaches – as classified by Huet. Also known as carp bream or bronze bream, it feeds on the bottom, eating worms, midge larvae, pea-mussels and snails. In winter it moves to the deeper waters and gathers in shoals of thousands. It also gathers to breed in May and June and the communal spawning can be a noisy affair, easily spotted from the bank. It readily hybridises with roach and silver bream. The silver bream *(Abramis bjoerkna)* is lighter in colour, more elegantly shaped and found in quieter parts of the river, mostly in the east of England.

EEL *(Anguilla anguilla)*

SIZE: 42–100 cm (female), 29–51 cm (male)

HABITAT: Widespread throughout fresh water habitats from estuaries to high-level trout streams, huge lakes and tiny ponds

IDENTIFICATION: Snake-like, no scales, covered in mucus. Small head. Dark goldish-brown with bronze underside when arriving in river systems; grey with silvery underside when leaving

SIMILAR SPECIES: Lamprey (in general shape only)

The eel is born in the warm Sargasso Sea, between the W. Indies and Bermuda, some 5600 km (3500 miles) south-west of Britain. Over a period of 3 years, the larva is swept north-east with the help of the Gulf Stream and the general flow of the Atlantic current. It then metamorphoses into an elver (10 mm shorter than the larva) and enters our waterways between January (in the south-west) and April (in the north-east). It spends 5–10 years in fresh water, feeding on insect larvae, small fish, crayfish, frogs, mussels and snails. Eventually, it changes from yellow to silver, its eyes grow, its jaws diminish and its intestine shrinks, its body hardens with fat and it is ready to return to sea, to breed and die. In this migratory form it has lived unfed in an aquarium for 4 years. The largest eel caught in Britain weighed 5.05 kg and was 1.35 m long.

PIKE *(Esox lucius)*

SIZE: 130 cm (female), 95 cm (male)

HABITAT: Widespread in deep, calm weed-choked waters: lakes, gravel pits and slow-flowing rivers

IDENTIFICATION: Distinctive. Marbled green and brown markings, streamlined with long snout, huge mouth, and broad tail

SIMILAR SPECIES: None

The fearsome pike attacks almost anything – including the angler careless enough to get within range of those terrible teeth. Tales of huge pike leaping out of the water to take ducks, dogs – even little children – are rife, although largely fanciful. In many a deep, murky pond there is said to be a monster that has defied capture for hundreds of years. In fact, pike do live for 30 years or more and get very large – up to 35 kg – but only very exceptionally. It hunts alone, ambushing its prey – fish, frogs, ducklings – in a lightning strike over just a couple of metres: it is not a good chaser and waits until the victim is close. Adults will cannibalise young pike and several times two pike have been found dead, the smaller jammed into the maw of the larger as its backward-pointing teeth will not allow a pike to disgorge an over-ambitious mouthful.

PERCH *(Perca fluviatilis)*

SIZE:	20–30 cm (up to 60 cm)
HABITAT:	Lowland lakes, ponds and rivers with clean waters; also brackish water near estuaries and occasionally in trout streams. Absent from Scotland
IDENTIFICATION:	Generally brownish or yellowish-green with 5–7 barred streaks across sides. Rounded, slightly humped body with narrow tail 'wrist' and two dorsal fins, the first large with heavy spines. Pectoral, anal and pelvic fins orange–red
SIMILAR SPECIES:	Others in the perch family vaguely similar

The perch likes to lurk around bridges, landing stages and heaps of dead branches where it can easily pick off young fish taking refuge from the strong currents. It moves about in shoals of mixed age, although where numbers are high some of the youngsters are at risk of being eaten by the older perch. The female lays long, sticky strands of eggs which she drapes over rocks and plants. These have a thick mucous covering which, after fertilisation, swells in the water and offers good protection, producing high hatching rates. Given that the female might lay 300,000 eggs, this can lead to overpopulation which in turn leads to a stunting of the growth of many perch. This condition of dwarfism is on the increase in many areas. The perch is a popular angling fish as, like its cousins the zander and black bass, it puts up a spirited fight.

BARBEL *(Barbus barbus)*

SIZE:	30–40 cm (up to 100 cm)
HABITAT:	Moving about on the bottom of the official 'barbel zone' – fairly wide rivers with powerful currents and rocks interspersed with sand or gravel banks. Mainly in E. and S.E. of England
IDENTIFICATION:	Brown to bronze–green with gold highlights, spindle-shaped body and large fleshy-lipped, downward-pointed mouth with four barbels, two above and one at each corner
SIMILAR SPECIES:	None in Britain

This is a brave fighter on the end of a line and thought a worthy catch by many anglers but, although tasty and well worth eating (if somewhat bony), it is advisable to steer clear of any roe found inside. This is slightly poisonous and was used in folk medicine as an emetic – not a nice end to a good meal. The barbel feeds on the bottom, feeling through the stones and sand with its barbels and soft lips for worms, insect larvae and pea-mussels, but also taking young gudgeon and sometimes plant debris. It moves upstream in shoals to breed, the female laying 3000–9000 eggs, which are washed down between stones by the current. Each female is usually closely watched by four or five males who rush to fertilise the eggs. The barbel takes 4–5 years to mature.

DACE *(Leuciscus leuciscus)*

SIZE:	15–20 cm (up to 30 cm)
HABITAT:	Cool running waters, lakes and brackish water near rivermouths. Absent from Scotland
IDENTIFICATION:	Bland grey spindle-shaped body, like a slender roach, with yellowish eyes and deep notch in the tail
SIMILAR SPECIES:	Roach

Apart from its absence in Scotland and northern Scandinavia, the dace is found all the way round mid- and northern Europe and Asia as far as Siberia, where it is an important food fish. It likes clean water and is very susceptible to pollution, so numbers can fluctuate according to local river conditions. Its territory extends from the trout zone right down almost into estuaries, but it does prefer fast water. It feeds both at the bottom on worms and small snails, near the bank on bits of plant, and at the surface on water insects and flies. In fact it is not unknown for dace to take an angler's trout fly, and bringing in a large one takes just as much expertise as landing a trout. It will not tackle young fish as its mouth is too small. Dace form compact schools, moving as the water takes them and coming close to the bank at night.

CHUB *(Leuciscus cephalus)*

SIZE:	30–40 cm (up to 60 cm in rare cases)
HABITAT:	Streams with strong currents but also lakes. Absent from much of the West Country, Wales and Scotland
IDENTIFICATION:	Brownish-silver, spindle-shaped body, sometimes with gold highlights, and black-edged scales
SIMILAR SPECIES:	Dace

Whereas the carp has been 'taught' to eat a variety of things by anglers, the chub does so naturally and is the most omnivorous of our freshwater fish. It not only takes trout fry, worms, molluscs, fish eggs, plants, seeds, and flying and water insects but has also been known to have a go at the fruit fallen from overhanging trees. Having such an eclectic taste ought to make it easy to catch with hook and line. Quite the opposite. It is extremely wary, touring round any offered bait and inspecting it very closely before nibbling cautiously. It is hardly worth catching for eating as it is full of bones, but anglers say it puts up a good fight. You should be able to see the chub in its favourite haunts near natural or artificial obstacles like piers, bridges, dead branches and gravel embankments, where it moves in groups near the surface.

GRAYLING *(Thymallus thymallus)*

SIZE: 30–40 cm (up to 60 cm)

HABITAT: Tumbling, well-oxygenated waters with a pebble bed, deep holes and stones: classified as second, or grayling zone. Wales, Midlands and S. England

IDENTIFICATION: Long silvery-bronze body with distinctive lengthways arrangement of scales and high, long dorsal fin

SIMILAR SPECIES: Powan (excepting dorsal fin)

This is a lovely fish, the last remaining member of the Thymallidae family, which is being newly introduced to many rivers or restocked where it has been wiped out by pollution. Its huge dorsal fin, which in the male turns blue in the mating season, is an instant identifier, although the only characteristic it shares with other salmonids is the adipose fin. Otherwise, with its small mouth and large aligned scales, it is very similar to the powan or whitefish *(Coregonus lavaretus)*. The grayling is carnivorous, feeding mainly on small water invertebrates: caddis-flies, molluscs, mayflies, dipteras, earthworms, etc., often coming to the surface with a highly characteristic, swaying rise to take a drifting insect. It is extremely sensitive and impossible to transport live for artificial rearing and restocking.

TROUT *(Salmo trutta)*

SIZE: 25–40 cm (up to 60 cm)

HABITAT: Sea trout: highly oxygenated, cold, fast-flowing streams for spawning although passing through larger, slower, warmer rivers on migration. Brown trout: clean freshwater rivers or lakes

IDENTIFICATION: Stout body with dotted markings on upper side. Colours vary (see below). Blunt head, eye ahead of rearmost part of mouth (see Salmon p. 320). Back margin on tailfin, fairly straight, thick 'wrist' at tail

SIMILAR SPECIES: Many different trout sub-species, Salmon

There are trout that live entirely in rivers and lakes, hatching, maturing, spawning and dying within a couple of kilometres, and there are those that live in the sea, migrating upriver to spawn. They are essentially the same fish. The trout family is divided into a complex variety of forms and sub-species determined by environment and behaviour rather than genes. In Lough Melvin (N.W. Ireland) there are at least three varieties of brown trout *(S. t. fario)* and colouration of all subspecies can vary from dark brown to flashing silver with various dotted markings. The brown trout (with white-rimmed red dots on its flanks) does not migrate, but the sea trout (silvery) moves upriver to spawn in the winter, usually several times in its life. Both are highly regarded by anglers who do invaluable work to improve the water environment.

WATER VOLE *(Arvicola terrestris)*

SIZE: 18–22 cm excluding tail

HABITAT: Streams and river banks

IDENTIFICATION: Dark brown or black fur, long tail about 10 cm

SIMILAR SPECIES: The large Bank vole on Skomer Island

In *The Wind in the Willows*, Ratty was a water vole, a rather more endearing creature than a rat. Unfortunately, it is now extinct in many parts of Britain where it was abundant, probably because of the introduction of mink which escaped from fur farms from the 1950s onwards. If you do disturb a water vole as you walk beside a river, you will probably hear a 'plop' as it dives into the water and then see it swimming away with only its head above the surface. It burrows into banks, making entrances both above and below the water line. Inside the network of tunnels there are usually at least two resting places, each lined with shredded grass or pith from rushes. Sometimes there is an exit a metre or so inland, indicated by a 'feeding lawn' of closely cropped grass nearby. Aquatic vegetation and small animals also contribute to its diet.

MINK *(Mustela vison)*

SIZE:	Body 40 cm, tail 20 cm
HABITAT:	Marshes, lakes, rivers, coastline. Widespread in Britain, absent from some islands
IDENTIFICATION:	Dark brown, almost black, thick glossy fur. Pointed snout, small eyes and ears, long furry tail. Gives off distinctive acrid smell when alarmed.
SIMILAR SPECIES:	Otter (distinctly larger)

The mink is a pest we could well do without, but will never be rid of. Beautiful as it is, it is also an indiscriminate, wanton killer of wild birds, fish, small mammals and domestic poultry. The mink escaped from fur farms from the 1950s onwards and has thrived. With no natural predators, this great survivor has ousted the otter from many areas and has devastated ground-nesting birds, particularly in the Scottish Highlands and Islands. A £1.65m, 5-year, multi-agency scheme to eradicate the estimated 10,000 mink from the Outer Hebrides was launched in 2001 following concerns that it would wipe out internationally important bird colonies on the island of North Uist. It was also said to be causing £$\frac{1}{2}$m worth of damage to crofting communities and fish farms each year. It is a strong swimmer and will tackle fish almost as large as itself.

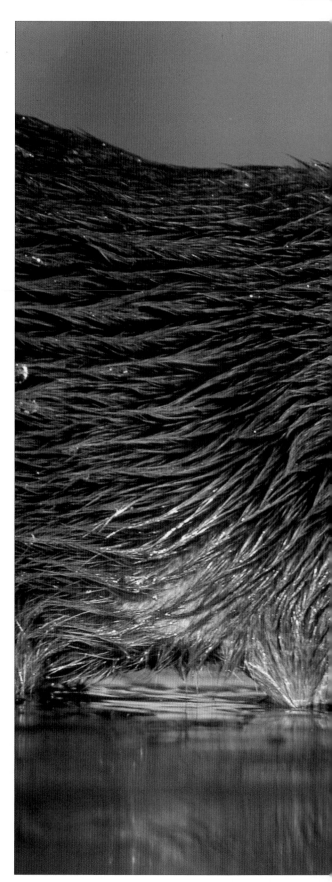

OTTER *(Lutra lutra)*

SIZE:	Up to 90 cm excluding tail. Up to 135 cm total length
HABITAT:	Rivers, lakes and coasts
IDENTIFICATION:	Sleek, tapering body and tail, brown fur with paler underside
SIMILAR SPECIES:	American mink which is smaller and darker

Once hunted as a pest, the otter is now a protected species and the one most people say they would like to see. Perhaps Henry Williamson's *Tarka the Otter* endeared this shy creature to us. Unfortunately, 95% of traditional otter territory in England and Wales is no longer occupied, so the west coast of Scotland or the Scottish islands are the most likely places to see one in the wild. Since otter hunting was banned in the 1960s, pollution, loss of habitat and road casualties have been the major causes of decline. During the floods of 2001, the fast-flowing water under bridges forced otters to cross roads, with fatal results.

In the more remote parts of Scotland each otter is able to stake its claim to about 19 km of clean river or coastline. Strongly territorial, it uses its droppings or spraints to mark its domain. The male, or dog, might have two or more females (bitches) living within his territory and rearing his cubs.

The holt is built by the bitch between the roots of a waterside tree or under a rocky cairn, often with an underwater entrance, and lined with grass or moss. She has a single litter of two or three cubs, born blind and helpless. After 2–3 months, when they have their waterproof coat, she teaches them to swim and, if they are reluctant to enter the water, pushes them in. The otter is naturally playful and the mother frolics with her cubs in the water. The otter also makes slides on snow or muddy banks and toboggans on its chest.

With its streamlined body and webbed hind feet, the otter is a superb aquatic hunter. It chases fish under water, staying down for several minutes then bringing them ashore to eat. Eels are a favourite food, but frogs and birds sometimes add variety to the diet.

Sea
and
Seashore

Where the sea meets the moon-
    blanch'd land,

Listen! You hear the grating
    roar

Of pebbles which the waves
    draw back, and fling,

At their return, up the high
    strand,

Begin and cease, and then
    again begin,

With tremulous cadence slow

DOVER BEACH
MATTHEW ARNOLD

SEA BUCKTHORN *(Hippophae rhamnoides)*

SIZE:	Up to 10 m tall but usually much shorter bush
HABITAT:	Widespread on coastal dunes
IDENTIFICATION:	Narrow, silvery-greyish leaves like willow. Thorny twigs. Small green female flowers producing clustered orange berries. Male flowers on separate bushes
SIMILAR SPECIES:	None

Like the willow, the sea buckthorn was one of the first plants to recolonise Britain after the Ice Age and there is evidence of it having been around almost 10,000 years ago. It spreads by suckering – sending out new plant shoots from its root system – and the resulting mass of growth stabilises surrounding soil. The dense thickets of thorny bush resist the depredations of grazing animals and tidy-minded humans, so once established it is hard to eliminate. Sea buckthorn can grow into quite a tall tree but, because it is found in windswept coastal settings, it usually keeps low to the ground. It is a soil improver, having the ability to fix nitrogen in the ground like members of the bean family. Sea buckthorn seed and the pulp and peel of the berry have high contents of special oils and fatty acids, which have been shown to alleviate dermatitis.

TAMARISK *(Tamarix anglica)*

SIZE:	Up to 6 m tall but usually a smaller shrub
HABITAT:	Widespread on coasts, sand dunes
IDENTIFICATION:	Abundant, alternate leaves, tiny and closely packed like scales on each twig. Small pink or white flowers clustered round twigs with reddish-brown bark. Feathery, drooping branches making dense canopy
SIMILAR SPECIES:	*Tamarix gallica*

The name probably comes from the Hebrew *tamaris* meaning broom and tamarisk can sweep all before it once established. It is a listed noxious weed in the western United States where selling its seeds is banned. There it out-competes native plants for water. With a single, large plant transpiring up to 1100 litres of water a day, tamarisk can create total local desiccation. It causes no such problems in Britain, where it was introduced from the Middle East in 1582. With a long history in its native lands as a medicinal plant it was used here to treat spleen disorders, rheumatism and bruising. It spread to coastal areas, where it thrives on poor, saline soil (it is also known as the salt cedar) and is cultivated as an ornamental shrub. *Tamarix gallica*, our other naturalised species, oozes an edible, honey-like substance when cut.

Marram Grass (Ammophila arenari)

Size: 60–120 cm

Habitat: Sand dunes

Identification: Stiff stems, long, narrow, greyish–green leaves.
                        Creamy flowers in a dense spike from June to August

The coastline is constantly changing as winter storms can erode entire beaches or redistribute sand to extend dunes into the sea. Windblown sand settles where it meets an obstacle, whether natural or artificial, forming the beginnings of a new dune. Country children living on the coast are taught not to pick or disturb the marram grass as it is often planted to stabilise the sand dunes. Its creeping underground stems form large patches and the stems become partly covered as the sands are blown by the wind. If completely covered by sand, the stems lengthen producing a new layer of roots and the plant emerges so that it can continue to grow. This is why the seaward side of the dunes shows the most vigorous growth. The coarse, scratchy leaves curl up in dry weather showing their bluish undersides.

Marram grass grew around the earliest British settlements and was used to make mats to cover earth floors or to hang as partitions within the dwelling. It is an ideal weaving material being pliant and hard-wearing. In parts of Anglesey it is still harvested in late summer using a purpose-made hook to cut the grass well below the level of the sand. After drying, it can be made into brooms, seats or woven into a loose, breathable mat to cover and protect crops. The mats are usually made from plaited strips using much the same method as that used by central African tribes.

THRIFT *(Armeria maritima)*

SIZE: Up to 20 cm tall

HABITAT: Sea cliffs, salt marshes

IDENTIFICATION: Narrow fleshy leaves, round pink flower heads from April to August

SIMILAR SPECIES: None

This familiar coastal perennial forms dense cushions on cliff-tops throughout Britain. Rocks above the tide line with very little soil can be seen supporting a clump or two of thrift. It can tolerate the salty sea winds and sends its roots far down to seek water. It is said to get its name from the fact that it can survive these inhospitable conditions and remain green all year. The plant is occasionally found on salt marshes and on some mountains. The flower heads vary in shades of pink but are always impressive as they are carried well above the foliage. The flowers, which are sometimes called sea pinks or rock roses, can be picked and dried for use in 'everlasting' flower arrangements.

SEA BINDWEED *(Calystegia soldanella)*

SIZE: Creeping up to 50 cm

HABITAT: Sand dunes and shingle

IDENTIFICATION: Trailing stems, kidney-shaped leaves, pink trumpet-shaped flowers from June to August

SIMILAR SPECIES: Hedge bindweed

Sand dunes form where wind-blown sand meets an obstacle and settles. Marram grass is usually the first plant to take root and, once the dune stabilises, other plants begin to find a foothold. One of these, often seen on an otherwise bare dune, is the sea bindweed. This creeping perennial is common around the coastline of England and Wales but scarcer in Scotland. The kidney-shaped leaves with their prominent veins and long stalks are easy to identify, but it is the flowers which are most eye-catching. The pink trumpets can be 40–50 mm across and usually have five, well-defined, white stripes. Unlike the other bindweeds, sea bindweed does not climb up other plants, but creeps along the ground.

ROCK SAMPHIRE *(Crithmum maritimum)*

SIZE:	15–30 cm tall
HABITAT:	Cliffs and rocky coasts
IDENTIFICATION:	Grey–green branched stems, narrow, fleshy leaves, yellow umbels from June to September
SIMILAR SPECIES:	Marsh samphire

Rock samphire is no relation of marsh samphire and they are found in very different habitats. However, both are edible. The fleshy leaves and stems can be boiled or steamed and eaten like the leaves of artichokes, leaving the tough stringy veins behind. Rock samphire is most common in the south and west of Britain, where it grows on cliffs and used to be collected at the same time as gulls' eggs. In *King Lear*, Shakespeare described the gathering as a 'dreadful trade', probably because so many gatherers fell to their deaths. It grew abundantly on the Isle of Wight in the 19th century and was sold in London for up to four shillings a bushel. Rock samphire was often pickled and, in 1699, John Evelyn recommended gathering it at Michaelmas, or in the spring, and soaking it in sea water or brine before pickling it in vinegar.

SEA ROCKET *(Cakile maritima)*

SIZE:	15–30 cm
HABITAT:	Sandy shores, occasionally dunes or shingle
IDENTIFICATION:	Straggly plant with shiny lobed leaves, clusters of pink flowers from June to August
SIMILAR SPECIES:	Common scurvy-grass, Danish scurvy-grass

The high tide line on a sandy beach is usually marked by seaweed and other flotsam and jetsam, but for one or two wild flowers this is their ideal habitat. The prettiest of these is sea rocket with its pale grey–green leaves and delicate flowers. In keeping with others in the cabbage family, the flowers have the usual four petals and colours can be white or lilac as well as the usual pink. A line of these flowers along the top of the beach with no other plant in sight can be quite spectacular. The scurvy-grasses have similar flowers, usually white but sometimes lilac, particularly the Danish scurvy-grass. They are not grasses but are other members of the cabbage family. They grow on sea cliffs or salt marshes and were valued for their vitamin C content as this was useful for preventing scurvy in sailors.

SEA ASTER *(Aster tripolium)*

SIZE: 15–75 cm tall

HABITAT: Salt marshes and sea cliffs

IDENTIFICATION: Sturdy, upright stems with narrow fleshy leaves, clusters of lilac flowers from July to October

SIMILAR SPECIES: Michaelmas daisy

In estuaries and sheltered bays there is often an area of low-lying land which is covered by the sea at high tide. The plants that grow here in the salt marshes must either be able to excrete the salt or limit its concentration. One such plant is the sea aster, which can be seen on salt marshes throughout the British Isles. The clusters of flowers are 10–20 mm across and have a central yellow disc surrounded by lilac–blue ray florets. It is usually at its best around September 29th which is St Michael's Day. The Michaelmas daisy found growing wild is obviously closely related but originally came from North America, introduced as a garden plant before escaping to grow in the wild.

SEA HOLLY *(Eryngium maritimum)*

SIZE:	30–90 cm tall
HABITAT:	Sand and shingle beaches
IDENTIFICATION:	Blue–green prickly leaves, round, blue flower heads from June to September
SIMILAR SPECIES:	None

This handsome, thistle-like plant has spiny, blue–green leaves with fine, white veins – their thick outer skin protects the plant from the salt sea spray. The metallic blue globular flower heads are unmistakable. Sea holly is one of the first plants after marram grass to become established as sand dunes form. Its long roots can go down as deep as 2 m to tap the water supply below the sand. These roots were dug up and candied in the 17th century and sold as sweetmeats called eryngo roots. They were reckoned to be an aphrodisiac in addition to being used to combat indigestion and were an essential ingredient in the Elizabethan marrowbone pie. Sea holly grows on shingle beaches as well as on sand dunes, but is rare in the north east and is not found in northern Scotland.

BLADDERWRACK *(Fucus vesiculosus)*

SIZE:	Up to 1 m long
HABITAT:	Rocks up to middle shore line and in estuaries
IDENTIFICATION:	Brown branched seaweed with conspicuous air bladders
SIMILAR SPECIES:	Egg wrack, Spiral wrack

Bladderwrack is a familiar seaweed around our shores. Its tough, brown fronds have pairs of oval air bladders along its length. Children pierce the bladders with their fingernails to hear them pop, leading to its other common name of popweed. It is edible, although more often grazed by sheep than picked for human consumption. In the Channel Isles and on some Scottish islands, it is gathered from the shores after storms and used as a soil improver or to speed up decomposition of the compost heap. In the egg wrack, or knotted wrack as it is sometimes called, the bladders are round rather than oval. Spiral wrack does not have gas bladders, but the swollen reproductive bodies at the tip of the fronds have a similar appearance.

Sea Purslane *(Atriplex portulacoides)*

SIZE:	Up to 80 cm
HABITAT:	Coastal sites, salt marshes
IDENTIFICATION:	Sprawling shrubby plant with silvery-green, spoon-shaped leaves. Yellow flowers in branched racemes from July to October
SIMILAR SPECIES:	None

Formerly known as *Halimione portulacoides*, meaning 'daughter of the sea' from the Greek word halimione, sea purslane can be seen from afar, its silvery foliage forming large masses alongside muddy creeks. On closer inspection, the leaves are covered in papery, scale-like salt glands. If these are scraped off, the plant looks much greener. The whole plant can be submerged by the incoming tide leaving more salt on the leaves as it recedes. Eventually the salt laden leaves are cast off and can sometimes form a strandline at the top of the marsh. Sea purslane is not frost hardy so is more common in southern Britain and western Scotland. The fleshy leaves are edible, although reports vary on how palatable they are. They can be eaten raw but are less salty when cooked.

Red Valerian *(Centranthus rubra)*

SIZE:	30–80 cm
HABITAT:	Cliffs, walls, old chalk pits and waste ground
IDENTIFICATION:	Upright plant with hollow, smooth stems. Stalkless leaves joined in pairs around the stem. Clusters of flowers, usually rich crimson but occasionally pale pink or white, from June to August
SIMILAR SPECIES:	Common valerian, marsh valerian

A native of Mediterranean countries, red valerian was introduced as a garden plant in the 16th century but has now become naturalised. It is common in southern England, particularly the coastal areas of the south west. The bold, sweet-scented flowers attract butterflies and other insects with tongues long enough to reach the nectar in the bottom of the flower tubes. The plant is sometimes known as 'red-spur valerian' referring to the slender spur at the base of each flower. The leaves can be eaten in salads and the roots made into soup quite safely as this variety does not have the sedative properties of common valerian.

Common valerian is now known as 'the Valium of the 19th Century', its calming effects being well known since the Middle Ages. It was used to treat shell-shock victims during the First World War and today is an alternative medicine used to treat insomnia and anxiety. Although not the only plant to have the common name of 'all-heal', this does reflect herbalists' claims that it lowers blood pressure, promotes wound healing, relieves cramp and balances the nervous system.

OARWEED *(Laminaria digitata)*

SIZE:	Up to 2 m long
HABITAT:	Rocky shores at low water mark or below
IDENTIFICATION:	Long oval stem, broad brown blade dividing into fronds
SIMILAR SPECIES:	Curvie

Oarweed is one of the most common kelp seaweeds, which are all called tangleweed in Scotland. This dark olive-brown weed, with its long flexible stem and branched holdfast can often be seen washed up ashore after stormy weather. It is the rough weather that makes the blades split into their characteristic fronds. Off the West coast of some Scottish islands, huge kelp forests protect the shore from the full force of the Atlantic by absorbing some of the wave energy. In the 19th century, kelp was collected and burned to provide a rich chemical ash used in a variety of products, including gunpowder and medicines. This boom industry collapsed with the arrival of synthetic chemicals. Oarweed is edible and tasty because of its sodium glutamate content. It is used today to wrap fish before baking to add flavour and keep the meat moist.

LAVER *(Porphyra umbilicalis)*

SIZE:	Up to 40 cm long
HABITAT:	On rocks on sandy beaches
IDENTIFICATION:	Thin, purplish-brown fronds
SIMILAR SPECIES:	Sea lettuce

Laverbread, as it is known in Wales, is not a bread at all but is one of our most delicious edible seaweeds. It is common all round Britain's coast, especially in the west. The transparent fronds are green when young, turning to a purplish-brown as they mature. Where the tide has gone out leaving them exposed to the sun, the fronds look almost black. The Japanese cultivate laver and use the thin fronds to cover rice balls. In south-west England and Wales, cooked laver can be bought from food shops or markets. However, it is easy to gather it yourself but it must be washed several times to get rid of any clinging sand. It is then simmered for several hours, seasoned with vinegar and strained before rolling it in oatmeal and frying it in bacon fat.

BLACK-HEADED GULL

(Larus ridibundus)

SIZE:	36–38 cm
HABITAT:	Widespread in almost all environments apart from heaths and woodlands
IDENTIFICATION:	Light grey upper parts, white below with very dark brown head and dark red bill (winter plumage without dark head)
SIMILAR SPECIES:	Little gull

You will see this 'sea-gull' as far from the sea as it is possible to get in Britain. It has always been more of a landlubber than the other gulls, but is now largely so, with only a quarter of the population living near the sea. Incredibly, it was near extinction in the 19th century but has bounced back to almost 500,000 pairs. In the north, colonies of thousands of birds are found in boggy sites around lakes; in the south, more congregate at the seaside, on salt marshes and among the dunes. Other nesting sites include gravel pits and sewage farms. Farmers are familiar with the black-headed gull. Flocks follow the plough, picking up exposed insects, while making a harsh, raucous scream which, when several hundred birds are together, can be unbearable. It eats almost anything, which is why so many are found around refuse tips.

GREAT BLACK-BACKED GULL

(Larus marinus)

SIZE:	65–80 cm
HABITAT:	Around all coasts, but mainly N. and W., all year, moving inland in winter
IDENTIFICATION:	White head, neck and under parts, black wings, pink legs. Heavy bill with red smudge on lower bill. Heavy build
SIMILAR SPECIES:	Lesser black-backed gull

If a big black-backed fixes you with its baleful eye, it might just be considering whether you are worth the trouble of killing and eating. This voracious opportunist will overpower anything weak or injured, from another gull's chick to a newborn lamb, to add to its diet of fish waste, carrion and rubbish dump gleanings. Its more wholesome menu includes crabs, molluscs, eels and other marine creatures, but when these, or a mouse or puffin or fulmar, are not available, it turns to whatever its heavy, curved bill can stab, smash or shake into pieces small enough to swallow. It is not a nice bird and its numbers are increasing. The lesser black-backed gull *(L. fuscus)*, is smaller with yellow legs and mainly a summer visitor, although many over-winter. It shares its larger relative's eating habits and is more likely to breed inland on fresh water.

HERRING GULL *(Larus argentatus)*

SIZE: 55–66 cm

HABITAT: Widespread around coasts, moving inland in winter

IDENTIFICATION: Pale grey upper parts, white beneath with black tail tip and pink legs. Distinctive red spot on lower bill

SIMILAR SPECIES: Glaucous gull (rare winter visitor)

The angry-looking gull dips its chin down to its chest, arching its neck high, draws breath and, throwing back its head and opening its red-tipped bill to the sky, howls a strident, mocking laugh across the seafront: 'kyee-arrk-warrk-warrk-warrk!'. It can only be a herring gull. Whether picking cold, discarded chips from a tattered piece of paper, perching on a trawler's mast or making 'bombing runs' on bathers, this is the quintessential seaside bird. Although called a herring gull it will eat absolutely anything and the population has boomed with the growth in the number of civic dumps and rubbish tips. It is a very enterprising scavenger and has learned to drop hard-shelled food such as mussels (and tins and boxes) from a height to split them open. A natural cliff-dweller, it was first noted nesting on buildings in seaside towns in the 1920s and it will happily make its home on rooftops, where it fouls buildings and adds unwanted noise. Unfortunately for those who object to it, it has a very high breeding success rate and lives a long time – up to 30 years or more. Where it has ousted less robust, and more popular, birds such as puffins and terns from their breeding sites on islands, dunes and cliffs, it has had to be culled. Its raucous call is augmented by a tender little mewing sound made as it potters about with nothing much to do and particularly by the female during the mating season as she 'begs' food from her mate. This plaintive sound has earned it the name cat gull in parts of Scotland. First-year birds are brownish with speckled tails ending in a dark band and it is several years before full adult plumage is reached.

COMMON GULL *(Larus canus)*

SIZE:	40 cm
HABITAT:	Widespread all year in Scotland, spreading throughout Britain in winter, together with European visitors
IDENTIFICATION:	Light blue–grey above, white below, black-and-white wingtips, yellow–green bill and legs
SIMILAR SPECIES:	Kittiwake, Herring gull

Along with the kittiwake, the common gull is one of the more delicate, pretty gulls, although it shares some of the herring gull's eating habits, taking birds' eggs, chicks and even small adult birds if it gets the chance. It will also harry other seabirds to make them drop their catch. It was probably named for being 'common', that is, unexceptional, in looks rather than in distribution as it is not as widespread as other gulls. It tends not to come inland very much, but will come to scavenge for grain, worms or insects on farmland when winter cereals are being sown or when the ground is being ploughed (in Devon it is known as the barley bird and in Roxburgh as the seed bird). In Scotland it can be found on inland waters as well as coasts and it nests on shingle beaches, small islands in lochs or boggy grassland or moors.

CORMORANT *(Phalacrocorax carbo)*

SIZE:	90 cm
HABITAT:	Widespread round coasts all year; and common inland near water, especially in winter
IDENTIFICATION:	Browny-green upper parts, black below, black neck and head with white cheek patches and chin. Long yellow bill. White thigh patch when breeding
SIMILAR SPECIES:	Shag

The cormorant has long had an unjustified reputation for greed – it eats no more than any other seabird of its size. However, it is human's greed which leads to this oddly primeval-looking bird being persecuted for stealing fish. Most people first see a cormorant at a reservoir or lake, often standing with its wings spread out to dry. It also haunts power station outlets, looking for mashed fish from the cooling systems, and certainly does take the occasional unguarded trout from a farm. It is also blamed for depleting salmon and trout from rivers but, as it actually prefers eels and flatfish, this is unlikely. In China, cormorants on long 'leads' are used to hunt fish, with rings put round their necks so they cannot swallow the catch. In literature and the arts it is historically associated with the devil and all things sinister.

FULMAR *(Fulmarus glacialis)*

SIZE:	47 cm
HABITAT:	Widespread along coastline all year, nesting on cliffs, some winter visitors
IDENTIFICATION:	Light grey back, white head, neck and under parts. Straight long wings in gliding flight. Tubular nostrils on top of hook-tipped bill
SIMILAR SPECIES:	Manx shearwater

Fulmar feathers in your pillow, fulmar oil to fuel your lamps, fulmar skins to make your shoes and fulmar meat to feed you. If this sounds like your cup of fulmar broth then life on St Kilda, the furthest west of the Outer Hebridean islands, would have been for you. For more than 1000 years, until the last inhabitants left in 1930, St Kildans lived off seabirds: mostly fulmar but also puffin and gannet. The men risked their lives scaling the highest sea cliffs in Britain to gather eggs and capture birds. Each islander ate more than 80 eggs a week and 125 birds a year. Catching a fulmar is messy. The name comes from 'foul maa' or foul gull: it squirts evil-smelling, sticky slimy oil over intruders who try to steal its solitary egg. Fulmar numbers have soared in the last 200 years, probably due to the increase in discarded trawler waste.

MANX SHEARWATER *(Puffinus puffinus)*

SIZE:	36 cm
HABITAT:	Clifftops and islands around the W. and N.W. coast, breeding on W. coast only
IDENTIFICATION:	Sooty black above, white below. Black crown, white chin and throat. Tubular nostrils on top of dark bill. Nests in burrows
SIMILAR SPECIES:	Fulmar

Watching a shearwater skimming the waves, its wingtips often cutting through the very tops of the spume with no apparent effect on the flight path, it is not difficult to see how it got its name. It flies with virtually no wing beats, using the wind to give impetus to glides lasting several minutes. Although a brilliant flier and excellent swimmer, it is a dreadful walker and comes to land only to breed, when it stumbles in and out of its nesting burrow on its stumpy legs. When feeding young, it comes back to the nest only once a day, usually just before midnight, when vast flocks assemble and make a terrible din, crowing and cackling: it is known as the mackerel cock in parts of Scotland and the baakie craa (barking crow) in Shetland. It bred on the Isle of Man, its traditional 'home' island, in 1967, after a 150-year absence.

SHAG *(Phalacrocorax aristotelis)*

SIZE:	76 cm
HABITAT:	Widespread along Britain's coast, mostly in the W. in summer and spreading to E. in winter
IDENTIFICATION:	Glossy black plumage with iridescent green tinge in breeding season. Base of bill yellow. Short crest in breeding season
SIMILAR SPECIES:	Cormorant

Although the well-known nonsense poem begins: 'The common cormorant or shag/Lays eggs inside a pager bag…', these birds are different (and, of course, bags do not feature in their nesting arrangements). The shag is smaller and black all over with a little crest at breeding time. It, too, stands and hangs its wings out to dry and has an even more dazed, half-witted expression. When gathered on the rocks, they look like crowds of puzzled, black-suited businessmen wondering when the next train is coming along. There are four times as many shags as cormorants, with a population of 35,000 or more, all on the coast and very seldom more than a few miles inland. It nests on sea-cliff ledges and, if approached, will swing its head from side to side and croak gloomily – before launching an all-out attack with its hook-tipped bill.

TERNS

Terns are beautiful and graceful. While seeking food, they flap about daintily as if suspended on wires, head down scanning the sea. When prey is spotted, they might go into a brief hover before diving, or make a sudden dart into the water to pluck out a sand eel or sprat.

The **Arctic tern** (*Sterna paradisaea*), 36 cm, is tough. It makes the longest migration of any bird: a round trip of up to 40,000 km. It arrives in May from wintering in the southern oceans and breeds in the north-west of England and in Scotland. The nest is a scrape in the ground, vulnerable to predators but fiercely defended, to the extent of drawing blood from human intruders. The Arctic tern has a sharp all-red bill, very short orange–red legs and black forehead and 'skullcap'. It is very light grey above, white beneath. The twin-pointed tail streams out like a swallow's tail. About 44,000 pairs breed, but the British population trend is down with big failures in the last 15 years, partly due to a lack of sand eels.

The **common tern** (*S. hirundo*), 36 cm, is less common than the arctic with just over 14,000 breeding pairs in Britain, widely scattered across eastern England, Scotland and eastern Ireland. It is so similar to the arctic that even experts can struggle to tell them apart. It has a black tip on the crimson-red bill, longer legs and head and a shorter tail that does not protrude beyond the wing tips. In flight, the dark outer primary feathers contrast with the pale inner ones. Although less numerous, it is the most commonly seen tern, as it comes further inland to breed by lakes, gravel pits and rivers as well as on coastal shingle banks.

The Groucho Marx of the family is the big, bulky **Sandwich tern** (*S. sandvicensis*), 41 cm, with its shaggy crown, drooping wings and harsh nagging call. It is seldom seen inland and breeds fairly commonly but locally, mostly on the east coast in protected reserves.

About 2400 **little terns** (*S.albifrons*), below, 24 cm, breed in a number of small coastal colonies, mainly in south-east England and East Anglia. It can be seen at Rye Harbour, Sussex, and at Blakeney Point, Norfolk. Apart from being smaller than other terns, it has a very short tail, a jerky, frantic wing beat, white forehead and black-tipped yellow bill.

The **roseate tern** (*S. dougalii*), 38 cm, is one of Britain's rarest seabirds. In 2000, just 53 pairs nested in the UK. The RSPB set up a special 'stronghold' for it on Coquet Island, Northumberland, to help safeguard its future which, like that of other terns, is threatened by huge reductions in the sand eel population. The roseate gets its name from a pink flush on its breast feathers in the spring. It winters as far south as South Africa, but its precise winter movements are still not fully known.

The **black tern** (*Chlidonias niger*), 24 cm, is a regular passage bird, most common on south-east and eastern English coasts, but also on lakes and reservoirs in the Midlands. It breeds rarely in Britain, but can be seen in large numbers at sites like Hornsea Mere, Yorkshire. Apart from its black, and slightly fatter, body it has broader, more rounded wings, a squarer tail and a relatively shorter bill than other terns.

little tern

GANNET *(Sula bassana)*

SIZE: 90 cm (wingspan 180–90 cm)

HABITAT: All around British coastline, commonest in N.W. Breeds in scattered island or seacliff colonies, mostly in N. Represents 60% of world population

IDENTIFICATION: Large white bird seen diving into sea. Yellowish head and nape, black wingtips, long bill, black legs

SIMILAR SPECIES: None

A gannet circles high above the sea, balanced on vast wings, dagger-like bill tilted down as it scans for fish; a dark sliver catches its eye, wings twitch and, quarry confirmed, it tilts over, starts to tuck its wings and plunges. As it draws its wings closer, it accelerates until, at the moment of entry, it is a perfect spindle, from sharp beak, through streamlined body, to fine, black wingtips, slamming into the sea with a mighty splash. Moments later, up it bobs, having swallowed its prey. A quick shake, a grating quack then a heavy, dragging effort to get airborne and back on patrol. Gannets nest in huge colonies, or gannetries, of up to 60,000 pairs, where they are noisy and aggressive. Young gannets, known as *gugas*, are harvested each September on the island of Sulisgeir by men from the Isle of Lewis in the Outer Hebrides, where they are considered a delicacy.

KITTIWAKE *(Rissa tridactyla)*

SIZE: 40 cm

HABITAT: Breeds on rocky islands, cliffs and sometimes coastal buildings. Winters at sea and around coastal waters

IDENTIFICATION: Similar to common gull but smaller, with black feet and a lemon-yellow bill. Black wingtips with no white spots, inner wing darker than very pale outer wing. Dark grey legs

SIMILAR SPECIES: Common gull

The kittiwake is Britain's commonest, and noisiest, breeding gull with an estimated 500,000 pairs that gather in huge colonies and make an unbelievably loud din at nesting time with their cries of 'kitti-kitti-wa-a-ak'. Even so, this prettiest of European gulls is not immune to environmental threats. In 1999, its breeding success rate on the Isle of May in the Firth of Forth was hit by a shortage of sand eels, its principal food. This was deemed so important a gauge of the sand eel stocks that a major part of the North Sea fishery area, the Wee Bankie, was closed to trawlers. The kittiwake is now used as a 'litmus test' of the European sand eel stocks, and further drops in breeding rates trigger fishery closures. This is a far cry from Victorian times when the bird was slaughtered for sport and to provide feathers for ladies' hats.

SHELDUCK *(Tadorna tadorna)*

SIZE: 60 cm

HABITAT: All round British coastline all year, moving inland in winter. Often nests in rabbit burrow or other hole in dune or bank

IDENTIFICATION: Dark, glossy green head, white breast and flanks, rusty-coloured breast band, wide dark stripe beneath.
Male has large knob on base of red bill, female does not

SIMILAR SPECIES: None

Shelduck parents take great care to lead their brood to safe waters after hatching – sometimes shepherding the fluffy ducklings a couple of kilometres. Then, after a few days, they effectively abandon them, pulled by the call of the moult migration. But no matter, shelduck society has an answer to this: the duckling crèche. Several broods unite, even if from different areas, under the supervision of one or more adults, thought to be failed or non-breeders. The size and composition of the crèche is forever changing, normally 20–40, but sometimes hundreds. A crèche of almost 200 shelducklings, some less than a week old, others almost free flying, was recorded in The Wash after a successful breeding season, attended by 12 adults. Broods are often large, as 'cuckoo' females without nests lay their eggs in the nests of others.

EIDER DUCK *(Somarteria mollissima)*

SIZE:	58 cm
HABITAT:	On coasts and islands around Scotland and far N. of England all year, winter visitor further south
IDENTIFICATION:	Male with white upper parts, breast and head. Breast has rosy tint. Black cap and green nape. Black belly, rump and flight feathers. Greenish bill with yellow along top. Female mottled brown
SIMILAR SPECIES:	None

Eiders often nest along with terns on small islets around northern shores. They benefit from the terns' aggression towards intruders. Both birds, however, have a disadvantage when it comes to human visitors because their nests, eggs and even chicks are so well camouflaged that they are easily trodden on. Anyone visiting an eider/tern colony in nesting season (not advisable) needs to keep a sharp eye out. Even the large females blend into the stony, seaweedy background and vacate their nests only at the last moment, leaving a clutch of beautiful, big mottled-olive eggs, snug in their cradle of down – the same as used in the best pillows and duvets, carefully plucked from the breasts of farmed birds. Only the drakes, with their glorious colouring, catch the eye. Eiders dive for molluscs or crabs and are happy in the roughest of seas.

COMMON SCOTER *(Melanitta nigra)*

SIZE:	48 cm
HABITAT:	Winter visitor round all coasts, some all year in N. Scotland.
IDENTIFICATION:	Male with all-black plumage, yellow bill patch and knob at base of bill; female browner with pale cheeks, no bill patch or knob
SIMILAR SPECIES:	Velvet scoter

Scoters arrive for the winter in big flocks, strung out in wavering lines, skimming low over the sea and settling into huge 'rafts' which ride the waves 100 m or so offshore. It is entertaining to watch hundreds of scoters doing synchronised 'duck dives' through wave after wave of huge rollers. It is our only all-black duck so it is easy to identify, although it can be confused with the velvet scoter *(M. fusca)*. The velvet, a scattered winter offshore visitor, is larger with a white crescent behind the eye, a white wing bar and orange–yellow sides to its bill. Both are nimble swimmers and good divers, unique in that they open their wings when under water, using them as stabilisers, while the powerful webbed feet thrust them down to reach their favourite mussels. Fewer than 200 pairs of common scoters breed in Britain, nesting by inland lochs.

GUILLEMOT *(Uria aalge)*

SIZE: 42 cm

HABITAT: Breeds on cliffs and rocky coasts, mostly N. and W. Winters at sea and all around the British coast

IDENTIFICATION: In summer: very dark brown above, white below, distinctive streaked flanks. Some with thin white line behind eye. Dark, sharp bill. In winter: pale throat and cheeks, dark line behind eye

SIMILAR SPECIES: Black guillemot, Razorbill

Few seabirds have such a variety of names as the guillemot, indicating its ubiquity and also the general affection felt towards this perky auk. Names include wil-duck, murre, eligny, spratter, lavy, frowl, sea hen, maggie and tarrock. The derivations are various, some obscure, but many, like murre and murse, refer to the deep, wailing murmur made by groups of nesting or swimming guillemots. Skuttock has a more earthy derivation: it is a variant of 'shite' and refers to the messy, smelly, guano-covered ledges left at the end of the breeding season. Breeding colonies can be vast, with up to 70,000 birds. The black guillemot *(Cepphus grylle)* breeds on rocky coasts, mainly in north-west Scotland, and winters at sea. It is uniformly black with a white wing patch. Guillemots dive for fish, groups often submerging simultaneously.

GREAT NORTHERN DIVER

(Gavia immer)

SIZE:	75–85 cm
HABITAT:	Around northern and western coasts in winter, a few breeding in N.W. Scotland
IDENTIFICATION:	Bulky with heavy bill. Head flat-topped with steep forehead. Summer plumage spotted on back, brilliant white below, dark green head, distinctive light and dark patches around neck; traces still visible as dark half-collar in winter when plumage is dullish grey above, white below
SIMILAR SPECIES:	Black-throated diver

The great northern ghosts in from the Arctic in winter, bringing with it one of nature's most spine-chilling sounds and a host of myths and legends. Up to 3000 of these big, dark birds haunt the coast of Scotland and a few places further south, curling their eerie howls and moans across the grey waters. Once heard, never forgotten. Also known as the loon or the rain goose, it features in folklore from Alaska to Norway, from Orkney to Siberia. Many stories tell how it takes on human form, how it flies with the souls of the dead, how it brings bad weather, how it helped create the world. Eskimos carried divers' heads as charms, and apocryphal tales about it were rife, particularly the one that said it hatched its young in a special hole under its wing. A pair bred on a loch in Wester Ross in 1970 and a few others have bred since then in Scotland.

RAZORBILL *(Alca torda)*

SIZE:	40 cm
HABITAT:	Breeds on cliffs and rocky coasts, mainly in N. and W. Winters at sea and around all coasts
IDENTIFICATION:	Black head, throat, upper breast and back, white elsewhere. Rectangular bill with two white lines, one vertical, one horizontal. Stockier and longer-tailed than guillemot. In winter, chin throat and chest all white, black mask extending down below eye level
SIMILAR SPECIES:	Guillemot, Black guillemot

The razorbill, widespread offshore in winter, is very particular about where it nests in summer. Although tending to be in the same general vicinity as the guillemot, it chooses more private, protected sites and is far less gregarious. There are no colonies south of Flamborough Head because of a lack of suitable cliffs, and similarly none on the south coast between Dover and the Isle of Wight. Courting pairs have a delightful ritual in which one bird stretches its head up and makes ecstatic little grating noises, while its partner nibbles gently at its throat with the tip of that razor-sharp bill. Other typical behaviour during the breeding season includes mass simultaneous display diving by groups of birds. The razorbill, like all sea-dwelling birds, is susceptible to oil spills and corpses are sometimes washed up *en masse*.

PUFFIN *(Fratercula arctica)*

SIZE: 30 cm

HABITAT: On remote grassy coastal cliffs and islands all round
                    Britain but mainly N. and W.

IDENTIFICATION: Distinctive. Huge, multi-coloured bill,
                    stocky build, white face with black forehead, cap
                    and nape, black back and white under parts.
                    Orange, webbed feet on short legs

SIMILAR SPECIES: None

You have to go out of your way to see a puffin – to a remote island or an almost inaccessible headland – unless, of course, it comes to see you. The puffin spends most of its life at sea but is prone to being blown inland by big storms. A puffin famously walked down The Strand in London in 1935, and in 1996 one was found in a field in Buckinghamshire. Written reports of inland puffins date back at least as far as the 16th century, adding to the public fascination with this characterful bird. It nests in a shallow burrow dug in a grassy cliff or taken over from a rabbit or shearwater and colonies number thousands of pairs. Both parents feed their single chick for about 40 days so they need a plentiful supply of sand eels and sprats. The puffin is an extremely good diver and can gather as many as ten small fish in its red, blue and yellow bill, holding them sideways.

It is shy but very trusting and inquisitive, which made it easy prey for the bird hunters of St Kilda (see Fulmar p352). Dogs were used to drive the birds from their burrows onto their familiar grassy slope, where the hunter had laid a length of rope with anything up to 40 little horsehair nooses tied to it. The first bird would get a leg snared in a noose and this would attract the attention of others who, waddling up to investigate, got snared in turn. Each hunter could catch up to 50 puffins a day like this and the birds were split and hung out to dry ready for the pot. In 1876, about 89,000 puffins were taken by the islanders and not one was wasted – they even had a recipe for puffin porridge.

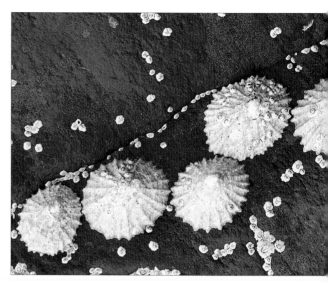

ACORN BARNACLE *(Semibalanus balanoides)*

SIZE:	Up to 15 mm wide
HABITAT:	On rocky shores around coast, mostly in the north
IDENTIFICATION:	Six greyish-white shell plates with diamond-shaped aperture
SIMILAR SPECIES:	Star barnacle

Barnacles soon make themselves known to bare-footed bathers, who learn to avoid the sharp-edged shell plates which cause painful grazing. Apart from some areas in the south west, the acorn barnacle is widespread and commonest in the north. It is found in a zone around the middle tide line, sometimes so densely packed that the rock beneath is hidden. Where populations are this crowded, it can affect the shape of the barnacle, which grows upwards to become tubular instead of its natural conical shape. The star barnacle, found mainly in the south and west, usually occurs higher up the shore than the acorn, but the two can overlap. The star barnacle's central opening in its volcano-like shell is oval and the tissue inside is bright blue with brown and black markings.

COMMON LIMPET *(Patella vulgata)*

SIZE:	Up to 6 cm shell diameter
HABITAT:	Rocky coasts all round Britain
IDENTIFICATION:	Conical ridged, greyish-brown shell
SIMILAR SPECIES:	China limpet, Black footed limpet

These tough limpets of varying size cling like grim death to rocks between mid- and high-tide levels. Try to move one and you would be forgiven for thinking that they spend their whole time anchored securely to one place. But, in fact, they move off to feed, always returning *precisely* to their home base by following a mucous trail. Sometimes this trail can be seen at low tide. Limpets can live for up to 16 years, their ridged shells clearly showing growth lines. Older shells are often seen encrusted with barnacles and algae. Limpets are edible, although a bit chewy. A recipe for 'limpet stovies' from the Isle of Colonsay suggests boiling and shelling them, removing their tough feet, then layering with potatoes and seasoning before baking for 2 hours.

KELP FLY *(Coelopa frigida)*

SIZE:	7–8 mm
HABITAT:	Seashore, especially sandy beaches throughout the British Isles
IDENTIFICATION:	Black bristly fly
SIMILAR SPECIES:	Other species of seaweed fly

During the autumn gales, huge quantities of kelp and other seaweed are torn from the rocks or seabed and thrown up in banks along sandy and rocky shores. As it starts to rot down, the female kelp fly can be seen choosing what is, in her opinion, the sweetest smelling spot to lay her eggs. When they hatch, the larvae feed on the seaweed, helping to speed the decaying process. They are often washed away during spring tides and float out to sea, providing an unexpected treat for fish such as mullet and bass. Rotting seaweed is not the only smell to attract the kelp fly (or seaweed fly as it is sometimes known). It also seems drawn to the scent of the industrial solvent trichlorethylene and, in 1954, there was a mass migration inland when the flies from the south coast invaded dry cleaners, factories and garages as far north as London.

COMMON WINKLE *(Littorina littorea)*

SIZE:	Up to 30 mm high
HABITAT:	Rocky coasts all round Britain except the Channel Islands and Isles of Scilly
IDENTIFICATION:	Dark brown snail-like shell with concentric ridges
SIMILAR SPECIES:	None

These shellfish are occasionally seen ready-cooked in fishmongers or even offered for sale in London pubs, complete with a wooden stick or pin with which to prise them from their shells. They are very easy to find and cook for yourself, although you do need patience and perhaps a little skill to extract the tiny spiral of flesh. Winkles, or periwinkles as they are sometimes called, frequent the middle to low tide lines and are abundant around weedy shores, especially where fairly sheltered. They are herbivores, grazing on seaweed, which also acts as cover to hide them from their predators. They reproduce by dropping egg capsules straight into the sea.

A tranquil inlet lined with oarweed

COMMON MUSSEL *(Mytilus edulis)*

SIZE: Up to 9 cm wide

HABITAT: Rocky shores

IDENTIFICATION: Bivalve with bluish-purple shiny shells

SIMILAR SPECIES: Zebra mussel, freshwater pearl mussel

Mussels have a world-wide culinary reputation, from the French moules à la marinière to the humble mussel suet pudding. The delicious pink–orange flesh has been called the poor man's oyster and the salty, smoky flavour is a wonderful addition to fish soups and stews. However, they should not be picked within sight of human habitation as filter-feeding molluscs can ingest organisms causing shellfish poisoning.

Mussels affix themselves to rocks, piers or wooden structures with their byssus or beard and this makes them relatively simple to cultivate. They are farmed on rafts with hanging ropes to cling to or on wooden poles driven into the seabed. In the wild mussels attach themselves to rocks and form dense colonies where they can live for up to 15 years. They open their shells to feed, filtering food from the 45 litres of seawater they each pump through themselves each day.

Unable to escape predators, mussels make a tasty meal for starfish, which pull the shells apart to reach the meat. Lobsters and crabs use their claws to crush the shells and gulls can be seen dropping mussels on to a hard surface to break the shells, flying higher and higher until they get the desired result. The thickness of the shell is dependent on wave action, so those from stormy shores give the gulls the most problems. It is only against the dog-whelk that the mussel retaliates. As it takes some time for the dog-whelk to drill through the shell, the mussel and its neighbours can launch their own attack. They attach their gluey byssus threads to the dog-whelk's shell in such quantities that it becomes immobilised.

Zebra mussels were first discovered in Britain in 1830. These small freshwater shellfish can cause serious problems to industry as numbers of up to 100,000 per square metre can block pipes and drains.

The freshwater **pearl mussel** *(Margaritifera margaritifera)*, is now a rare species, found mainly in Scotland, and was protected in 1998 by the Wildlife and Countryside Act. Pearls are formed in both sea and freshwater mussels as the creature coats any irritating foreign matter with layers of nacre – the same 'mother of pearl' that coats the inside of its shell. It can take 3 years for the pearl to become large enough to be commercially valuable.

COMMON SEA URCHIN

(Echinus esculentus)

SIZE:	Up to 15 cm diameter
HABITAT:	Deep water around the coasts or in rock pools
IDENTIFICATION:	Pinkish-purple round ball covered with spines
SIMILAR SPECIES:	Heart urchin

You will not often find a live sea urchin as you wander along the shore, but you might come across an external skeleton or 'test'. This in itself is rather beautiful and a whole one is a worthy addition to a favourite shelf at home, along with treasured shells and driftwood. The sea urchin is a delicacy, not only for humans but also for otters and gulls. When gulls find them, they take them a couple of metres up and drop them on the rocks, smashing them open to reach the flesh and leaving only broken tests for walkers to find. It is the roe that is valuable and in 1995, trials were carried out to assess the viability of harvesting sea urchins around the Shetland islands and sending the roe to London for Japanese sushi bars. Although the roe satisfied seven out of eight criteria, the colour was not considered attractive enough for the Japanese.

COMMON WHELK *(Buccinium undatum)*

SIZE:	Up to 11 cm
HABITAT:	Around Britain's coast from low tide line to the continental shelf
IDENTIFICATION:	Tall spiral, greyish-brown shell with ridges and grooves
SIMILAR SPECIES:	Red whelk

The whelk is carnivorous, often scavenging on dead sea creatures. It is regarded as a pest by lobster fishermen, who might find several of these low-value creatures in a creel, having eaten all the bait. But it is edible and can be found ready-cooked in fishmongers. If you are desperate for food, you could try slicing whelks thinly and frying or grilling them. When you find a whelk shell in a rock pool it is more likely to be occupied by a hermit crab (p369), using this tough, spiral shell as its adopted home. If you walk along the shore line, you might come across something looking like a mass of white, dry frog's spawn. This is a cluster of whelk egg cases that have floated ashore after the dispersal of the eggs. The inedible red whelk is a similar or larger size with a white outer shell and a red interior.

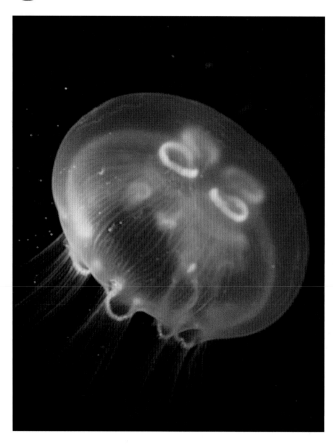

COMMON JELLYFISH *(Aurelia aurita)*

SIZE: 5–40 cm diameter

HABITAT: Coastal waters all round the British Isles

IDENTIFICATION: Translucent yellow or purplish jellyfish with four darker gonad rings

SIMILAR SPECIES: None

The common jellyfish, or moon jellyfish as it is sometimes known, is the commonest species of jellyfish around the UK. After gales, it can often be seen stranded on the seashore. The umbrella-shaped upper body has four frilly mouth-arms and many small marginal tentacles. It swims by pulsating its upper body through the water, keeping close to the surface, and can be seen in large swarms from April to September. It moves on to warmer waters as winter approaches, using the sun as a compass. Food, such as plankton, fish eggs and small fish, is collected on its outer surface and 'shuffled along' to the stomach through eight radial canals.

LUGWORM *(Arenicola marina)*

SIZE: Up to 18 cm long

HABITAT: Sandy beaches and muddy estuaries

IDENTIFICATION: Reddish-brown segmented worm

SIMILAR SPECIES: Ragworm

Fishermen around Britain's coast have perfected the art of digging for lugworms as they make excellent bait, especially for catching bass. The worm burrows fairly deeply in muddy sand, which it passes through its body digesting micro-organisms as it goes. It can be located by the spiral cast of disgorged sand with, nearby, a shallow depression around the blow hole. The lugworm, or blow lug, will be somewhere between the two features in its U-shaped burrow. As the tide goes out, long-billed waders like curlews will try to beat the fishermen in their search for this valuable source of food. The estuary ragworm, with a flatter, flabby body of up to 100 segments, is also dug for bait, but does not have the casts and holes of the lugworm. The ragworm can be green, yellow or orange with a distinctive red blood vessel down the middle of its back.

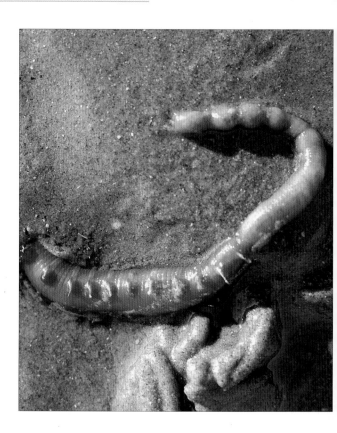

COMMON STARFISH

(Asterias rubens)

SIZE:	Up to 50 cm diameter
HABITAT:	Rocky or sandy seashore and estuaries all round Britain's coast
IDENTIFICATION:	Dark yellow or orange star shape with five arms
SIMILAR SPECIES:	Sand star

The rubbery but surprisingly firm common starfish is frequently seen around our coasts and lives happily on nearly all types of substratum from mid-tide level to about 400 m offshore. The colour of the flattened, star-shaped body can vary, sometimes with a brownish-purple tinge. It is carnivorous, feeding on small crustaceans and bivalves like mussels. You might come across a starfish with irregular arms; this is probably because it has lost one at some stage and is in the process of growing a new one. There are many species of starfish around our coasts. One rather attractive creature is the brittle-star, which has a tiny central disc and five long, thin flexible arms. As its name suggests, it is very fragile and will break easily if touched.

COMMON RAZOR SHELL

(Ensis ensis)

SIZE:	Up to 13 cm long
HABITAT:	On sandy shores all round Britain's coast
IDENTIFICATION:	Long, narrow white shells with glossy brown exterior membrane
SIMILAR SPECIES:	Pod razor shell, Grooved razor shell

If you are old enough to remember cut-throat razors, it is easy to see how this shellfish got its common name. It is widespread around Britain's coast but abundant on some sandy beaches, or even just part of a beach, and absent on others. It is unusual to see one alive as it lives in a deep vertical burrow between low tide line and shallow waters. Known as spoots in Orkney, this shellfish is very good to eat. However, it is renowned for being very difficult to catch. It can only be found at low tide and, at the slightest vibration, will use its powerful foot to dig itself further into the damp sand within seconds. As the shell is open at both ends, the razor shell will not live long out of water, which makes it almost impossible to market live in the same way as mussels.

BEADLET ANEMONE *(Actinia equina)* ▲

SIZE: Up to 50 mm high

HABITAT: Rocky shores and rockpools

IDENTIFICATION: Red cylindrical column with flower-like tentacles *(see above)*

SIMILAR SPECIES: Strawberry anemone

A familiar sight in rockpools everywhere, these carnivorous marine animals can be seen waving their tentacles in search of food. When disturbed or dry, the tentacles are retracted, leaving a jelly-like blob. Sea anemones attach themselves to rocks with a basal sucker or by burrowing into softer substrata. The beadlet anemone can tolerate fluctuations of temperature, so is found on exposed coasts as well as in sheltered bays. Both the male and female disgorge juveniles. The strawberry anemone, found lower down the shore, can be almost twice as big as the beadlet and is easily recognised by its distinctive pale spots, resembling a strawberry. Another interesting relative is the dahlia anemone which may be various shades of red, green or grey and has pieces of shell or debris sticking to its adhesive warts.

YELLOW SCALES *(Xanthoria parietina)*

SIZE: Spreading

HABITAT: Coastal rocks and walls

IDENTIFICATION: Patches of wrinkled, leafy, yellow scales

SIMILAR SPECIES: *Xanthoria aureola*

On rocky shores, barnacles usually form a dividing line between the brown seaweeds clinging to the rocks and the higher levels where lichens grow. Immediately above the barnacles, a dull black lichen dominates and above this is the colourful growth of yellow scales. It flourishes where there are mineral salts in the atmosphere and is often found on farm buildings in coastal areas. The scales are deep yellow or orange with narrow, deeply cut lobes, often overlapping. The similar *X. aureola* is common on rocks and walls. Its surface is covered with rod-like outgrowths. Lichens are extremely sensitive to air pollution and changes in the environment. A classic example of this is the 'canine zone' on suburban trees: this zone, at cocked-leg level, supports *Xanthorion* lichens, but higher up the trunk a different species grows.

HERMIT CRAB *(Eupagurus bernhardus)*

SIZE: Up to 9 cm

HABITAT: Rocky and sandy shores

IDENTIFICATION: Reddish brown head, pincers and legs seen protruding from whelk or other suitable shell

SIMILAR SPECIES: Many different species of hermit crabs

This crab has no shell on the hindmost part of its body, so it has to find, or even steal, one to protect its soft and vulnerable abdomen. It seeks out the shell of a whelk, winkle or whatever seems a good fit. Its abdomen is bent so it can curve around the corners of the snail-like shells. It even has two tiny pairs of legs to hold on to the inside of the shell. As it grows, it discards the shell and moves to a larger home, snatching out the original occupant if it is still inside. When threatened, the hermit crab withdraws far inside the shell, protecting the entrance with its right pincer, which is considerably larger than the left. These crabs are often seen in rockpools, and larger species live below the low tide line up to 80 m offshore.

SHORE CRAB *(Carcinus maenas)*

SIZE: Up to 7 cm wide

HABITAT: Seashore, estuaries and saltmarshes

IDENTIFICATION: Dark green carapace,
sometimes with yellowish patches

SIMILAR SPECIES: Velvet crab

Lift a rock by the seashore in the summer and you might see, scuttling away to safety, one or more shore crabs of varying sizes, from a few millimetres to several centimetres wide. The shore, or green, crab tolerates low salinities so it can be found far up estuaries and in the upper reaches of saltmarshes. It is also a denizen of rockpools and the crab most commonly captured by young explorers. But they should mind their fingers. The French call this the crabe enragé, or angry crab, and part of its scientific name, maenas, means frenzied. Although it will usually try to run and hide, if it is cornered it will put up a fierce struggle to show how it got its names. Despite its size, the shore crab can give a nasty nip with its pincers. Researchers have recorded the pressure of its grip at 2 kg – nearly 30 times the weight of its body – whereas the maximum power of a man's grip is only about two-thirds of his weight.

The crabs breed in the summer after the female has moulted off her old shell and before her new one has hardened – a process that usually takes about 24 hours. Each female lays about 850,000 eggs, which can stay attached to her for several months before hatching into planktonic larvae. Adult crabs move offshore in the winter.

The shore crab is edible but being so small is usually only used in soups. A more popular small crab for the kitchen is the reddish-brown, equally fierce, velvet crab *(Necora puber)*, which has fine silt-filled hairs on its carapace. This is caught in large numbers off the Scottish coast and is transported to Europe, mostly Spain, where it is highly regarded. Its carapace is slightly less wide than the shore crab and its eyes are a devilish red.

The edible crab *(Cancer pagurus)* is much larger with a distinctive 'piecrust'-edged carapace and is less likely to be found on the shore as it prefers to stay below the tideline.

SANDHOPPER *(Talitrus saltator)*

SIZE:	Up to 25 mm long
HABITAT:	Sandy shores around all coast of the British Isles
IDENTIFICATION:	Shiny sand-coloured segmented body
SIMILAR SPECIES:	Many different species of sandhopper

This amphipod is nature's beach scavenger, living above the high tide line under the strand line debris. If you lift some rotting seaweed away from the sand, dozens of these active little creatures will hop or jump out of the way. In the mid-1990s, local councils in North Cornwall carried out mechanical beach cleaning in order to win Clean Beach Certificates and attract more tourists. This made sandhoppers extinct on some beaches and a 'Strand Line Group' of the Cornwall Wildlife Trust was formed to protect the species. The group was successful in persuading the council to reduce its mechanical cleaning and sandhoppers were reintroduced to the beaches where they had become extinct.

SEA SLATER *(Ligia oceanica)*

SIZE:	Up to 30 mm long
HABITAT:	Rocky shores on all Britain's coasts
IDENTIFICATION:	Grey, flat, oval segmented body with two long antennae
SIMILAR SPECIES:	Other species of sea slater

The sea slater is a primeval-looking creature – even more so than its smaller relative, the woodlouse. Like a tiny, flat armadillo, it is commonly found under rocks and in crevices above the high water mark. It shelters from its predators by day and becomes active, and surprisingly fast moving, after dark. Although usually grey, the sea slater can change colour to blend with its surroundings and becomes pale at night. Even more oddly, it lies in the sun to get cold. In hot weather it has been seen emerging from its hideaway and settling on a rock, sunbathing. This is because, in the moist atmosphere of its refuge, it is unable to secrete moisture and becomes overheated. Outside in full sun, moisture is evaporated through its permeable cuticle and this evaporation reduces the dangerously high temperature.

COMMON LOBSTER *(Homarus gammarus)*

SIZE:	Up to 50 cm
HABITAT:	Rocky coasts around Britain
IDENTIFICATION:	Dark blue segmented body with two large pincers
SIMILAR SPECIES:	None

When we say 'as red as a lobster' we are referring to the cooked one on the fishmonger's slab or restaurant table. Straight from the sea and before being boiled, the lobster is a beautiful, lustrous dark blue with yellowish markings. Larger specimens live in deep water, but sometimes smaller ones are spotted tucked away in rockpools or crevices. It has a high value as seafood and numbers are dwindling as a consequence. If it can escape the creels, the lobster has a lifespan of 15–20 years and can weigh up to 5 kg. The small or young might fall prey to predators, but a large lobster can look after itself quite well. The stalked eyes give early warning of danger and it can retreat backwards at an extraordinary rate with a few flaps of its powerful tail. However, if it needs to fight, the claws are a formidable crushing weapon – to be avoided.

BROWN SHRIMP *(Crangon crangon)*

SIZE:	Up to 6 cm long
HABITAT:	Fine muddy sandy shores and estuaries
IDENTIFICATION:	Brownish translucent body with dark spots
SIMILAR SPECIES:	Many other shrimps and prawns

In Morecambe Bay, Lancashire, shrimp fishing used to be a thriving business, and at one time fishermen could be seen working the flats on horseback. The cost of labour and decreasing stocks have now sent this industry into decline. Shrimping is still a favourite pastime of children on holiday, wading in the shallows with D-shaped nets. The shrimps and prawns come close inshore during the summer, but move out to sea at the first sign of bad weather. The common shrimp is very difficult to see because it changes its colour to blend perfectly with the background and will burrow into the soft sand, leaving only its antennae protruding. Shrimps are boiled for a few minutes and, in France, are eaten whole. It is usual in this country to shell them and to extract the morsel of meat from the tiny tail.

LESSER SAND EEL

(Ammodytes lancea or *A. tobianus)*

SIZE:	Up to 20 cm
HABITAT:	Widespread and abundant around coastal waters, often buried in sand or shingle by shore, from mid-tide level to shallows below low tide line
IDENTIFICATION:	Long, thin body, green on back, silvery-white below with yellowish tinge
SIMILAR SPECIES:	Greater sand eel

The humble sand eel is an essential link in the food chain – eaten by commercial fish, seabirds and dolphins – but numbers are threatened by quite different creatures: pigs and chickens. Billions of sand eels are taken from the North Sea by Danish trawlers each year to feed factory-farmed animals. The surplus is used to fuel power stations. In 1993, the UK government dismissed concerns about sand eel numbers but in 1998, responding to falls in seabird numbers, the European Commission set a catch limit of one million tonnes, 960,000 of them, on Denmark. The sand eel swims in shoals but its silvery colouring makes it almost invisible. The greater sand eel *(Ammodytes lanceolatus* or *Hyperoplus lanceolatus)*, up to 32 cm, has a bluish body with a distinct dark spot in front of its eye. Its jaw does not protrude as in the lesser sand eel.

ROCK GOBY *(Gobius paganellus)*

SIZE:	Up to 12 cm
HABITAT:	Rock pools and among shoreline rocks. All round Britain except on east coast
IDENTIFICATION:	Stout, dark reddish-brown body with short tail stalk and prominent dorsal fins. Obvious band across top of first dorsal and protruding eyes. Much lighter colour if living over sand
SIMILAR SPECIES:	Black goby, Common goby, Sand goby

There are several goby species, but the rock goby is the one most often found under rocks at low tide. Young fish, about 45 mm long, are more common on the shore than adults. Like all gobies, it has a pelvic fin that is fused to form a weak suction cup. It eats tiny shrimps and worms and rarely tackles anything it cannot swallow in one go. The black goby *(Gobius niger)* looks very similar but is slightly larger with a more pointed dorsal fin. The common goby *(Pomatoschistus microps)* is the tiny fish (64 mm) you see darting about when you loom over or disturb a sandy-

bottomed rockpool. It is difficult to see because it blends in with the sand. It feeds on small crustaceans. It only lives for 1 year and is sometimes found in estuaries. The almost identical but larger sand goby *(Pomatoschistus minutus)* is found in pools nearer the low tide mark.

LESSER WEEVER *(Echiichthys vipera)*

SIZE:	Up to 15 cm
HABITAT:	On clean, sandy bottoms from low water to shallows below low tide line. Widespread round Britain
IDENTIFICATION:	Short, deep, yellowish body. Protruding eyes set high on head, upturned mouth. Short, black first dorsal fin supported by 3–6 sharp spiny rays. Long spine on gill covers
SIMILAR SPECIES:	Greater weever

The weever fish is a puzzle. It seems designed specifically to give an extremely painful sting – far beyond the needs of self-defence against smaller predators – to the naked feet of unwary swimmers, yet we are not really a threat. In any case, by the time we have trodden on it and been stung it has probably been crushed to death. Its dorsal fin and the spines beside its gill covers, both deliver quite a powerful venom. Fortunately it is not very common on the shore and generally lives in the shallows below the low tide mark where it buries itself almost completely in the sand. It has very sharp teeth and eats worms, shrimps and small fish. The greater weever *(Trachinus draco)* grows up to 40 cm but lives in deeper water. It is widely used as food in the Mediterranean but is rarer in northern waters.

LUMPSUCKER *(Cyclopterus lumpus)*

SIZE: Up to 60 cm (female), 50 cm (male)
                   but usually smaller

HABITAT: Bottom living from very shallow to
                   deep offshore waters all round British coast

IDENTIFICATION: Distinctive deep, rounded body with thick,
                   fleshy, wavy-edged dorsal fin and sucker disc
                   on belly. Rows of bony plates running
                   length of body. Blue–grey above and pale
                   orange–red below

SIMILAR SPECIES: None, very distinctive

The lumpsucker, or sea hen, is more common in the north and Scotland, and is the biggest fish you are likely to come across along a shoreline. It can be very big – up to twice as large as a football and almost as round. Most probably, though, you will find the remains of a lumpsucker left on a rock, its stomach eaten away by an otter and the rest left virtually intact. The best time to find one is from February onwards when it moves inshore from the deep waters to breed. At this time, the sea can be very rough, even in the English Channel, so the male guards the eggs on the shore, sticking himself to the rocks with the strong sucker on his belly, formed from the modified pelvic fins. The young hatch from an orange egg mass, emerging as brown-and-green pea-sized blobs in the mid-tide pools. These are the first fish larvae of the year to come onshore.

COMMON BLENNY OR SHANNY
(Lipophrys pholis)

SIZE:	Up to 16 cm
HABITAT:	Widespread under rocks and in crannies on rocky shores all round British coastline
IDENTIFICATION:	Small green fish with elongated body, large, blunt head, large eyes and thick lips. Soft, slimy skin. Dorsal fin extending along most of body
SIMILAR SPECIES:	Several within blenny family

Also called the sea-frog, the blenny is commonly found hiding among rocks at low tide. It often rests out of water on weeds and jumps back into the pool with a plop when disturbed. It uses its sharp teeth to chew barnacles off rocks and munch into dead crabs and pieces of carrion it cannot swallow whole. The adults breed inshore in early spring, the male guarding the eggs in the large pools. It has a strange, snake-like swimming motion and is distinguished from the gobies by its long dorsal fin. Other blennies found between the tides are the larger tompot blenny *(Parablennius gattorugine)*, brownish-orange with two aerial-like tentacles on its head, and Montagu's blenny *(Coryphoblennius galerita)*, similar but covered in pale blue dots and with a flap of skin on its head. Montagu's blenny is only found in the south-west of Britain.

BUTTERFISH *(Pholis gunnellus)*

SIZE:	Up to 25 cm
HABITAT:	Widespread under rocks on lower shore and extending into deeper water on rocky, sandy or muddy bottoms. All round Britain's coast
IDENTIFICATION:	Distinctive golden-brown, eel-like body with dorsal fin extending almost whole length. A dozen or so white-rimmed black spots running along base of dorsal fin
SIMILAR SPECIES:	Eel pout

No one could justly be called a butterfingers for not being able to keep hold of a butterfish. This well-named little wriggler is almost impossible to get to grips with when found under a rock at low tide. Rockpool hunters are advised to use a net if they want this specimen in their jars. It cannot fail to attract their attention with its lovely golden colour and dramatic dark spots. These spots act as 'false eyes' to fool a predator into thinking it is dealing with a much larger fish – or even several fish. The butterfish, or gunnel, eats worms and small crustaceans and comes into shallow waters to lay its eggs. In common with many small shoreline fish, the male guards the eggs until they hatch. The eel pout *(Zoarces viviparus)*, slightly larger, lacking the black spots and with a pointed tail, is found among the weeds or buried in the sand.

SEALS, DOLPHINS AND WHALES

Our marine mammals are rarely sighted but much loved. Whales, dolphins and porpoises have serenity and dignity and seals have a plump cuddliness which makes them irresistible (not that cuddling up to a foul-breathed seal is recommended).

The **common seal** (*Phoca vitulina*) is quite small (up to 2 m) and when it is swimming along with just its head above water, it looks a bit like an earless dog. It is not as common as the grey seal and is seen mostly off northern and eastern coasts and in the Wash, between Norfolk and Lincolnshire. A good place to see it is at Blakeney Point, Norfolk. It eats crustaceans, molluscs and fish and hauls out of the water onto beaches, sandbanks and rocks.

There are few things more unnerving for a canoeist than having a huge and inquisitive, **grey seal** (*Halichoerus grypus*) paying close attention. It can grow enormous – up to 3 m long and 350 kg – especially when feeding off offal and fish waste in harbours. Its numbers are high around Scotland where fish farmers are allowed to shoot it as a predator and it can now be seen off most British coasts except the south-east. It is much bigger than the common seal and has a longer, flatter head. It hauls ashore to breed and the pups have a white coat for the first 2–3 weeks. Its scientific name comes from the Greek meaning 'hook-nosed sea pig' – an apt description of the larger specimens.

If you want to see a **common dolphin** (*Delphinus delphis*) your best bet is to keep watch off Strumble Head in Wales, one of its regular haunts. Despite its name, it is not all that common and rarely seen from the shore but it does follow boats. Most people see their first dolphin or whale from a ferry, particularly on the Irish, Scottish and Scilly Isle runs. The common dolphin, a fish-eater, grows up to 2.5 m and has attractive wavy yellow, grey or brown marks on its flanks. It has a long, narrow beak and an upright triangular dorsal fin. It is very vocal, making high-pitched squealing noises, which can sometimes be heard above the surface.

The dolphin you see in films and at sealife parks is the **bottlenose dolphin** (*Tursiops truncatus*). It is larger (up to 4 m) and more uniformly grey than the common with a short snout, a steep forehead and a more backward-curving dorsal fin. It rides in the bow wave of boats (and even large whales) but can be seen from the shore, sometimes very close in, particularly off Land's End in Cornwall, Durlston Head in Dorset and around the Shetland Isles. It eats fish but has been seen (by horrified dolphin lovers) eating baby seals after 'playing' with them as a cat plays with a doomed mouse. Some researchers think it can stun its prey with loud noises. As a way of promoting understanding and welfare for these creatures, the Whale and Dolphin Conservation Society has an 'adoption' scheme featuring animals resident in the Moray Firth, Scotland.

bottle-nosed dolphins

Female **bottlenose dolphins** live longer than males, sometimes for 50 years or more, but not that long in captivity. A bottlenose mother's milk contains 14% fat – more than four times the amount in human or cow's milk.

The *common* or *harbour porpoise* (*Phocaena phocaena*) is the only member of the porpoise family found in European waters and comes quite close to shore, surfacing in a smooth, slow black arc several times before diving for a few minutes. Its reappearance is marked by a fairly loud 'blow' and it breathes at each subsequent rise. Schools of up to a dozen or so will patrol like this, hunting for fish, often in a bay or narrows between the mainland and an island and they have been known to swim up rivers. It has a blunt head and a stubby, triangular dorsal fin and grows to about 2 m.

Its inshore habits make it vulnerable to pollution and to being caught as a trawling 'by-catch' and as many as 2000 each year are thought to be drowned in fishing nets in UK waters. Quite apart from this threat, harbour porpoises are the shortest-lived cetacean, rarely surviving more than 12 years. Consequently, the females start to breed at 4 years, far younger than other cetaceans. In early 2003, the UK Government launched the By-catch Response Strategy for small cetaceans, an initiative aimed at tackling the killing of dolphins and porpoises by fishing trawlers. The strategy proposed that acoustic deterrent devices, or 'pingers', should be installed in nets and that research should be done on reflective nets and special separator grids and escape hatches to keep the cetaceans from being ensnared.

Our only commonly seen whale is the **minke** (*Balaenoptera acutorostrata*), the smallest and most abundant rorqual, which is found mostly off the west coast of Scotland. It sometimes comes quite close to shore, especially off the Hebridean islands, but is more often seen from boats. It grows up to 10 m long and can be distinguished from other rorquals at close range by the white bands on its flippers. From further away you won't see its indistinct 'blow' but you should see its pronounced, backward hooking dorsal fin. It can stay underwater for up to 20 minutes between blows.

Instead of teeth it has hundreds of baleen plates hanging down 20–30 cm from the top jaws, which sieve fish and krill from the water. It has 50–70 pleats running from its throat to just past its flippers and these stretch apart, allowing it to take in huge volumes of water to filter. It is itself a main meal for killer whales and is still hunted by people from the coast of Norway.

ACKNOWLEDGEMENTS

The publisher would like to thank Oxford Scientific Films for kindly providing the photographs for this book. We would also like to thank the following for their kind permission to reproduce their photographs:

Key: b = bottom   t = top   r = right
           c = centre   l = left

Alan & Sandy Carey 330; Alan Hartley 130, 190, 163; Alastair Shay 65t, 79t, 178, 263, 292; Andrew Plumpton 346b; Anthony Nyssen 24b; Archie Allnutt 78t; Arthur Butler 73, 78tl, 113b, 184t, 206t; Barry Walker 138; Barrie E Watts 114t, 277; Barry Watts 71,104b, 362tr 367b; Ben Osborne 123; Bill Pattern 140; Bob Fredrick 70, 71t; Bob Gibbons 17, 25t, 96, 98, 100t, 114b, 122t, 183, 221t, 223 265t, 271, 342; Bomford & Borrill 340; Breck P Kent 152b; Brian Kenny 355; Brand/Okapia 135; Bruce Harrod 167; C E Jeffree 347t; Carlos Sanchez Alonso; 215b, 235b; Chris Knights 44b, 36b, 171, 257, 281b, 301b; Colin Milkins 181b, 279t, 305t, 308b, 309, 311tl, 315, 322b, 328t, 329t, 368; Conrad Wothe 113t; D G fox 72t; Daniel J Cox 333; David Boag 52, 317t, 341; David Cayless 212, 160; David Fox, Back of jacket centre, 142t, 148t, 182b, 203, 275t, 276b, 345; David M Dennis 80b, 205; David M Morris 55t; David Thompson 49, 369; David Tipling 129t, 129b, 194, 218, 251t, 261, 283, 290b, 297b, 302, 336, 337, 350, 361; Deni Bown 18t, 18b, 21, 24tl, 111, 117t, 122b, 174, 179b, 201b, 226, 227t 228t, 251b; Dennis Green 66b, 233t, 237t; Derek Bromhall 51b; DJ Sanders 127, 191bl, 195b, 351t; Doug Allan 234t; Dr F Ehrenstrom 376b; Dr John Cheverton 185l; Eric Woods 132t, 217, 240, 296b; Frances Furlong 141, 233b; Frithjof Skibbe 68t, 227b, 365t; G & T Andrewartha 164; G I Bernard 20b, 54t, 61b; G A Maclean 20t, 46b, 66t; Gallo Images 93; G M Bernard, 19; Geoff Kidd 14, 94,101t, 104r, 104l, 105t, 106b, 107bl, 107br, 115t, 115b, 120, 121t, 172, 182t, 186, 188r, 232, 266b, 276, 279, 340t, 343, 344r; George Reszeter 299t; Gordon Maclean 12t, 15, 95t, 95b, 102tr, 108t, 107t, 118, 132b, 204, 222t, 265b, 268, 273b, 275b, 280t; Gunter Zuccki 16t; Hans Reinhard 13t, 187, 125t, 213, 316,323, 325, 327; Harold Taylor Abipp 22, 46b, 51, 56t, 60, 62t, 74b, 83b, 146t, 221b, 286; Harry Fox 56b, 246, 278r; Ian West, Jacket flap, 87, 97, 100b, 108b, 102l 121b, 139, 161r, 185r, 231, 272, 274, 284, 289b, 343t, 344l; Irving Cushing 74t, 184b, 192, 188l, 199, 206b; J A L Cooke 60t; Jim Hallett 119, 125b; Jo Frohlich/Okapia 146b; Jo McDonald /Okapia 281t; John Downer 91, 222t, 285; JS and EJ Woolmer 144; John Woolmer 145; Jos Korenromp 45, 236, 293r, 346t; K G Volk/Okapia 48, 112, 184t; Karen Gowlett-Holme 366t; Keith Ringland 124, 234b, 300, 320; Ken Cole 136; Kenneth Day 297t,

360b; Konrad Wothe 54b; Larry Crowhurst 59, 64, 68b, 147, 202b; Liz & Tony Bomford 152t; Lon E Lauber 166t; London Scientific films 46t, 83t, 362tl, 371t; Manfred Pfefferle 247b, 312; Marianne Wilding 151; Mark Hamblin 3, 8, 26, 27t, 27b, 28, 31, 32, 33, 34, 35, 39, 40, 41, 42, 43, 50b, 81, 84/5, 92 103, 109, 131tl, 117b, 128, 131b, 137t, 150, 157, 176, 168,186tl, 191bl, 192t, 193, 198t, 209, 211, 216, 225, 235t, 238tl, 239, 242t, 242b, 243, 244, 245, 248, 254, 255, 256, 360t, 280b, 282, 290t, 291, 293bl, 294, 298, 301t, 314b 349t, 353, 357, 359, 375; Martyn Chilmaid 148b; Max Gibbs 318, 331; Merlet/Okapia 324, Michael Brooke 13b; Michael Richards 166b; Michael Foaden 181t; Michael Richards 29b; Michael Leach 7, 88, 110t, 134, 153, 154, 156t, 198b, 208, 224t, 229; Michael Sewell 303; Mike Birkhead 50t, 69, 241; Mike Linley 55b; Mike Slater 179t, 220; Muzz Murrey 79b, 273; Neil Bromhall 202t; Niall Benvie, Back of jacket right, 4, 162, 224b, 266t, 346b, 358t, 335; Norbert Rosing 259; OSF 57t,65, 76, 142b, 143b, 161l, 189, 200b, 250, 304, 305b, 329b, 358, 363t, 365b, 370, 373b; Owen Newman 75; Paul Franklin 149, 247t, 264, 311r, 313; Paulo de Oliveira 47, 53, 63, 328; Paul Kay 348, 363b, 364, 367t, 372, 373t, 374, 376t; Peter Clarke 366b; Peter Gathercole 317b, 322t; Peter O'Toole 116; R L Manuel 61t; Raymond Blythe 80t; Raymond Parks 57b; Raj Kamal 99; Richard Day 253; Richard Manuel 308t, 269; Richard Packwood 37, 143t, 158, 195t, 319, 349b, 352t, 352b, 356t, 356b; Robin Redfern 29t, 155, 215t; Roland Mayer 258; Ronald Toms 10, 249, 270; Roy Coombes 299b; Rudie Kutter 62b; S. Stefanovic/Okapia 267; Sophie Evans 23t; Steen Drozd Lund 306t; Stephen Warman 278l; Stephen Dalton 159; Stuart Bebb 23t; Steve Littlewood 330, 354; Stuart Bebb; 23b; T C Nature 207; Terry Andrewartha 131t; Terry Button 2, 180, 295t; Terry Heathcote 82, 106t, 169, 173t, 175, 196b, 228b; Tim Shepherd 12b, 16b, 25b, 177, 170b, 314t; Tom Edwards 130; Tom Leach 95b; Tom Ulrich 289t; Tony Bomford 295b; Tony Martin 296t; Tony Tilford 30, 36t, 44t, 89, 126, 133r, 137b, 189b, 194, 196t, 197, 332; W. Wisniewksi/Okapia 288; William Gray 72b
Front of jacket image by Mark Hamblin

The Publishers would like to thank the following for their kind permission to reprint copyright material:
The Society of Authors as the literary representatives of the estate of A E Housman
(A Shropshire Lad - A E Housman)
Faber and Faber Ltd
(Crow Hill - Ted Hughes)

This book would not have been possible without the help of
Ruth Blair and the research team at Oxford Scientific Films, Julie Crane, Gabi Hellas, Jackie Dobbyne,
Sue Neate, Trevor Bunting, John Dunne and Guy Nettleton

BIBLIOGRAPHY & REFERENCES

Allen, Gwen; Denslow, Joan; Whiteley, Derek: Insects (OUP, London) 1974

Animal Aid: www.animalaid.org.uk

Arcarti, Kristyna: The Language of Flowers (Hodder & Stoughton, London) 1997

Arlott, N; Fitter, R; Fitter, A: Collins Complete Guide, British Wildlife (HarperColliins, London) 1993

Bennett, Stuart M: www.the-piedpiper.co.uk

Birdguides Online: www.birdguides.com

Birds of Britain: www.birdsofbritain.co.uk

Brightman, Frank H: The Oxford Book of Flowerless Plants (OUP, London) 1966

British Arachnological Society: www.britishspiders.org.uk

British Deer Society, The: www.bds.org.uk

British Marine Life Study Society: http://ourworld.compuserve.com/homepages/BMLSS

British Naturalist's Association: www.bna-naturalists.org

British Ornithologists' Union Online: www.bou.org.uk

British Wild Boar: www.britishwildboar.org.uk

Brown, R.W; Lawrence, M.J.; Pope, J: Animal Tracks, Trails and Signs (Hamlyn, London) 1993

Burton, Dr Philip; Ginn, Howard; Gillmor, Robert; Parmenter, T.W.; Parslow, John; Walker, Cyril; Wallace, D.I.M.: Field Guide to the Birds of Britain (Reader's Digest, London) 1981

Burton, John A.: Wild Animals (HarperCollins, London) 1998

Burton, John: The Oxford Book of Insects (OUP, London) 1973

Butterfly Conservation: www.butterfly-conservation.org

Chinery, Michael: Garden Wildlife of Britain & Europe (HarperCollins, London) 1997

Country Life: www.countrylife.co.uk

Creature Creations: www.creature-creations.com

Davidson, Alan: North Atlantic Seafood (Penguin, London) 1980

Deer Commission of Scotland, The: www.dcs.gov.uk

Deer UK: www.deer-uk.com

eFishBusiness: www.efishbusiness.co.uk

Environment Agency, The: www.environment-agency.gov.uk

Eurobirding: www.eurobirding.co.uk

Exotic Scottish Animals: www.bigcats.org/esa

FishBase ICLARM: http://ibs.uel.ac.uk

Fishbase: www.fishbase.org

Flowerdew, John: Mice & Voles (Whittet Books, London) 1993

Fritter, Richard; Blamey, Marjorie: Wild Flowers (HarperCollins, London) 1980

Gilbert, Oliver: Lichens (HarperCollins, London) 2000

Glasgow Zoo Park: http://glasgowzoo.inyourcity.com

Greenoak, Francesca: British Birds, Their Folklore, Names and Literature (C. Helm (Black), London) 1997

Harris, Esmond; Harris, Jeanette: Field Guide to the Trees and Shrubs of Britain (Reader's Digest, London) 1981

Hatfield, Audrey Wynne: How to Enjoy Your Weeds (Frederick Muller, London) 1977

Hayward, Peter; Nelson-Smith, Tony; Shields, Chris: Collins Pocket Guide, Sea Shore of Britain & Europe (HarperCollins, London) 1996

International Dolphin Watch: www.idw.org

Mabey, Richard: Food For Free (Fontana Collins, London) 1975

Magnan, Didier: Freshwater Fish of Europe (Könemann, Cologne) 2001

Mammal Society, The: www.abdn.ac.uk/mammal

Marine Life Information Network: www.marlin.ac.uk

McNeill, F. Marian: The Silver Bough, Vol 1: Scottish Folklore and Folk Belief (William Maclellan, Edinburgh) 1997

Muus, Bent J.; Dahlstrom, Preben: The Freshwater Fishes of Britain and Europe (Collins, London) 1971

Nichols, David; Cooke, John; Whiteley, Derek: The Oxford Book of Invertebrates (OUP, London) 1971

Over The Garden Gate: www.overthegardengate.net

Press, J.R.; Sutton, Dr D.A; Tebbs, B.R.: Field Guide to the Wild Flowers of Britain (Reader's Digest, London) 1992

Royal Society for the Protection of Birds: www.rspb.org.uk

Schofield, Bernard: A Miscellany of Garden Wisdom (HarperCollins, London) 1991

Skinner, Bernard: Colour Identification Guide to Moths of the British Isles (Viking, London) 1998

Species 2000: www.sp2000.org

Sterry, Paul: Collins Complete British Wildlife Photoguide (HarperCollins, London) 1997

Tolman, Tom: Butterflies of Britain and Europe (HarperCollins, London) 1997

UK Biodiversity: www.ukbap.org.uk

UK Safari: www.uksafari.com

Waller, I.J.: The Butterflies of Northumberland and County Durham: www.ijwaller.demon.co.uk

Warwickshire Amphibian and Reptile Team: www.wartsoc.co.uk

Wharam, Helen: Eurasian Badger, Information and Guide to Resources: www.bath.ac.uk/library/msc/1997/11747/badger.htm

Wild Hearts: www.wildhearts.org

*All web references as at 01/01/2002

INDEX